African Americans
Reviving Baseball in Inner Cities

Sharon T. Freeman, Ph.D.

AASBEA PUBLISHERS
2300 M STREET, NW
SUITE 800
Washington, DC 20037
Phone: (202) 332-5137
Fax: (202) 293-3083
Email: INFO@AASBEA.COM
Web: WWW.AASBEA.COM

Freeman, Sharon T.

African Americans Reviving Baseball In Inner Cities

Sharon T. Freeman, Ph.D.

ISBN 978-0-9703463-9-1

1. African Americans & Baseball
2. Bascball
3. Baseball, Sports & Recreation
4. Negro League Baseball
5. African Americans & Community Development
6. African Americans & Economic Development

I. Freeman, Sharon T. II. Title.

ISBN 978-0-9703463-9-1 (Trade Paper)

Publisher:

AASBEA Publishers
All American Small Business Exporters Association, Inc.
2300 M Street, NW, Suite 800
Washington, DC 20037
Email: INFO@AASBEA.COM
Web: WWW. AASBEA.com
Phone: (202) 332-5137
Fax: (202) 293-3083

Cover design and Graphic layout by Gene Hansen Creative Services
Chester, Maryland

Table of Contents

LIST OF TABLES

LIST OF BOXES

Foreword

Dear Readers:

My motto is: "It starts at the bottom." Therefore, I am pleased to have this opportunity to forward this important book that starts at the bottom--at the grass roots level--to understand why the participation of African Americans in baseball has declined and to offer practical recommendations for reversing the tide.

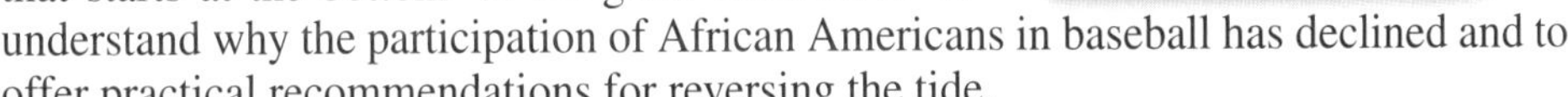

As I have often stated, I have been blessed with the opportunity to play Major League Baseball for a number of seasons. Baseball has given me opportunities to positively influence others, provide for my family, and to compete against some of the best athletes in the world. If it were up to me, I'd encourage everyone to play baseball regardless of race, ethnicity, height, weight, age, and even ability level.

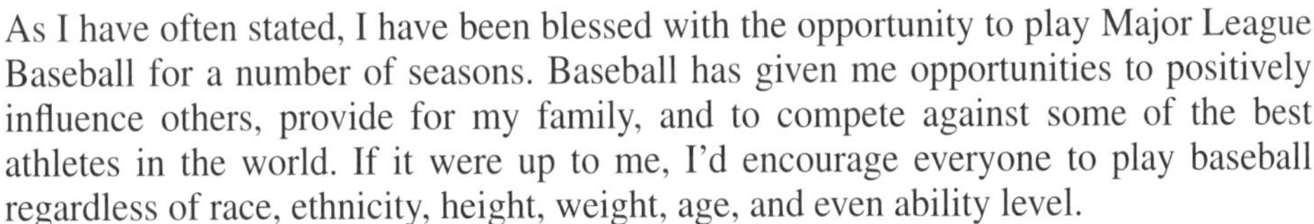

I am passionate about encouraging African American youth to play the great game of baseball!

My success in baseball, and that of my Major League friends, did not start at the Major League level; it started during Tee-Ball and little league, and in backyards. The opportunity to play baseball never starts at the top, it starts from the bottom up.

As stakeholders—players, mothers, fathers, community organizations, and others, we must re-double our efforts to encourage kids to play the game of baseball in the inner cities, where so many kids are overlooked and have limited resources and opportunities. It is important to encourage kids to play the game, to enjoy the competition, and to learn the character lessons that baseball helps impart.

On my part, I have put my money where my mouth is and have initiated a program, *The Torii Hunter Project*, which helps address the problem. Through the project, I have reached an agreement with Little League Baseball International to help sponsor two nationally known events. The first is a program that affords African American youth the opportunity to participate in the *Little League World Series*, one of the most highly regarded competitions in youth sports. The second event is affiliated with the *Little League Urban Initiative Jamboree*, which is part of *Little League's Urban Initiative* program. The program started in the year 2000 and has grown to 268,000 players. It encourages kids to play the game, to improve, and most importantly, to continue playing baseball in high school and college.

Through *The Torii Hunter Project*, I also support inner city baseball initiatives such as the RBI *(Reviving Baseball In Inner Cities)* program, which was founded by John Young, and which supplies baseball equipment, gear, baseballs and other forms of assistance to help urban youth stay in the game.

I am committed to helping increase the participation of African Americans in baseball, and to contributing in practical ways that touch the lives of kids who need and want help.

There are many practical things that can be done to help; this book, for instance, makes a practical contribution by helping to ignite revived enthusiasm for baseball in inner cities.

I encourage readers to read this book and to discover the role they can play in reviving baseball among African Americans in the inner cities.

Torii Hunter
Los Angeles Angels

Message from District of Columbia Mayor Adrian M. Fenty

Greetings

The District of Columbia is now home to a state-of-the-art stadium for the Washington Nationals. This facility will bring together generations of baseball fans to again enjoy America's pastime. Meanwhile, the Nationals and the DC Sports and Entertainment Commission are working to bring sports into the neighborhoods of the District.

Our nation's capital has a proud history of African American contributions to baseball. I encourage players and spectators alike to stay in the game.

Adrian M. Fenty
Mayor, District of Columbia

Message from Baltimore Mayor Sheila Dixon

SHEILA DIXON
Mayor
250 City Hall
Baltimore, Maryland 21202

Dear Friends:

It is my great pleasure to extend insight on the important subject of reviving baseball for our youth in inner city communities. Baseball is more than a game; it is part of the legacy of our country.

I am proud to say that some of the greatest contributors to the game, such as Frank Robinson, the first player to win the Most Valuable Player in the National and American Leagues and Cal Ripken, baseball's Ironman, both Baseball Hall of Fame Inductees had illustrious careers in Baltimore. Sadly, over the decades we have witnessed a decline in participation in the game among African Americans, but the time has come to reverse the tide.

The African-American aesthetic not only changed baseball, but has been a catalytic force behind the sport's growth in popularity and profitability over the years. Many believe the participation of African Americans has plummeted dramatically over the last three decades. However, African Americans are rising to the occasion and playing an important role in many aspects of civic life.

All of the baseball leagues in Baltimore provide an outstanding example of developing our youth through a never-ending process of self-study, education, training, and most importantly of all, experience. If we continue to build rich community networks and encourage youth involvement in our neighborhoods, we continue to develop our future leaders of tomorrow.

Best wishes,

Sheila Dixon
Mayor
Baltimore City

SD:cc

phone: 410.396.3835 fax: 410.576.9425 e-mail: mayor@baltimorecity.gov

Message from James Brown CBS Sports *The NFL Today*

James Brown

Dear Readers:

I am pleased to have this opportunity to weigh in on the important subject of reviving baseball in inner cities among African Americans.

Baseball, my first love, meant a lot to my entire family and community when I was growing up. My grandfather, Milton Barnes, was not only a fan; he was one of the pioneering Black baseball entrepreneurs who formed the "*Hattiesburg Black Sox,*" in Hattiesburg, Mississippi.

Growing up in Washington, DC, I can remember hearing the roar of the crowd when the Washington Senators played, and I remember the stories my family shared about great Negro League players like Satchel Paige, whose "Hesitation Pitch" was the talk of the town, when he and other Negro League greats came to town to play the Homestead Grays.

Today, as part of the Washington Nationals minority ownership team, I can say unequivocally that once again, we will soon hear the roar of African American crowds in our new stadium.

This book comes at an auspicious time; it's about *going beyond the ballpark* to reach into inner cities throughout America to get the African American crowd back in the game. It's also about changing the paradigm from limited "outreach" to intensifying the "reaching in" and "reaching down" strategy to ensure that there is urgency and immediacy of efforts by all stakeholders—starting from the bottom up—to revive baseball again among African Americans whose presence in the game has always mattered.

This book is a clarion call.

James Brown

James Brown
CBS Sports, *The NFL Today*

How to Order Books From AASBEA Publishers

By Credit Card: www.AASBEA.COM [PayPal ADD TO CART]

By Direct Purchase: Mail check ($19.99 + $5.00 S&H) to:
AASBEA Publishers
2300 M Street, NW, Suite 800
Washington, DC 20037
Email: INFO@AASBEA.COM
WEB: WWW.AASBEA.COM

By "Special Order" at all Major Bookstores: ISBN 978-0-9703463-9-1

Books by AASBEA Publishers:

- **Gems of Wisdom for Succeeding in the 8(a) BD Program—*and Beyond*** (Freeman, S.T., & Kruvant, M. C., 2007)
- **Africa's Youth Define Leadership** (Freeman, S.T. & Williams, W. A., 2007)
- **How To Sell Into The U.S. Market From Pakistan: A Practical "How To" Guide for SMEs** (Freeman, S.T., 2006)
- **African Leaders Reach Out to Africans in the Diaspora** (Freeman, S. T., 2004)
- **Making It In America: Conversations With Successful Ethiopian American Entrepreneurs** (Gebre, P. H., 2004)
- **Conversations With Powerful African Women Leaders: Inspiration, Motivation, and Strategy** (Freeman, S. T., 2002)
- **Recipes From the Road: Favorite Global Recipes of Washington, DC's Global Women** (Freeman, S. T., 2002)
- **Exporting, Importing, and E-Commerce: A "How To" Guide For Minority, Immigrant and Women-Owned Firms** (Freeman, S. T., 2001)
- **Conversations With Women Who Export: Inspiration, Motivation, and Strategy** (Freeman, S. T., 2000)

Some Also Available on Amazon.com

Acknowledgments

There is a steep learning curve to understand baseball, and mine was perhaps steepest of all. There were many people who helped me climb the curve and I thank them all most sincerely.

First, I would like to thank Anheuser- Busch Companies, Inc. for its generous financial support of this publication.

I thank Torii Hunter of the Los Angles Angels who graciously provided the foreword to this book. When I contacted him he was in free agency, and in the midst of negotiating with his new deal with the Angels. Despite his busy schedule, and all that was on his mind, he took time out to speak with me, to encourage me, and to offer his kind assistance. That is what we are talking about when we talk about "African Americans Reviving Baseball in Inner Cities."

I thank Cal Ripken, Jr. who has done more single handedly to help keep baseball alive in the inner city than perhaps any other, and for adding his voice to the back cover for this book. One thing is for sure: If you want to see a smile on anyone's face, just mention the name Cal Ripken, Jr., he exemplifies everything good in baseball, and all of the good that can continue to come after the end of one's playing career on the field. Today, he's a player off the field and is everywhere in Baltimore helping to keep baseball alive.

I also sincerely thank CBS NFL Sports Analyst James Brown for providing a wonderful and encouraging message to readers, and I am deeply grateful to the Mayors of Washington, DC and Baltimore who are doing everything in their power to encourage African Americans to stay in the game of baseball.

I thank my friend, Faye Fields, one of the minority owners of the Washington Nationals, first, for being my friend over the years. No one could have a better friend. I also thank her for helping me along the way in this book in many ways, and for inspiring me to look at the sport of baseball in the first place to see what I could see. I also thank William (Ike) Fields for all of his words of encouragement; if he wants to encourage you, you will definitely be encouraged because no one could be more generous in their gift of praise.

I express my deep gratitude to George Eccles, President of Black Diamond, and to Joe Durham, former Negro League and Baltimore Orioles player, who have been among my most ardent supporters throughout the writing of this book. They have introduced me to people, driven me around, attended countless meetings with me, and encouraged me in every possible way. There was never a week that went by in over a year that George and Joe didn't check in to ask, "Hey, Doc, how's the book coming—you need anything?" This has been music to my ears, and when I have felt tired, and wondered why I was pushing myself so hard to complete this book, they gave me the answer: It was for people like them who actually cared.

I thank my fellow Carnegie-Mellon alumni and volunteer James Mosher Little League Coaches, Lawrence (Chris) Cager, and Thelphs Evans, Jr. Thank you for sharing your knowledge with me for this book, and thank you even more for all of the years you have spent as volunteers helping the kids of Baltimore progress in baseball and in life.

I thank my friend Mamie "Peanut Johnson, the last remaining female player in the Negro Leagues, who is a source of inspiration for all women proving that anything is possible when one has the desire.

A special note of gratitude is conveyed to the whole Baltimore-based James Mosher Little League organization whose support for this book was boundless. From meeting with me, to introducing me to others, to convening meetings, this little league institution showed me how organizations like theirs are the first line in the grassroots movement to revive baseball in inner cities. A special note of thanks is given to Mike Singletary, President of the James Mosher little league organization: Mike, you are my man. I also thank Alan Meachum, Sr., and William Neal for their generous help and inputs.

There are many baseball stakeholders in Baltimore who helped with this book. While there are too many to name, I have to especially thank Coppin State University Head Baseball Coach Harvey Lee. No one could have more enthusiastically supported me in this endeavor, and no one is more committed to making a great baseball team than you. I also thank Coach Reginald Smith, Randallstown High School, Coach Travis Chapman, Carver High School baseball, and Coach Ruffin Bell at Baltimore City Community College.

I acknowledge and thank Baltimore Recreation and Parks Jim O'Connor who introduced me to many people and who took time with me to identify baseball stakeholders in Baltimore.

I also thank the Baltimore Orioles organization for its support and acknowledge Scout Dean Albany, former Orioles player Al Brumbry who provided information, insights, and contacts.

Nancy Paterson, one of the first little girls to serve as an umpire in the little Leagues, who then took that expertise and shared it with the Harlem Little League, I thank you for your insights, your interest, and for taking me up to Cooperstown to the Baseball Hall of Fame to get the photos for this book.

John Horne, Jr., Photos Library Associate at the National Baseball Hall of Fame and Museum, thanks so much for helping me with the photos and for introducing me to your friend Dr. David Ogden.

Dr. David Ogden thanks so much for providing your insightful chapter on "Pied Pipers for Baseball." You have been a longtime advocate of keeping baseball alive among Black inner city youth, thank you for that, and for all of your excellent scholarly work on the subject over the years.

Diane Grassi, you know how much I appreciate you, your work, and your support of my efforts in writing this book. Specifically, thanks for bringing information to my attention, thanks for the great work you contributed to this book, and thanks for your constant efforts in keeping the public informed of what's going on in baseball. Importantly, thanks for making sure no one forgets the connection between African Americans and baseball.

John Brewer of the Pittsburgh Courier, thank you for searching your files for excellent Negro League era photos. You certainly have one of the best collections out there.

Glen Harris, thank you for hosting me on your News Channel 8 Sports Talk program to give me a shout out even before the book was ready. Thanks also for the excellent insights you shared with me for this book.

Saving the best for last, thank you to my husband, Peter Hagos Gebre, who was enthusiastic about me writing this book from day one, and who never faltered in his support of me in this endeavor. Thank you for reading and commenting on the chapters, thanks for attending stakeholder meetings with me in Baltimore, and thanks for believing that although I had never written about baseball, that there was a common thread between my experience as an economic development specialist and the subject of reviving baseball in inner cities.

About the Author

Dr. Sharon T. Freeman

As an African American what I am most concerned about is making sure that our people have opportunities. I look at baseball as an opportunity.

After working in over 100 countries over the past thirty-five years to promote economic development

overseas, I recognize that inner city America is in as much need of development as poverty stricken countries abroad.

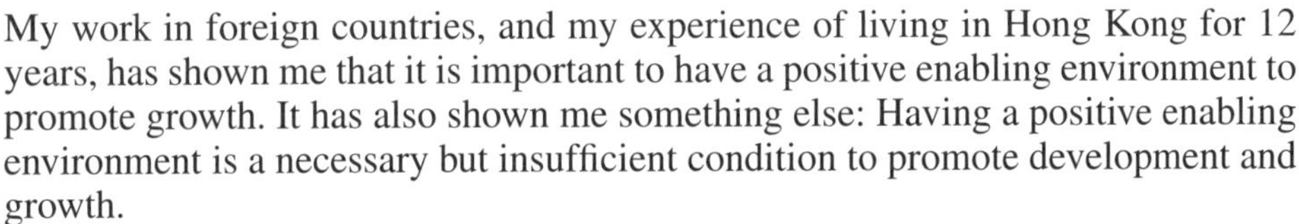

My work in foreign countries, and my experience of living in Hong Kong for 12 years, has shown me that it is important to have a positive enabling environment to promote growth. It has also shown me something else: Having a positive enabling environment is a necessary but insufficient condition to promote development and growth.

The missing ingredient is always leadership. It takes leaders to help people have a vision and to rise up to take advantage of opportunities. Reviving baseball in inner cities is at its core a leadership challenge that involves complex social and economic dynamics.

To write this book took I drew on over thirty years of experience as an Economic Development professional. My career began in 1975 as a Senior Management Consultant with Booz, Allen & Hamilton. It is an experience that showed me the importance of building solid and sustainable institutions. As a Diplomat in Hong Kong starting in 1981, I learned from the Chinese that all things are possible with good leadership and hard work, and from my work abroad, I learned that countries that have failed did so because they lacked good leadership.

As an entrepreneur and President of three firms, I have learned that to successfully play any game in life one must always stay focused on the money. When the Negro Leagues were formed, they were formed as businesses. Today, it's equally important to realize that reviving baseball in inner city America is also about creating opportunities, not just for ball players of the game but also for economic players in the game.

Through my firms, Lark-Horton Global Consulting, the All American Small Business Exporters Association (AASBEA), which is the publisher of this book, and the International Foundation for Trade and Investment Skills Development, a 501 (c) (3) non-profit, I have learned how to be an agent for change. My goal in writing this book is to once again be an agent for social change right here in my own backyard. Though my professional domain is primarily focused on international development, development is development and the same dynamics apply in any situation.

My development credentials include a Ph.D. in Applied Management and Decision Sciences from Walden University (1998), a Masters of Science from Carnegie-Mellon University in Public Policy and Management (1977), and dual Bachelor of Arts degrees from Carnegie Mellon in Cognitive Psychology and History (1974). I also currently serve in the following advisory capacities: Advisor to U.S. Secretary of Commerce and U.S. Trade Representative on *Trade Policy Matters Affecting Small Business*, Advisor to the U.S. Trade Representative's *Trade Advisory Committee on Africa*; Advisor to the U.S. Department of Energy's *Small Business Advisory Committee;* and, Advisor to the U.S. Small Business Administration's *Washington DC Metropolitan Advisory Board*. I also served as Advisor to the U.S. Export-Import Bank in 2006 and 2007.

My work has been recognized by the U.S. Small Business Administration's (SBA) *Small Business Journalist of the Year* (2007); the SBA Region III's *Minority Small Business Advocate of the Year* (2004); by DC Chamber of Commerce's *Crystal Leadership Award* (2002) and *Women's Leadership Award* (1997), and *Walden University's Alumna of the Year* (2006) See *http://realpeople.waldenu.edu/video-sharon.cfm*.

I am especially proud of Walden University's recognition of my work and to be featured in its national advertising campaign. The advertisement, shown on the following page, has been featured in magazines such as Newsweek, Oprah, Real Simple, Black Enterprise, among others.

At the end of the day, education is the key that unlocks all doors, and is also increasingly the gateway to entry into Major League Baseball (MLB).

Contact:

EMAIL: INFO@AASBEA.COM
WEB: WWW.AASBEA.COM

Introduction

Absence of African - Americans in baseball: Crisis or Fact of Life?

C.C. Sabathia - the only African-American player on last year's [2006] Cleveland Indians' roster - looks around the Indian's locker room (and baseball fields everywhere) and observes something painfully obvious: "There aren't very many African-American players, and it's not just in here, it's everywhere. It's not just a problem -- it's a crisis."

The Cleveland pitcher contends that the problem is not limited to major league rosters:

"I go back home to Vallejo [California] and the kids say, 'What's baseball?' It's not just an issue for my hometown; it's an issue for the whole country. I think Major League Baseball should do something about it. I don't know exactly what they could be doing, but I know it's not enough."

Neither a crisis nor merely a fact of life, this book shifts the paradigm and lends another perspective: "**A clear and present opportunity exists to increase the participation of African Americans in baseball**."

Who should do something about it?

As African Americans are the biggest beneficiaries of a revival of baseball in their inner cities they should take the lead in igniting the revival. Rather than relying on top down approaches, African Americans must *"reach down"* into their on communities to spark a *"bottom up"* revival.

Just as the U.S. Presidential election campaign of Barack Omaba showed the world that it is possible to come from nowhere and yet go somewhere, against all odds, it's also possible for African Americans to take the lead in reviving baseball in inner cities.

In the new paradigm, Major League Baseball would transcend beyond current *"outreach"* approaches to develop new *"reach in"* strategies to work more closely with inner city stakeholders in reviving baseball in inner cities.

Why should African Americans care about reviving baseball in inner cities?

Baseball presents an additional option, and having more options is better than having less options.

What is the state of African Americans in baseball?

Succinctly put, baseball in inner city America is scattered in one million little pieces. It's hard to follow the ball when the left hand doesn't know what the right hand is doing.

Baseball is happening in inner city America, but in scattered, disjointed, and sub-optimal ways. As time goes on, each feeder link in the baseball chain is becoming weaker and weaker. One day, it will simply break down altogether.

The snapshot of where African Americans stand in baseball given in the University of Central Florida's, *2006, Racial and Gender Report Card:Major League Baseball* (Lapchick, Ekiyor, & Ruiz, 2006), shows that the number of African Americans playing the game as of the year 2006, at 8.4 percent, is the lowest percentage since the Report was initiated in the mid-1980's. It is precisely that, a snapshot: It is not a moving picture.

This book endeavors to go behind the statistics to understand the whole picture in motion.

Accordingly, there are seven chapters in this book, with each "chapter frame" contributing a unique portrait within the overall moving picture. Chapter One, *The Perfect Storm*, sets the stage. It identifies critical factors that have a bearing on leading African Americans to baseball and to leading them away from baseball. Chapter Two, *Decoding Cool: Loving Baseball From The Inside Out*, tackles the issue of whether baseball is cool, and how anything gets to be designated as cool. The message is that in order to capture the hearts, minds, and "soles" of young African Americans, the MLB must figure out how to send the message that baseball is cool.

One of the most important chapters in the book, Chapter Three, *From Home to Home Plate*, examines the case of baseball in inner city Baltimore to identify what the internal and external barriers are to baseball for African Americans. This knowledge is important as input for formulating strategies to remove barriers. Chapter Four, *Diamonds Are Girl's Best Friend*, shines a spotlight on the important role of African American women and the stake they have in baseball. As single African American women head the majority of inner city African American households, this chapter demonstrates that in order to revive baseball, the first order of business is to revive the interest of African American women in it.

Chapter Five, *Gold In the Diamond*, draws attention to the money in baseball. It underscores that a lot of people are making a lot of money in baseball, and that African Americans shouldn't pass on the opportunity. Moreover, it stresses that the opportunities in baseball are not just for players on the field; they are for players off the field as well. It reminds readers that to play the game, one must be in the "real" game.

Chapter Six, *It Takes A Pied Piper*, raises the voice of stakeholders who are in the broader "village" as supporters of African Americans in baseball. Dr. David Ogden, a well-known baseball scholar and expert on African Americans in baseball, lends his voice to the Clarion Call to re-engage African Americans in baseball.

Finally, Chapter Seven, *Revival Strategy*, puts forward a stakeholder-driven "game plan" for reviving baseball in inner city America.

The Perfect Storm

The Perfect Storm

Heart thumping, captivating, mesmerizing, thrilling, exhilarating, spellbinding, action packed.

Baseball? No—not to the uninformed observer.

Those in the know understand and appreciate the skill level involved in the game, however.

For baseball players nothing is more riveting than having a ball come at their faces at over 100 miles per hour. In a fraction of a second they have to think quickly and make one of two choices: either to hit that speed demon ball or get out of its way. The problem is that the action happens in a split of a second and only those involved in it can see it and appreciate the amount of skill it takes to make and execute the right decision.

It's like "turkey spotting." Only a small select highly trained number of young girls in the world—from Thailand—know how to "spot" the difference between male and female turkeys. Their eyes have to be trained to be able to "spot" the difference before they are eight years old; after that it is too late. Every year the U.S. turkey industry imports an army of "turkey spotters" from Thailand to differentiate between the male and female turkeys for Thanksgiving tables. Many attempts have been made to get around this necessity, but there is no way around it: One has to be trained from an early age in the special techniques of eye coordination and orientation that are required to master the skill. What are they seeing to be able to discern the difference, can't others be trained to do this; can't we train a robot to do it? These are among the questions that have long plagued the U.S. turkey industry, but alas it turns out that there is only one way to master this skill; one has to "go through it to get to it"—in others words the investment has to be made in the child at an early age to develop that child's ability to master the art.

Similarly, to be a good baseball player, one has to be trained from an early age to master the art and science of "spotting" and deciphering the movement of a 100+ mph ball. It takes a lot of skill to discern its physics, and to develop the reflexes and coordination required to hit it or to move out of its way. It also takes a lot of experience to remove the fear associated with the speed and ferociousness of the ball.

The problem for spectators of baseball is that the action is so fast and so skillful that it takes the equivalence of a "turkey spotter" to see it.

It is not that baseball isn't action packed; the problem is only a well trained eye can spot the action in baseball. A famous landscape artist said, "It is necessary to cultivate one's perception so as to comprehend the essence of the object seen." And so as in baseball, it is necessary to cultivate both the audience and young players.

It doesn't take a "turkey spotter" to see that there's an 800 lb. gorilla on the field. How can the thrill of baseball be communicated to an audience that can only appreciate blunt "in your face" action such as a goal line dance on the football field or a *slam dunk* on the basketball court?

Though it takes years of training to truly master the game of baseball, parents and neighborhood friends in the African American community used to reach across the diamond to explain to young kids how to "see" and appreciate baseball. As the numbers of Black males who are knowledgeable about baseball have declined, so has the interest of young African American kids who, today, don't understand the game and who have insufficient resources to appreciate and learn it properly.

It is an oversimplification to suggest that African Americans don't think baseball is "cool," or that it's boring. The real answer to the question of why more African Americans aren't playing baseball is far more complex and multi-faceted.

Just as there was a perfect storm of positive factors during the Negro League era, and for at least two decades after Jackie Robinson's integration of Major League Baseball, contributing to the growth of African Americans in the game, a perfect storm of factors has come together today to contribute to the declining participation of African Americans in baseball.

The Perfect Storm That Flooded The Baseball Field With Great African American Players

Living in rural areas in earlier generations with few alternative sports outlets other than baseball contributed to creating a positive enabling environment for baseball to grow among African Americans.

Courtesy of The Library of Congress

Generations of Blacks in one family and in the neighborhood who played baseball, and passed down the game, contributed to creating the perfect storm. Fathers living in male-headed households and baseball legends living in the community were also positive factors that promoted baseball.

Black entrepreneurs and baseball titans who ensured that there was an economic trickle down of benefits to the community associated with the game was a decisive factor, as was the hunger of Blacks to be accepted as first class citizens through baseball. For them, baseball, as America's national pastime, was a part of the acculturation process. The lack of ascendancy of alternative sports and the belief that one of the few viable routes to empowerment was through the sport of baseball also contributed to creating the perfect storm. Importantly, the influence of Black newspapers that promoted baseball within the Black community was a major contributing element. Limited opportunities to pursue higher education, and therefore, the lack of connection between sports and higher education, as contrasted with the situation today, was yet another element. The list goes on.

But to be sure, there were many heart thumping, captivating, mesmerizing, thrilling, exhilarating, spellbinding, action packed episodes in the baseball experience of Black players and fans. During such times, crowds were roaring and the "against all odds factor" was in play. The satisfaction and reward was instant, and the opportunity for individualized showmanship was there, and so were Black fans.

Courtesy of the National Baseball Hall of Fame Library, Cooperstown, NY

Stealing bases was one aspect of the style of play among the Negro League players that created a lot of excitement; exciting pitching was another.

> Take for instance Satchel Paige's "*Hesitation Pitch*," reportedly banned by the MLB. It has been suggested that anyone who saw Satchel Paige deliver fastballs had to be impressed. Well past his prime when he came over to the Browns from Cleveland, Paige was still awesome. Night games showcased his fastball. It came in like a white streak. Paige had a new wrinkle he started with the Browns. It was the "Hesitation Pitch." The mechanics were that he delayed the pitch for an instant when his left foot came through the windup. The pitch confounded batters already jumpy looking at his "High Hard One." He took down lots of good hitters with it.

Then, of course, there was Josh Gibson, who mesmerized and thrilled audiences. Baseball historians consider Gibson to be among the very best catchers and power hitters in the history of any league, including the Major Leagues. Elected to the Baseball Hall of Fame in 1972, Gibson was known as the "Black Babe Ruth." He never played in Major League Baseball because, under its unwritten "gentlemen's agreement" policy, non-whites were exlcuded from the game.

As the Negro Leagues flourished over two decades in the 1930s and 1940s, as the talent among Blacks became evident, and as opportunities to capture and monetize the Black fan base came into sharp focus, it was just a matter of time before the "gentlemen" who signed onto the "Gentlemen's Agreement" placed economic considerations over social considerations and absorbed the Negro Leagues and its talent into Major League Baseball. (See Appendix 2: Index of Negro League Teams)

The baseball color line, sometimes called the "Gentleman's Agreement", was the policy, unwritten for nearly its entire duration, which excluded African American players from organized baseball in the United States before 1946. As a result, various Negro Leagues were formed, which featured those players not allowed to participate in the major or minor leagues.

Just as civil rights activist Rosa Parks was the perfect choice to demonstrate the folly of denying Blacks the right to sit at the front of buses in the south, Jackie Robinson was the perfect choice to demonstrate the folly of excluding Blacks from major league baseball.

When Jackie Robinson broke the color line in Major League Baseball (MLB) in 1947, it was ranked—then and still now—by Blacks as one of the greatest victories of the 20th century. Not surprisingly when African American journalists were asked by the *Journal of Higher Education* in 1999 to name the ten most important events of the 20th century, Jackie Robinson's integration of major league baseball ranked ninth. Whereas White contemporaries chose events such as Neil Armstrong's moonwalk, the discovery of penicillin, and the Wright brother's flight of 1903, virtually all Black respondents listed events that were important in the struggle for Black equality.

Courtesy of the National Baseball Hall of Fame Library, Cooperstown, NY

In March 1945, the white majors created the Major League Committee on Baseball Integration. Its members included Joseph P. Rainey, Larry MacPhail, and Branch Rickey. Because MacPhail, who was an outspoken critic of integration, kept stalling, the committee never met. Under the guise of starting an all-Black league, Rickey sent scouts all around the United States, Mexico and Puerto Rico looking for the perfect candidate to break the color line. His list eventually was narrowed down to three, Roy Campanella, Don Newcombe, and Jackie Robinson. On August 28, 1945, Jackie Robinson met with Rickey in Brooklyn where Rickey gave Robinson a "test" by berating him and shouting racial epithets that Robinson would hear from day one in the white game. Having passed the test, Robinson signed the contract which stipulated that from then on, Robinson had no "written or moral obligations" to any other club. By the inclusion of this clause, precedent was set that would raze the Negro leagues as a functional commercial enterprise.

Jackie Robinson's achievement was an undeniable and untainted victory in the struggle for Black equality, and every living Black person at the time was aware of it and applauded it. At last, the long battle to prove that Blacks had the talent to make it in the Major Leagues had been definitively won.

The question was asked and answered: Did Blacks have the talent to excel in Minor and Major League Baseball? They proved that they did, but today, a new question has arisen: Besides possessing the raw talent to play the game, are the other necessary inputs available in inner cities in sufficient measure to keep African Americans in the game?

Given the significant impact that Blacks have had on the game of baseball, and the impact it has had on Black America in turn, it is hard to imagine that the game has passed its time with African Americans. Moreover, given that Blacks can play baseball, and that it presents another alternative route for a professional career and success, why should Blacks pass up the opportunity? After all, not everyone is suited to play basketball or football. If there's untapped talent among Blacks in the inner city to play baseball that can be cultivated it's in the interest of African Americans, and in the interest of the game, to develop it. History has clearly shown that baseball can make a positive contribution to Black society and that Blacks can make a positive contribution to the game.

Courtesy of the Naticnal Baseball Hall of Fame Library, Cooperstown, NY

The Ethnic Presence of African Americans in the Game

From setting and breaking records, to innovating new styles of play, to expanding the fan base for baseball, the ethnic presence, personality, and signature of African Americans in the game has made the game more exciting and has been a contributing factor to its growth and popularity. At the same time, the accomplishments of Blacks in baseball have been an important socioeconomic barometer. In many regards, what has gone on in baseball is a mirror of American society, and what the mirror showed in the past was not a pretty sight.

Baseball's "race card" was in play from the late 19th century until it played out when Jackie Robinson broke the color line in 1947.

Courtesy of the National Baseball Hall of Fame Library, Cooperstown, NY

Examining the history of baseball reveals how the "race card" was played; it conveys a systematic trail of development, prominence, and in some cases dominance, laid down in chronological order by specific groups of Americans.

"If one wanted to know America, one had better know baseball," it has been claimed. More to the point, from an

Courtesy of The Library of Congress

historic perspective, "if you wanted to assimilate in America, play baseball." Germans, Irish, Italians, Jews, Slavs, African Americans, Latin Americans, and Asians did. On thousands of sandlots in cities and towns across the country, all became, unknowingly, a microscopic part of the stitching of the American game. Baseball was a common thread, with each group contributing its part to the stitching of American baseball.

First, there were those of English descent whose bat and ball games arrived in the cultural baggage of those who helped colonize the Massachusetts Bay colony in 1620. The twentieth century came with a systematic influx into Major League baseball of players representative of ethnic groups other than White Anglo Saxon Protestants. African Americans, Asians, and Hispanics followed players of German and Irish descent. Players like "Slide Kelly" personified the Irish connection to baseball. Joe DiMaggio was the embodiment of the Italian personality and connection to the game; while Sandy Koufax stitched in the Jews, and players like Stan Musial and Carl Yastrzemski offered as proof that those of Eastern European descent could also "make it in America."

Among the groups striving to "make it in America," the journey of African Americans in baseball has been particularly poignant. While it is true that from the very beginning the baseball field marked a small area where dreams seemed possible, for African Americans, there were two baseball fields.

Baseball in Black communities has historically embodied dualism, a "twoness." "One forever feels his 'twoness,'" wrote DuBois. "Two souls, two thought, two unreconciled strivings." Black baseball before integration fitted DuBois's remarks perfectly. But the "twoness" was more than a feeling: It was institutionalized by baseball's "Gentlemen's Agreement" that mandated racial separation.

During the separation, Negro professional baseball teams sprouted and took root on the urban Black field of dreams. The Black press kept the ground fertile. Black businessmen reaped the benefits, and Black players became heroes. It was indeed a tale of two baseballs worlds made one: "*It was the best of times, it was the worse of times, it was the epoch of incredulity...*"

The "twoness" ended when Jackie Robinson integrated the Major Leagues in 1947 and the Negro Leagues folded. But, suddenly, the whole of the "one" didn't equal the sum of the parts: The eradication of the separate Negro League teams also eradicated economic opportunities for Black baseball entrepreneurs.

Early 19th Century Black Baseball

An examination of defining events in the Black experience in baseball demonstrates just how much the game meant to the Black community. According to the Negro League Baseball Players Association's (NLBPA) description of Blacks in baseball: "Blacks played baseball throughout the 1800's, and by the 1860's, notable Black amateur teams such as the Colored Union Club of Brooklyn, and the Pythian Club of Philadelphia, had formed. All-Black professional teams began in the 1880s, among them the St. Louis Black Stockings and the Cuban Giants (of New York). Reflecting American society in general, amateur and professional baseball remained largely segregated."

"During the 1890s, most professional Black players were limited to playing in exhibition games on "colored" teams on the barnstorming circuit. Players on major league teams also barnstormed in cities and towns after the regular season was over. In some places Black teams and White teams played each other, and some Blacks played for all-Black teams in otherwise all-white leagues." There were many important milestones and accomplishments of Blacks in baseball from the late 1800s onward, that built the connection between Blacks and baseball, but it was on February 14, 1920 that everything changed. It was then that that Rube Foster organized the first Black professional baseball league (Negro National League) consisting of eight teams: Chicago American Giants, Chicago Giants, Dayton Marcos, Detroit Stars, Indianapolis ABC's, Kansas City Monarchs, St. Louis Giants, and the Cuban Stars. For the next thirty odd years, no sport was more meaningful in the lives of Blacks than baseball.

The Negro League Era

For decades, baseball was the national pastime in the United States. As one of this country's central institutions, baseball has long mirrored the complex and generally painful issue of race in the United States. Baseball was actually a forerunner in the realm of race relations, as the integration within the major leagues predated early civil rights landmarks. The Negro Leagues served as a proving ground and paved the way for the integration.

The Negro Leagues arose in response to the segregation policies of the major leagues. Implicit in the existence of the Negro leagues was the belief that the Black community produced athletic talent worthy of professional status that should be developed and displayed.

The Negro League story is the penultimate *"Little Engine That Could"* story in American history. In sandlots across the country, Blacks demonstrated that they could not only play baseball, they could knock the ball out of the park. The power, majesty and accomplishments of Negro League players are legendary and well documented.

Less is known, however, about Black baseball as entrepreneurship; about the role the Black press played in promoting Black baseball; and about the Black community's participation in baseball. While by its nature any conundrum contains a complex set of variables, an examination of the aforementioned three issues sheds light on important clues for solving the mystery of what has led to the declining participation of African Americans in baseball today.

The Negro Leagues As Entrepreneurship

The enterprising spirit and determination of the captains of Black baseball presented a symbolic challenge to the flawed foundations of segregation.

> "Negro National League's President, Rube Foster, who also owned and managed the Chicago American Giants team, took pride in what he and his fellow Black team owners were able to accomplish with their scant resources, particularly when compared to their counterparts in the major leagues. Where big league owners had wealth counted in millions, Foster told the *Chicago Defender*, he and his fraternity had only the faith in the weather man…we are willing, know what can be done, but have nothing to do it with."

Negro League baseball wasn't only a route for cultural assimilation: it was a path with multiple feeder roads for Black entrepreneurship. The Negro Leagues not only provided an opportunity for talented Blacks to play baseball, it was also an important entrepreneurial endeavor that was reported to be the third or fourth largest Black-owned business at the time.

Not surprisingly, a priority during the early phase of the Negro League's existence was establishing baseball's businesses on stable terms, which entailed keeping control of the sport within the Black community.

With so much at stake, a rivalry between the Negro League and Major League Baseball (MLB) was inevitable. To challenge the MLB, the Black press and Black businessmen partnered. The Negro League operated under the motto, "We are the ship; All else is the sea." Despite the almost uniform support from large Black newspapers and the

Courtesy of The Library of Congress

unwavering support of sports critics, success didn't come easy, nor was it lasting for Negro Leagues when confronted by MLB's post 1947 strategy of "**Embrace, Enhance, and Extinguish**."

Imagine, in the early 20th century, Sunday attendance at a Negro League baseball game in larger cities was around 10,000, according to Fort and Maxcy (2001), while the average for a Major League Baseball (MLB) game for the 1921 season was around 7,100 per team.

In *The Demise of African American Baseball Leagues*, Fort and Maxcy (2001) explain that organized African American baseball was the longest-lived rival to Major League Baseball (MLB) in history. Thriving from the 1920s to the early 1950s, it posed a serious threat to the MLB until baseball was integrated, after which time the MLB simply raided the Negro League of its best players.

To appreciate the extent to which Blacks supported baseball in the past, it is important to examine the evidence presented by Fort and Maxcy (2001), shown in Box 1, which also demonstrates what was at stake in the rivalry between the Negro Leagues and MLB.

As Effa Manley, owner of the Newark Eagles stated in *Our World* in August 1948, "…there's a potential two million Negro fans to draw from. Any baseball businessmen would be 'looney' not to see that." Accordingly, as Fort and Maxcy (2001) show, the success of the Negro Leagues did not escape the attention of the MLB.

Box 1

The Demise of African American Baseball Leagues: A Rival Explanation

Rodney Fort, Washington, State University and
Joel Maxcy, SUNY-Cortland

...At the [Negro] league level in the 1923 season, net revenue represented a 21% return on total expenses. On average, each team's net was nearly $5,000. Aggregate financial data for in MLB for the years 1939, 1943, 1946, and 1950 reported to Congress in 1951 (House of Representatives, 1951, p.965) showed that it only hit the AAB rate of return in 1946.

Moving later into the 1920, Peterson (1970) reports that Rube Foster's Chicago American Giants averaged $85,000 annually from league games over the 1920 to 1926 period. The Kansas City Monarchs were somewhat lower at $41,000, and the bottom end average was in the $10,000-$15,000 range (Peterson, 1970, p.89).

In the second competitive episode of the Negro Leagues (NNL2), teams had almost $2 million in total revenues, and most teams at least broke even. From 1942 to 1945, every team cleared at least $25,000 profit each year. (Ribowsky, 1995, p.265). The Kansas City Monarchs routinely cleared $100,000 profit in this period. By 1942, AAB teams combined to spend $500,000 in operating expenses compared with $175,000 in the late 1930s. Indeed, with 12 to 15 teams in two leagues, the $2 million figure yields a minimum of $133,000 per team in total revenues; up from a $20,000 or so average team total gross revenues in 1923.

Most Negro League teams played in MLB parks at a steep rate, another indicator of profit. For example, the Cuban Stars leased the Cincinnati Reds Redland Field off time for $4,000, collected at a rate of half the gate until paid in full. (Peterson, 1970, p.86). By 1938, Yankees Stadium rented for $3,500 per game. In 1939, the League switched booking agents to Eddie Gottlieb (an owner and founding father of the NBA), and rent fell to $1,000 per game. Teams playing games there averaged profit of $16,000 in 1939. (Ribowsky, 1995, p.239).

Post-season play was also profitable. The Negro League All-Star Game version outdrew its MLB counterpart seven times from 1933 to 1950, and for three straight years, from 1942 to 1944. Hearing data indicate that the All-Star Game was worth hundred $110,000 on average, over the 1951 to 1956 period.

Wages were high in the AAB relative to the opportunity costs of African Americans at the time. In 1923, Rube Foster made just under $10,000, an amount that must be considered relative to the alternatives facing an African-American businessman in 1923. The Negro League players also did well, especially considering their alternatives (general wages during the 1920s and 1930s were about $80 per month).

Crowds of 12,000 to 15,000 were common in 1946, but by 1947, the bottom began to fall out. Newark Eagle's home attendance dropped from 120,923 in 1946 to 57,000 in 1947

and was down to 35,000 in 1948, a 71% decline in 2 years. By 1949, the Negro Leagues were all but dead.

The MLB pursued an "**embrace, enhance**, and **extinguish**" pattern in respect to raiding the Negro Leagues of its best players.

Most of the big league clubs didn't pay the Negro league teams by buying up the player's contracts, as they did when they hired a player away from a minor league team. Even Branch Rickey, who signed up to 16 players for the Brooklyn Dodgers organization, had an excuse for this theft of talent. Many Negro League owners were numbers runners, Ricky told reporters. Therefore, the league was a 'racket' that wasn't entitled to compensation.

Effa Manley, Owner of the Newark Eagles, puts a different spin on Ricky's "racket" angle: "He took players away from the Negro leagues and didn't even pay for them. I'd call that a "racket."

There was no formal business relationship between the Negro Leagues and the MLB to govern player contract or territorial disputes. Therefore, disputes over compensation were between Negro League owners and players, not between the Negro League and the MLB.

Compensation for Negro League players was no more than a few thousand dollars per player. The New York Giants paid the Newark Eagles $5,000 for Monte Irvin; according to owner Effa Manely: "that started bargain-basement." All teams started grabbing Negro players for $5,000. Regarding the $15,000 paid to Effa Manley for Larry Doby's contract, Manley said: "You know that if he was a white boy you'd give me $100,000. In the end, Rickey never paid the Kansas City Monarchs a penny for Jackie Robinson, and Hall of Fame-caliber players were had for song.

Initially, Negro League owners hoped they might begin a lucrative business selling players to MLB, and the history of the MLB treatment of rival leagues seemed consistent with such hopes. MLB's economic treatment of early arrivals was replete with buyouts, expansion to make room for owners of previous rifle league teams, and artificially low-priced franchises to facilitate their assimilation into the MLB. But such was not to be Negro League owners and players. Only the New York Cubans ever entered into any formal agreement, and not until 1949. No other teams were signed this way. Furthermore, Negro League owners were offered a chance to either buy an existing MLB team or enter the league with their previous franchise in tact. The lack of any chance at cheap entry into the MLB clearly distinguishes the relationship between MLB and the Negro Leagues from MLB's treatment of all other rivals. The reasons for this different treatment are straightforward. First, unlike all previous rival league episodes, the Negro League had no ability to respond to MLB talent raiding with its own counterattack, and second, MLB had a lock-hold over baseball at the time. There was nowhere else to go.

Journal of Sports Economics, Vol. 2, No. 1, February 2001, pp. 35-49

The Negro Leagues and the Role of the Black Press

In the period of the 1920s to 1940s, the Black press had the power of all forms of Black media today rolled into one. Imagine having all available Black radio programs, Black television, and Black print media singularly focused on promoting Blacks baseball, without any competition from other sports. That is precisely the equivalent situation that existed to support and grow the allegiance of Blacks to baseball in the first half of the 20th century.

Now, imagine that no other media was reporting on Black baseball other than Black newspapers. It was a field day for Black newspapers and for Black players on the field. Leading Black newspapers considered themselves important partners with Black professional baseball as "overseers of uplift."

They had deep penetration into Black communities throughout America. For instance, by 1920, the *Chicago Defender*, the nation's largest Black weekly, distributed more than two thirds of its issues outside of Chicago, mainly by using Pullman car porters. This increasing national influence and awareness among Blacks dramatically expanded the impact of the crusading Black press. By 1925, the *Defender* had a circulation of 250,000, which set a new standard for Black newspapers. With an estimated pass-around readership of between four and five people, the true number of readers may have numbered more than a million.

> "The Pittsburgh Courier was against segregation in professional sports. Wendell Smith, who became the paper's sportswriter in 1938, used his column to denounce segregation in the major leagues. His efforts contributed to Jackie Robinson's signing with the Brooklyn Dodgers in 1947. In the early years of Robinson's baseball career, Smith traveled and roomed with Robinson on several Dodger trips, and arranged his travel and housing itinerary, because in some cities Robinson could not stay with the rest of the team in segregated hotels. The Courier was one of the few black newspapers to provide coverage of news in Africa as the continent moved towards independence."

The *Pittsburgh Courier* also had a significant national circulation and distribution network. Founded in 1910, the Pittsburgh paper was by the late 1930s the most widely read Black newspaper and remained so through the 1950s. In 1947, for example, the paper represented a $2 million business with a circulation of about 330,000. In the 1930s, the *Courier* operated 12 branches and published 14 editions.

When Black newspapers promoted Black baseball, the message rang out loud and clear and could be heard in every household within the Black community. The message was: "Black baseball was good for the Black community, it served as a point of pride for the Black community, and the community should get behind it." For its part, the Black press was firmly behind it, promoting it as a

minority-owned, minority-run business. It wasn't just about sports: it was about Black empowerment and entrepreneurship.

The Black press promulgated a "businessman-as-hero model" during the first phase of the Negro Leagues. In fact, emphasis in coverage on baseball as a business overshadowed reporting of wins and losses in the game. For instance, coverage by the Black press of the first "Colored World Series" in 1924 focused on gate receipts and the financial impact of the games, not on the performances on the field or on the outcomes of the games. Even holding the series was hailed mainly for its potential fiscal impact on the Black community.

Negro League owners viewed themselves as businessmen, community leaders, and as heroes. For instance, after the first *Colored World Series*, Rube Foster wrote in the papers that anyone could see the "mutual benefits to the whole race that come from the able and courageous business ability of the baseball leader."

Promoting the "business-owner-as-hero" model soon caused problems for the Black press, however, as doing so was in sharp contrast to mainstream sports writing of the period. Predictably, the close partnership between the press and Black baseball began to fracture by the late 1924 and 1925 period, especially as the Negro League's financial problems surfaced and as infighting between owners began to take a toll and force sports writers to pick sides.

By September 1926, the *Chicago Defender's* sports editor wrote that he was fed up with the Negro National League's dissension. He lashed out, challenging owners to "lay their petty ambition and jealousy aside, and get down to business." This criticism marked a significant shift in coverage and a break from the boosterism that characterized most of the first seven seasons of Negro league play.

At this point, the pendulum swung in the opposite direction. From then on, rather than give owners the benefit of the doubt in any dispute with players, Black press writers began to assume that the primary motivation for any action by an owner was greed and self-protection, and criticism became more frequent and increasingly personal.

The passing of the hero's baton from businessmen to the athlete could be seen in the illustrations that Black newspapers ran with their columns and stories. In the early 1920s, studio portraits of baseball team owners routinely appeared in the sports pages. An image of the American Giants' Rube Foster, regally sitting on a throne-like chair, wearing a three-piece suit, bowler hat, and gold watch and chain, and holding the type of cigar preserved for celebrating backroom business deals, frequently ran in newspapers. By the 1930s, images of the athlete striking heroic poses replaced images of the owners.

Never again would the Black team owners be able to use the Black newspapers as their personal soapboxes from which to strike out at adversaries and rivals. Just as the metropolitan dailies began to subscribe to the "get tough" school of journalism, the Black press, too, developed a sober strain in its Negro league coverage. From this point, the *Defender* and the *Courier* would cheer far less and instead make demands that Black baseball do better at organizing and consistently providing fans with a good product on the field.

During the same period, mainstream sports journalism was also being transformed becoming more objective, but the reasons were different. For mainstream papers, new competition for game accounts from radio placed increased emphasis on the athletes by relying more on pre-and post-game interviews.

Black newspapers, however, remained the exclusive source for Negro League game reports. The promise of more objective reporting coincided with the emergence of some of the biggest names in athletic history. The late 1930s introduced Black and White audiences to heavyweight fighter Joe Louis, and to the main hero of the 1936 Berlin Olympics, Jesse Owens. Add to this elite group Black baseball's Satchel Paige, who like Louis, had a personality to match the extraordinary athletic talent, and newspapers had impetus to begin showcasing athletes rather than owners.

Satchel Paige held his own in the fight for news coverage with hero Jesse Owens. Prior to Paige, newspaper coverage of games consisted of straightforward accounts of play, with little on individual players, and only a rare feature story on a player. Paige changed this, as his personality commanded attention both on and off the field. In fact, a content analysis revealed that Paige received more coverage doing the season than a majority of the teams. Thus, he became the Exhibit A in the case that Negro league talent belonged in the big leagues.

Paige served also as a precursor to Jackie Robinson. After Robinson broke into the major leagues in 1947, the Black press immediately shifted resources to coverage of Robinson and the Dodger organization and away from the Negro leagues. The Black

press realized what the White mainstream elite did not: The signing of Robinson cleaved baseball into two periods of "before" and "after," just as *Brown vs. the Board of Education* in May 1954 marked eras in the nation's schools.

It Takes a Village: The Negro Leagues and Community Participation

Viewed against the standard of Major League Baseball, the Negro Leagues were neither well organized nor financially stable. However, viewed in the context of the African American community at the time, the Negro Leagues represented a major success.

Negro League games, especially Sunday games, were important social events for the Black community and time to wear one's finest clothing, catch up on the news, and meet old friends passing through town. What spectators saw on the field was baseball that was every bit as good as the major league variety, but that was also different. Black baseball was faster, more stylized, and filled with crowd-pleasing showmanship. Paige, for instance, occasionally asked his fielders to sit for an inning while he brazenly proceeded to strike out the side.

As a social and cultural critic Amiri Baraka wrote, the Negro Leagues were:

> ...Like a light somewhere back over your shoulder as you go away, a warmth still connected to laughter and self love. The collective Black aura that can only be duplicated with Black conversation or music...these were professional ballplayers, legitimate Black heroes. And we were intimate with them in a way, and they were extensions of us, there, in a way that the Yankees and Dodgers...could never be. It was like we all communicated with each other and possessed ourselves at a more human level than was usually possible out there in the cold...

A firsthand account of that "*little light somewhere back of your shoulder*," is given by James Tillman, a former Negro League player, who was born in 1919 in Orangeburg, South Carolina, and who played with the famous *Homstead Grays* from 1941 to 1943. He was on the scene, and of the scene, and his face lights up when he tells his stories.

> Tillman experienced the thrill of playing in the Negro Leagues and the very special thrill of playing in Yankee Stadium. On the very first day he played with the *Homestead Grays*. From the time he was a little boy he loved baseball. No one told him to love baseball he just did; his parents didn't play baseball. He came to love it based on watching the local college play. When his family moved from South Carolina to Washington, DC in 1933, Tillman continued to seek out opportunities to experience baseball. He found them in the alleyways where he and neighborhoods boys made bats out of sticks and played where and when they could. His experience playing with the *Homestead Grays* was the greatest experience in his life, and though the crowds were

James Tillman

> roaring, he never heard them because he was so excited and so scared to fail that he could only hear his own heart beating out there on the field. On that first day at Yankee Stadium when he had to prove to the scouts "what he was made of," he showed them what he was working with: He hit a home run at his first time at bat.

The Black community was close during this time but segregation was part of the price paid for such closeness. Segregation during the Negro League era wasn't confined to the ball field: It also meant that Negro League baseball heroes lived in segregated Black communities. Because the players were a part of the community, kids got to interact with them on a regular basis. For instance, one might find Josh Gibson, Satchel Paige, or Cool Papa Bell playing a pick up game with the kids on the block. The degrees of separation between the hero and the worshipper were substantially fewer than today. As William C. Rhoden explained in "*Forty Million Dollar Slaves*:"

> ...In those days of suffocating, uncompromising segregation, we cheered Black muscle with a vengeance. The fate of Black civilization seemed to rest on every round and on every bat. "Knock his white ass out," or "Outrun his white ass," or "Block that white boy's shot." Or, worst of all: "You let that white boy beat you?"

Fighting Major League Baseball (MLB) was exhilarating in many ways. Negro League players knew they had the athletic ability to excel in the sport so it made the battle interesting. The stakes were high but the odds favored the underdog. Proving their ability in baseball was an important indicator of Black equality and competence.

Though baseball is a team sport, the embrace of it by Blacks has primarily been based on worshipping individual heroes on given teams. Satchel Paige and Josh Gibson were Exhibits A and B of what constituted the ideal hero in the Black community at the time: They demonstrated their athletic superiority by striking out the most hitters, running the fastest, stealing the most bases, jumping the highest, and putting on a good show in the process. When they played, the whole Black race joined together in a single chorus chanting, "See, I told you so, nah nah nah nah nah."

Courtesy of the National Baseball Hall of Fame Library, Cooperstown, NY,

Effa Manley, Top Row (R)

Stand-out-star-quality heroes whose style of play is singularly differentiated and whose star power the whole Black community can rally around are increasingly things of the past. African Americans are continuing to excel in the game, but they are doing so in relative obscurity, while a much louder chorus of applause is being reserved for individual heroes on the basketball court and football field. Today's baseball heroes do not command the attention they once did. For instance, the story of Barry Bonds breaking Hank Aaron's record was relegated to the sports page of *Jet Magazine*; it didn't even make *Jet's* cover story.

In the old days, baseball mattered in the African American community; it was more than a sport. It was integrated into the everyday lives and social fabric of the community. As visible and active members of the community, many Negro League members and sponsors contributed to the sponsorship of local contests and Black organizations, using their positions to promote social justice. For instance, Effa Manley, wife of Newark Eagles owner, Abe Manley, and later owner of the team in her own right, was especially active in the movement for civil rights during the 1940s. An active member of the NAACP, Manley frequently sponsored events to benefit that organization's operations. Eagles games raised thousands of dollars for the struggle to bring before the public the horror of lynchings in the South and to support the educational and political efforts of the NAACP.

In short, everywhere the Negro League operated, public visibility of Black baseball was utilized for the advancement of the Black image and the promotion of racial justice in America. Negro League players were not just ball players, they were players in the community and in the fight for justice and equality.

The Perfect Storm That Is Diminishing The Number Of African Americans On The Field And In The Stands Today

If it was hard to keep African Americas out of baseball, it's exponentially harder to get them back.

There are three critical perspectives to take into account in trying to understand what happened to diminish the interest and participation of Blacks in baseball since Jackie Robinson broke its color line. The first set of issues has to do with what's happening internally within the Black community; the second concerns what's happening in the game; and the third concerns factors outside of the game that have a bearing of how baseball is viewed vis-à-vis alternative sports.

Curve Balls Inside The Black Community

First things first: The Black community. At the outset, it's important to note that there is some question about how to define an African American.

> When recently asked to name five African American baseball stars, for instance, one African American little leaguer from Baltimore named Miguel Tejada, who is Hispanic, and another, when asked if he knew who the Black baseball player Derek Jeter was, said: "Derek Jeter isn't Black. He's "light skinned."

Table 1: Black Population in the United States, 2006	
Black or African American alone	37,051,483
Black or African American alone or in combination with one or more other races	39,151,870
Non-Hispanic Black or African American alone	36,434,530
Hispanic Black or African American alone	616,953
Foreign-born, Black or African American alone	2,903,618
Total U.S. population	**299,398,485**

Source: Jill H. Wilson, Brookings Institution
U.S. Census Bureau's 2006 American Community Survey

Nothing is straightforward in American society; everything is complex.

The concept of race as used by the Census Bureau reflects self-identification by people according to the race or races with which they most closely identify. These categories are socio-political constructs and should not be interpreted as being scientific or anthropological in nature. Furthermore, the race categories include both racial and national-origin groups. **Black or African American:** "A person having origins in any of the Black racial groups of Africa. It includes people who indicate their race as 'Black, African American, or Negro,'or provide written [Census] entries such as African American, Afro American, Kenyan, Nigerian, or Haitian."

Clearly, societal development and change encompasses all of a society, including its historical, cultural, ecological, economic, political, scientific, social, and technological aspects. To understand those changes, it's necessary to understand the contexts within which change takes place, the variety of forces that operate to bring about a myriad of change in different spheres; the consequences of change at different levels, and the role of social and cultural change agents.

Furthermore, to fully understand and appreciate the fast and complex nature of change within Black society, one must also examine theories, models, and ideas from perspectives as diverse as philosophy, ethics, sociology, psychology, economics, political science, anthropology, history, and others. While it's outside of the scope of this book to tackle all of these issues, it is useful to take a snapshot (Box 2) of where Black society has landed today, given the foregoing considerations.

Box 2
The African American Population At a Glance
As of Decennial Census 2002

- **38.3 million:** Estimated number of U.S. residents who were Black or Black in combination with one or more other races as of July 1, 2002. This race group then made up 13.3 percent of the total population.
- **$29,17:** The annual median income in 2002 of Black households.
- **23.9 percent:** Poverty rate in 2002 for Blacks.
- **8.8 million:** Number of Black families. Of these, 48 percent are married-couple families.
- **9 percent:** Black children who live in their grandparents' household--the highest rate for any race or ethnic group.
- **25 percent:** Blacks 65 or older living below the poverty rate.
- **52 percent: Black**s who live in the central city of a metropolitan area.
- **32 percent: Black** population under 18.
- **33 percent:** Black population under 18 living below the poverty rate.
- **28 percent:** Black men who are employed as an operator, fabricator, or laborer, and about **19 percent** in technical, sales, administrative support jobs, and service occupations.
- **36 percent:** Black women who work in technical, sales and administrative support jobs and about **27 percent** each in managerial and professional specialty.
- **41,000** employed Black physicians, **91,000** engineers, and **43,000** lawyers.

The foregoing indicates where the African American society is, but not how it got there. A closer look at three keys decades, from the 1960s to 1980s, provides insights.

The 1960s: Throughout the 1960s, Blacks advanced both socially and economically, making notable strides in a number of areas including educational attainment, voting rights, equal housing opportunities, earnings, and in employment. These advancements came about during a period of favorable economic conditions. It was a time of social change that saw the passage of the Civil Rights Act of 1964 and the establishment of the Equal Employment Opportunity Commission. This was a positive period for Blacks and their connection to the game of baseball intensified, but there were many negative things that happened as well, with the worse being the impact of the Vietnam War on the Black community.

> According to Department of Defense statistics, the percentage of black draftees serving in Southeast Asia during the war ranged from a low 10.5 percent in 1967 to a high 12.6 percent in 1969 and 1970. The percentage of blacks killed by hostile fire through the period ending June 1971 exceeded these percentages: 14.5 percent in the Army and 13.1 percent in the Marine Corps. Combined, black casualties between these two branches equaled 14 percent, a figure significantly in excess of the percentage of blacks in both these services. Stated differently, proportionately more blacks than whites served in the war zone and received assignments in combat units.

The 1970s: Blacks experienced the negative fall out in their communities (war casualties, drug addition, war-induced mental traumas, etc.) that was in part attributable to the Vietnam War. In addition, during the 1970s period, job opportunities and occupational mobility slowed considerably as the Nation underwent three recessions. With each contraction came periods of sustained and progressively higher levels of unemployment, accompanied by severe inflationary pressures which failed to subside over the course of the decade. Movement up the occupational scale for Blacks progressed more slowly during the 1970s, as the number of Black professional and craft workers increased only about half as fast as during the 1960s. Clearly, economic disruptions affected the occupational advancement not only of Blacks but of all workers as well. Still, Blacks continued to hang in there with baseball.

The 1980s: Things started to fall apart during the 1980s when something very sinister happened in the Black community: The crack cocaine epidemic.

The crack epidemic refers to a six year period between 1984 and 1990 in the US when there was a huge surge in the use of crack cocaine in major cities, creating crack-houses all over the USA. Fallout from the crack epidemic included a huge surge in homelessness, murder, theft, robbery, and long-term imprisionment. The first effects of the epidemic started in the early 1980s, but the DEA officially classifies the epidemic from 1984 to 1990. The epidemic affected all major American cities.

The impact of the 1980s period was devastating to the Black community. The resulting increased incarcerations of fathers, the increased incidences of homelessness, the increased crime rates, and the erosion of hard won economic gains combined to create an unfavorable environment for the family-oriented sport of baseball.

Today, new dark clouds loom over the economic stability of African American communities. One such threat is the long-term impact of predatory subprime mortgage lending practices employed in the African American community. An article written by *Baltimore Sun* reporter John Fritze on January 8, 2008 reports:

> "In a potentially groundbreaking lawsuit intended to stem foreclosures in Baltimore, Mayor Sheila Dixon's administration is suing a leading mortgage provider for what the city says has been a pattern of predatory lending in black neighborhoods. The lawsuit alleges that California-based Wells Fargo Bank sold higher-interest subprime mortgages to Blacks more frequently than to Whites and that the practice, known as reverse redlining, violates federal housing law. Baltimore's lawsuit could be the first in the nation in which a city is attempting to recapture costs associated with foreclosed homes that wind up vacant.

Dealing With the Fall Out of Bad Situations: Change in the Family Structure

Arguably, one of the most significant and detrimental impacts of the lost decade of the 1980s was the resulting change in the family structure within Black society. Current economic threats to the economic health of the African American community only compound the problem.

Unlike the traditional nuclear family composition involving a husband and a wife, who are the mother and father of their children, the structure and composition of the African American family today can vary according to the presence or absence of persons who are parents, children, and/or other adult or child family members. From a child's perspective, there is a greater likelihood that the child will live in a single-parent family and a dual-parent family. The prevalence of female and grandparent-headed households has implications for passing the game down from father to son. The demise of the dual parent household, and the dwindling number of qualified and available dedicated neighborhood Black coaches, also helps cut the ties between baseball and young Black boys.

The average, young African American, single female parent is not prepared to mentor her son in how to play the game of baseball, and this can pose a problem. As Stadler (2007) wrote in *The Psychology of Baseball: Inside the Mental Game of the Major League Player*:

> "Baseball is impossible without psychology--impossible to play, and impossible to appreciate fully as a fan. The physical demands of the game are intense, and the physical abilities of the players, extraordinary as they are, cannot by themselves meet those demands. Working alone, even the fastest reflexes would be insufficient. The reflexes must be supported by the player's intellect. The player's intellect, in turn, is shaped by those cognitive and emotional forces that are the province of psychology."

Fathers are the ones who are typically relied upon to help their young sons develop and hone essential cognitive and emotional assets. Indeed, nobody masters baseball alone; "it takes a village." When fathers are not available to play their expected roles, extraordinary measures must be taken within the community to bridge the gap and to help young African American males develop the mental assets they need to become winners.

Alison Gopnik (1999) lends another important perspective:

> "Imagine if we taught baseball the way we teach science. Until they were twelve, children would read about baseball techniques and occasionally hear inspirational stories of the great baseball players. They would answer quizzes about baseball rules. Conservative coaches would argue that we ought to make children practice fundamental baseball skills, throwing the ball to second base twenty times in a row, followed by tagging first base seventy times. Others would reply that the economic history of the reserve clause proved that there was, in fact, no such thing as "objectively accurate" pitching… But only in graduate school would they, at last, actually get to play a game. If we taught baseball this way, we might expect about the same degree of success in the Little League World Series that we currently see in science performance."

There's no way around the necessity of getting out onto the fields to play the game. Parents must play a critical role in encouraging their children to get out of the house and onto the baseball field to develop their skills, and this takes resources and time not just those of the parents and the child, but of the entire "village" support system for baseball. The city, which allots land, maintains parks, and provides instructional supports is in the "village." The parents who provide financing to support the child in the game are in the "village." The professional baseball club, the volunteers, the fans, the sponsors—all are in the "village." If any resource in the "village" is missing or is not optimally deployed, there's a problem, as there's no room for slippage. The future career of a potential great African American ball player can be derailed for want of a mere $35, or the fee associated with playing in a little league in a given year.

More Fallout: The African American Community Striking Out Multiple Fronts

According to the National Urban League's "*The State of Black America 2007*," the overall state isn't good. Salient factors, which combine in having a negative impact on the connection between Blacks and baseball, include:

- **Education**: Earlier in life, Black children excel until the middle-grades and high-school years when their achievement falls off significantly. A major disconnect, however, starts to occur after elementary school as Black students, especially males, begin to fall behind or drop out completely. The disparities in writing proficiency scores widen as Blacks grow older. At 4th grade, Blacks score at 87 percent of Whites, and by the time they get to 12th grade, the gap doubles to 26 percentage points with Blacks scoring at 74 percent of Whites. By the time they get into their teens, Blacks are more likely to have dropped out of high school than their white counterparts–15 percent compared to 12 percent for Whites. For Black males, the percentage rises to 18 percent compared to 14 percent of White males. But those numbers only measure the drop-out rates of students who are on the school rolls in the first place– not the ones who never show up.

- **Economics**: In terms of annual median income, Black men earned less than three-quarters of what White men earned ($34,443 vs. $46,807), roughly a $12,000 gap. Black women made 87 percent of what White women made and $5,000 less than Black men ($29,588 a year). Unemployment was highest among Black men – 9.5 percent compared to 4.0 percent for White men– a 5.5 percentage point gap. Black women experienced an unemployment rate of 8.5 percent, 4.4 percentage points above the 4.1 percent of their White counterparts.

- **Social Justice**: A higher percentage of Blacks (especially males) than Whites continue to be convicted and receive longer sentences, raising the question of bias in the U.S. Justice system. As a percentage of the population, seven times as many African Americans than Whites are in prison. Black men have an incarceration rate that is over 20 times that of Black women. Overwhelmingly, Blacks are more likely than Whites to die as a result of homicide. Overall, Blacks are five times more likely to be murdered than Whites and Black men under 25 years of age are 15 times more likely to die by homicide than their white counterparts. The murder rate for Black males over 25 is nearly seven times that of White males. The homicide rate for Black females is nearly three times that of White females.

A cloud also hangs over the health of the Black population. According to the Office of Minority Health of the U.S. Department of Health and Human Services, as of 2003, the death rate for African Americans was higher than Whites for heart diseases, stroke, cancer, asthma, influenza and pneumonia, diabetes, HIV/AIDS, and homicide.

Obesity is also a growing problem among African Americans. According to the national health report of 2005, obesity in Black women and Black men jumped almost 11 and 7 percentage points, respectively, between 1994 and 2002. Compiled by the National Center for Health Statistics and the Centers for Disease Control and Prevention, the report presents findings that from 1999 to 2002, 49.6% of Black females between the ages 20 to 74 were obese, and the figures have increased significantly: From 1988 to 2004, 39.1% of Black women were obese, compared with White females (23.3%) and Mexican women (36.1%). Overall, over 60% of Black males and nearly 80% of Blacks females are overweight.

> Not surprisingly, one typical overweight inner city African American little leaguer from Baltimore said the hardest thing about baseball was "running."

The problems don't end there as one thing leads to another. One of the profound negative impacts of the "lost decade" is the resulting loss of contact with sports heroes.

Quite simply, danger lurks in the inner cities.

The intimate ties that neighborhood Blacks used to have with their baseball heroes during the Negro League era have been broken, in part because of the danger that lurks in the inner cities.

Players no longer spend time in the community. On one hand, they are faulted for not stepping up to the plate to encourage young Black boys to play baseball, but on the other Black communities throughout the urban core of America must accept the blame for being crime ridden unsafe places in which to be. Today, many athletes find it necessary to travel with bodyguards and don't feel safe going into some urban areas, even if they originally hailed from such areas, or perhaps, especially because they hailed from such areas and know about the dangers of the ghetto firsthand.

The tragic November 2007 slaying of Washington Redskins football player Sean Taylor underscores the problem. One commentary on the tragedy raised the following questions:

> "What happens when the hope and tragedy of so many Black men in this country intersects? What happens when the fame and riches of sports that allures so many children intertwines with the reality of their everyday lives? What happens to Black boys when they see that even sports can't save you?"

One thing that happens is that people run away from the ghetto and when they do, they inadvertently draw up the bridge of hope for others who languish there.

Gang activity in inner cities is a huge problem that must be overcome. The prevailing wisdom about why gangs form is that youths join for safety, material access, status, a valued identity, and peer pressure. Gangs thrive in areas characterized by extreme

poverty and isolation, where social disorganization is accompanied by deteriorating homes, demographic change, and high immigrant populations. Because of isolation, competition, and conflict in such places, they are "naturally selected" for gang formation. Weak societal controls in socially disorganized communities allow gangs to flourish.

The bottom line is that many inner cities are dangerous and unwelcoming places to be. For baseball heroes with a lot at stake, it's risky going into such areas. In their absence, the caring face of baseball that Black players could provide to give kids a reason to like playing baseball again is absent throughout urban America. In the meantime, a cloud looms over the prospects to reconnect Blacks to baseball.

Curve Balls Thrown By Major League Baseball

Things have happened inside the Black community to cut its ties to baseball, and many things have happened with the game itself that have distanced Blacks, and others, from it as well.

Emphasis On Statistics: Substance Over Style

Surprisingly, the emphasis on baseball statistics is a factor that has had a negative impact on the way Blacks enjoy baseball.

Statistics play an important role in summarizing baseball performance and evaluating players in the sport, and since the flow of baseball has natural breaks to it, the game lends itself to easy record keeping and statistics. This makes comparisons between the performance of players on the field relatively easy and gives statistics more importance in baseball than in most other sports. That is the good news. The bad news is that the emphasis on statistics has had an impact on the style of play.

Emphasis on statistics, for instance, has diminished the use of stolen bases as a defensive weapon. Today, many of the best leadoff hitters are more apt to reach second base with a double gap than with a bunt and a steal. The thing today is to hit the home run; the stuff in between doesn't matter as much.

Baseball's Black Outs

The **1994 Major League Baseball Strike** was the eighth work stoppage in baseball history, as well as the fourth in-season work stoppage in 23 years. The 232-day strike, which lasted from August 12, 1994, to April 2, 1995, led to the cancellation of 938 games overall, including the entire 1994 postseason and World Series. The cancellation of the 1994 World Series was the first since 1904. Major League Baseball became the first professional sport to lose its entire postseason due to a labor dispute.

Through this strike, baseball lost its moral high ground. Whereas the game of baseball was an integral part of life in 20th-century America, the strike revealed that the game had moved from a quiet pastime to a multibillion dollar business. The strike cost a lot, and everyone paid the price from players to team owners to fans. A glimpse of how players paid a price is described in Box 3.

Box 3:
Everyone Pays The Price

The then-Montreal Expos' best season in their history was interrupted by the strike. They had the best record in baseball, 74-40, and were six games ahead of the Atlanta Braves in the NL East. Some baseball writers were considering the Expos as major World Series contenders.

Chicago White Sox star Frank Thomas, who wound up winning the American League's Most Valuable Player Award in 1994, said "I've had a career year, but I'm not going to finish it." Tony Gwynn had a chance to be the first to finish a season over .400 since Ted Williams, as he was batting .394 at the time of the strike. The strike also cost Matt Williams of the San Francisco Giants a chance to beat Roger Maris' single season home run record. When the strike forced the cancellation of the remaining 47 games of the season, Williams had already hit 43 home runs, well on pace to top Maris' single season record of 61 home runs. Cleveland Indians second baseman Carlos Baerga was unable to extend his record two-year streak of 20 home runs, 200 hits, and 100 RBI by a second baseman because of the strike.

Seattle Mariners star Ken Griffey, Jr., who led the American League with 40 home runs at the time of the strike summed it up best by saying, "We picked a bad season to have a good year."

By the third day of the strike, Cleveland Indians owner Richard Jacobs directed that all souvenirs being sold at the Indians' gift shop carrying the words "inaugural season at Jacobs Field" be sold at half price. The strike also led to an absurdity: Minnesota traded Dave Winfield to the Cleveland Indians for a player to be named later before the season was officially canceled, so no player was named. To settle the deal, the executives of the teams went to dinner, and Cleveland picked up the tab, meaning Winfield had been dealt for dinner.

Losing the moral high ground hurt the reputation of baseball; it used to stand for what was good in America—it was an ideal, not just a game.

Second Strike: Steroids and Doping Engulfing Baseball

Talking about losing its moral high ground and wholesome image, what could be worse than the steroid and doping charges in the past decade? The Associated Press report of the January 15, 2008 Congressional hearing on the matter says it all.

Box 4: Another Day Another Black Cloud Over Baseball

WASHINGTON (AP) – At a House Oversight and Government Reform Committee hearing [congressmen noted]: … "The illegal use of steroids and performance-enhancing drugs was pervasive for more than a decade, Major League Baseball was slow and ineffective in responding to the scandal, and the use of human growth hormone has been rising," said committee chairman Henry Waxman, a California Democrat.

"The Mitchell Report also makes it clear that everyone in baseball is responsible: the owners, the commissioner, the union and the players."

After standing and raising his right hand to be sworn in, former Senate majority leader George Mitchell [said]: "Now it's up to the commissioner, the clubs, and the players to decide how they will proceed."

[Commissioner] Selig vowed in his prepared statement to develop a program "to require top prospects for the major league draft to submit to drug testing before the (amateur) draft." He also reiterated his willingness to support use of a test for human growth hormone "when a valid, commercially available and practical test for HGH becomes reality, regardless of whether the test is based on blood or urine." The union has said in the past it would agree to a urine test, but it has not committed to a blood test.

"I want to be clear that I agree with the conclusions reached by Senator Mitchell in his report, including his criticisms of baseball, the union and our players," Selig said.

…In some ways, the mood was captured succinctly by Connecticut Republican Christopher Shays, who began his questioning time by noting, "This is almost surreal to me."

Mitchell's report connected more than 80 players to allegations about performance-enhancing drugs. The name that stood out was that of Clemens, who is scheduled to testify to the same committee Feb. 13, [2008] along with former teammate Andy Pettitte, and McNamee.

At the 2005 hearing, Palmeiro said under oath, "I have never used steroids, period." He was suspended by baseball later that year after testing positive for a steroid. When the committee looked into whether Palmeiro should face perjury charges, it spoke to Miguel Tejada, who at the time was a Baltimore Orioles teammate of Palmeiro's. Palmeiro said his positive test must have resulted from a B-12 vitamin injection given to him by Tejada.

In the Mitchell Report, Adam Piatt, Tejada's former Oakland teammate, said he provided Tejada with steroids and HGH in 2003. "Tejada told the committee that he never used illegal performance-enhancing drugs and that he had no knowledge of other players using or even talking about steroids," Waxman said. "Well, the Mitchell Report, however, directly contradicts key elements of Mr. Tejada's testimony."

What is a young person to think? The message is if you want to win you better cheat. This is very disappointing, especially at a time when many young African American single moms are looking to the game of baseball for positive role models and positive life lessons.

New Curve Balls: From Foreign Lands

Arguably, the investment in developing talent in foreign destinations has resulted in a disinvestment in urban America. There are a multitude of factors that have led to the investment in player development overseas. From the weather, to lower costs, to the lack of clear and present neighborhood danger, to MLB rule changes, there are a number of critical factors that have led to a perfect storm favoring overseas player development.

Among these factors, the famous Curt Flood decision has a significant bearing on the issue.

> Curtis Charles Flood (January 18, 1938- January 20,1997) was a Major League Baseball player who spent most of his career as a center fielder for the St. Louis Cardinals. A defensive standout, he led the National League in putouts four times and in fielding percentage twice, winning Gold Glove Awards in his last seven full seasons from 1963-1969. He also batted over .300 six times, and led the NL in hits (211) in 1964. He retired with the third most games in center field (1683) in NL history, trailing only Willie Mays and Richie Ashburn.

One of Flood's major claims to fame was becoming one of the pivotal figures in the sport's labor history when he refused to accept a trade following the 1969 season, ultimately appealing his case to the U.S. Supreme Court. Although his legal challenge was unsuccessful, it brought about additional solidarity among players as they fought against baseball's **reserve clause** and sought **free agency**.

> **The reserve clause** is a term formerly employed in North American professional sports contracts. The reserve clause, contained in all standard player contracts stated that upon the contract's expiration, the rights to the player were to be retained by the team to which he had been signed. Practically, this meant that although both the player's obligation to play for the team as well as the team's obligation to pay the player were terminated, the player was not free to enter into another contract with another team. The player was bound to either a) negotiate a new contract to play another year for the same team, or b) ask to be released.
>
> In professional sports, a **free agent** is a team player whose contract with a team has expired, and the player is able to sign a contract with another team. The term came into wide use in North America after sports leagues stopped using a "reserve clause" after much acrimonious collective bargaining, which

provided a repetitive option for the club to renew the contract for one more year, but did not allow the player to terminate the relationship with the team. The result of the reserve clause was abusive from the player's standpoint making the player essentially property of the team. Once in free agency, a player is in a "pool" of free agents, where teams can sign players who are able to drive hard bargains in the employment market place since the owners now must compete for their talents.

The economics of free agency are disadvantageous for team owners; it can lead to bidding wars: Increased player salaries means decreased owner profits. One solution for strengthening the owner's bottom line has been overseas player development. Many players have been trained in the Dominican Republic as a result. As of 2006, the approximately 1,521 Dominican Republic players signed to MLB organizations (of which 1,442 are minor leaguers).

Some, like Detroit Tigers Gary Sheffield, believe that the issue goes beyond economics; there are also other factors at play in favoring the development of foreign players over African American players. Sheffield suggests:

> Gary Sheffield (June 2007): In an interview with *GQ Magazine*...the typically outspoken Tigers designated hitter said Latin players have replaced African-Americans as baseball's most prevalent minority because they are easier to control.
>
> "I called it years ago. What I called is that you're going to see more black faces, but there ain't no English going to be coming out. ... [It's about] being able to tell [Latin players] what to do -- being able to control them," he told the magazine.
>
> "Where I'm from, you can't control us. You might get a guy to do it that way for a while because he wants to benefit, but in the end, he is going to go back to being who he is. And that's a person that you're going to talk to with respect, you're going to talk to like a man.
>
> "These are the things my race demands. So, if you're equally good as this Latin player, guess who's going to get sent home? I know a lot of players that are home now can outplay a lot of these guys."

Mamie Peanut Johnson, the sole surviving female Negro League baseball player, agrees with Sheffield. As a former baseball coach in her later years, she said that she gave up coaching "because the African American kids were too disrespectful, too undisciplined, and not committed to learning the game." By contrast, she notes, "players from overseas are totally committed to learning the game and are outstanding players as a consequence, which is why it's difficult to compete against them. Their devotion to the sport has lifted the bar of competition, and as a result, it is harder for African Americans to shine in the sport unless they put in comparable time and effort.

Mamie
Peanut Johnson

Baseball is down right hard to learn and to play at the highest levels. Some African Americans would rather take their chances in basketball, which is a whole lot easier," according to Mamie.

Box 5
Dominican Republic Baseball
By Bill Bathe

From the sugar mill towns of 'San Pedro de Macrois' and 'La Romana,' to fields all across the Dominican Republic, young, poor kids dream of someday playing major league baseball and bringing financial security to their families. The Dominican Republic has a passion for baseball far and above anywhere else.

From late October to January, when the sugar mills are slow, a baseball season is born in the Dominican Republic. It is the big leagues for Dominican ball players who dream of making it big. It's where their fantasies can come true-- to play well and to be seen by major league scouts. It is also a time when current major leaguers can come home and play in their winterball season.

Since the 50's when Ozzie Virgil made Dominican Republic baseball famous by playing in the major leagues, we have seen more and more players make the transition and do it well. The Alou brothers, Sammie Sosa, Manny Ramirez, Pedro Martinez, and more.

When the ten year war (1868-1878) in Cuba brought turmoil to the country, many Cubans fled their country and migrated to the Dominican Republic bringing with them the game called "Baseball" or "Beisbol. Dominicans were quick to learn the game and soon organized teams.

The national sport and passion of Dominican Republic is baseball or "Beisbol" as the Dominicans call it. No matter where you go on the island you will find a baseball stadium/ park, even in the poorest of towns. Today, more than one in six players in the American league is from Latin America, the majority of them coming from the towns located on the southeastern coast Dominican Republic

It's true that Latin American players hunger to excel in baseball. For them, baseball is a way off of the island. Their passion for baseball is boundless, and as was proven on sandlot after sandlot across America during the Negro League era, if there's a passion for the game, where there is a will there is a way.

What's happening inside the Black community, and what's happening inside the baseball organization are only two of the factors that have a bearing on the affinity of Blacks to baseball. Perhaps the most important issue is what's happening outside of the world of baseball to lure African Americans away from baseball.

Curve Balls From Alternative Sports

Over the years, the definition of excitement and fun has changed. As a result, two major external threats to baseball have loomed in importance: one is posed by alternative sports to baseball, and the other is posed by the draw of home-based entertainment.

Cars speeding and crashing against walls, the lone weekend cowboy in Las Vegas on a mechanical bull trying not to fall off, with a back drop of the roar of the crowd, gives the kind of "buzz" that comes close to emulating the thrill of staring into video games and having a simulated thrilling experience.

To captivate today's "video-reared and raised" young audience, sports action must either be thrilling, aggressive, or heart thumping. The stakes in the game for African Americans must be high. Arguably neither golf nor tennis would rise to the video heart-thumping test, but they don't have to because African Americans understand what's at stake for their heroes the Williams sisters and Tiger Woods. Their triumphs in the game are breaking new ground in heretofore White-dominated sports.

The opportunity to demonstrate individual mastery in a sport, whether real or simulated, is an important ingredient that must be present to captivate young people, especially young African Americans. The basketball dunk, the goal line dance, the NASCAR first place win, all have in common that defining moment when, as the young people say, "it's all about me."

"Yes, there is a team. Yes, my individual prowess helps the team to win, but there is no doubt about my superiority as a team member," are statements that echo the sentiments of today's Black youth.

Today, there is little appreciation for the African American athlete who is merely "also" on the team: that doesn't cut it. African Americans want to be winners and they want to win in style. If there is no opportunity in a given sport to shine, to stand out, and to express individual and unique style while breaking away from the pack, many won't be interested in that sport.

When Tiger Woods wins, he demonstrates his superiority over his White competitors and that sends chills up the spines of his Black followers. When he hosted his first championship in Washington, DC in the summer of 2007, there were more Blacks at Congressional Golf Club on that single day in the club's combined entire history. Why? Because Tiger Woods had risen to the challenge that is given to all Black athletes by other Blacks, which is to demonstrate individual athletic superiority against very high odds. Who would have thought that a poor Black boy would rise to become the greatest golf player of all times?

While the game of golf involves a great deal of technique, as does baseball, the difference is that the golf shot happens in an instant, in a single swing that is visible to the naked eye—either the player makes the hole or not. Importantly, a viewer can coordinate watching the game to tune into the moment when a particular hole is being played. The viewer wants to watch at that precise moment—and not on TIVO—to see if the hero makes the 18th hole; watching at that moment is almost as good as being there.

In both golf and tennis, television viewers are in charge. They can tune in at the critical moment to celebrate victory or to lament defeat. Knowing the outcome instantly is important. Basketball's slam dunk, football's goal line, soccer's goal line, the golf hole shot, the tennis net drop, all have one thing in common: It is a zero sum game, one does or does not prevail over the challenge in an instant. In terms of television viewership, in a busy world, the audience wants to engage in controlled program watching. Viewers don't want to watch the whole game. They just want to tune in for the "*hallelujah moment*" to scream, dance, and holler with friends at home.

Tiger Woods Becomes Nation's Favorite Sports Star as Michael Jordan Drops to Number Two for First Time in 13 Years
The Williams sisters top the list of favorite female sports stars

For the first time since 1993, an athlete, Tiger Woods has stepped up to claim the number one spot from Michael Jordan as the nation's favorite sports star. Venus Williams returns as the nation's favorite female sports star after a one-year absence, and sister Serena Williams is right behind her in the number two spot. These are the results of a Harris Poll conducted online by Harris Interactive® among a nationwide sample of 2,085 U.S. adults in May 2006.

Creativity, freedom, self-expression, instant reward, and high-pitched thrill are the draws that alternative sports hold. Not bound by rules, time or even a defined space, alternative sports emphasize performance and progression over winning or losing.

Recent studies of sports participation clearly indicate that sports and leisure preferences mirror an evolving society, reflecting not only explosive changes in the youth culture, but also the basic need for novelty and change.

Large gains in sports participation have come from new "extreme" sports, such as skateboarding, artificial wall climbing, wakeboarding, paintball, and snowboarding. That new action sports have gained ground at the expense of traditional American pastimes such as baseball, basketball, football is

undeniable. In the aggregate, team sports, including the trendier activities of soccer, lacrosse, and fast-pitch softball, continue to enlist a growing number of followers.

Despite the growth of alternative sports, baseball is holding its own so far. In fact, professional baseball has recently registered an all-time high attendance of over 100 million fans attending games at both the Major and Minor League levels. But baseball can't afford to rest on its laurels while other traditional and non-traditional sports are gaining ground. Information presented in Box 6 shows how other sports gained ground.

Box 6
The Harris Poll® #94 (December 27, 2005)
"Professional Football Continues to be the Nation's Favorite Sport Baseball is now a distant second in popularity followed by college football and auto racing"

Professional football continues to surge in popularity, as one-third (33%) of U.S. adults who follow at least one sport say it is their favorite sport. This is up three points from last year. Baseball slips slightly again this year, dropping to 14 percent, down one point from last year. Coming close on the heels of baseball is college football (13%) followed by auto racing (11%). While both of these have seen a rise in the past year, racing is up four points this year, most likely as a result of NASCAR's increasing popularity.

These are the results of a nationwide Harris Interactive® survey conducted online in December 2005 among 1,961 U.S. adults, of whom 1,402 follow at least one sport.

In the past 20 years, professional football and baseball have seen the most dramatic changes in popularity. Since 1985, professional football has risen nine points in popularity (from 24% to 33%), while baseball has dropped the same amount (23% to 14%). The next largest change in popularity is in auto racing, which has risen six points since 1985, from five to 11 percent. Men's tennis has seen a drop in popularity of four points in this same time period down to one percent from five percent in 1985.

Many competitor sports to baseball are competing for the African American dollar and for its talents and eyeballs. And though much has been made of the high cost associated with playing baseball and attending baseball games, African Americans have money to spend, and they spend it when and where they want to.

> "*The Buying Power of Black America*," which has been published annually for the past 12 years, is one of the most widely quoted sources of information on Black consumer spending. According to the report, Black households had $679 billion in earned income in 2004, an increase of 3.5% over the $656 earned in 2003. Among the products and services that showed the greatest one-year increase were sound systems (+127%), computer online services (+38%), sports and recreational equipment, among others.

The challenge for baseball is to figure out how to more effectively compete with other sports to win back African American fans. Doing so will depend upon a deeper understanding of today's African American culture and on crafting well-thought-out stakeholder driven strategies.

Kids, according to Nickelodeon's 2005 study of multicultural kids, have time to play outside, but many factors influence their choice of games to play.

In general, the majority of kids across ethnic groups find they have adequate time in their lives to satisfy their needs, obligations and wants.

US Multicultural Kids Study 2005

Have To's	Should Do's	Want To's
Go to school Study, do homework Keep bedroom clean Chores Personal hygiene	Help Mom/Dad Visit family Get exercise	Play outside Hang out with friends Watch TV Play video games Play on the computer Sleep late

Baseball must be seen as being fun again. Optimally, it would also be great if it could be seen as an uplifter of the race, as it was viewed during the Negro League Era. As William C. Rhoden wrote in "*Forty Million Dollar Slaves*:"

> …our cheering assumed a deeper meaning: we were cheering for our very survival. Black athletes became our psychological armour, markers of our progress, tangible proof of our worth, and evidence of our collective soul. Our athletes threw punches we couldn't throw, won races we couldn't run. Any competition or public showing involving an African American was seen as a test for us all; the job of the athlete was to represent the race. This was a heavy burden on one hand, but at the same time it represented a noble, timeworn responsibility. You always represented.

Courtesy of the National Baseball Hall of Fame Library, Cooperstown, NY

Vicarious and Virtual Thrills

In a chaotic, unpredictable, and increasingly dangerous world, sports begin to mimic reality, and it's not just sports. The pitch of everything has to be extremely high. Consider, for instance, cooking show host Emeril LaGasse. What is his tag line? It's "BAM," underscoring that even food programs have to have a "wow" factor.

Wham, bam, is how excitement is defined. It is the "decibel and danger" factor.

While the "decibel and danger" factor is perhaps the biggest draw for a competing sport today, it is nevertheless still possible to attract African American young and older audiences alike to cerebral quiet sports like golf and tennis, but under certain circumstances. In such cases, the attraction is the odds. The odds have to be stacked incredibly high against the probability that an African American player will excel in the sport, and when the player does, the whole Black community rallies around that player and the sport. It becomes another "see, I told you so moment."

One of the greatest "I told you so moments" for Blacks first came in baseball when famous Negro League player Satchel Paige played in a February 1936 tune-up against major league All-Stars before a sell out crowd in Oakland. "It was one of the greatest exhibitions of pitching witnessed in nearly a score of years," wrote White sportswriter Eddie Murphy. Paige struck out a dozen and allowed only three hits, one of them to New York Yankee great Joe DiMaggio, who later described Paige as the greatest pitcher he had ever faced. This was significant because one of White baseball's biggest stars and best hitters had hailed Satchel Paige as Black baseball's premier pitcher. It was the ultimate "I told you so moment."

Today, many such "I told you so moments" are experienced on television or the Internet.

Competing with the virtual world of thrill is no joke; it's even harder than competing against "real world" sports alternatives.

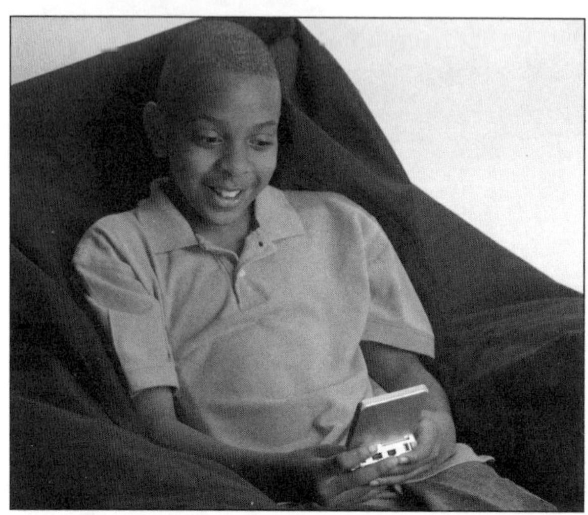

It's common knowledge, for instance, that the *EASports* franchise controls the sports video game industry. A quick search of its online store as of January 2008 reveals that while there is only one video game for baseball, on a Playstation[2] platform, there are over 28 for football on multiple platforms, and 12 for basketball on multiple platforms. These days, children are acquainted with sports first in the house before they ever get out onto any field.

At the end of the 1950s, seven of eight U.S. homes (87%) had a TV set and personal computers. Video game consoles had not been invented. As the century came to a close, 99% of children 2- to 18-years-old lived in homes with a TV set (60% lived with three or more TVs, and over half had a TV in their bedroom), 70% had video game consoles, and 69% lived in homes with a personal computer (Roberts, Foehr, Rideout & Brodie, 1999; also see Roberts & Foehr, 2004).

Television and the Internet are not the only culprits in stealing away the attention of the Black community from baseball; all forms of media are to blame. The Kaiser Family Foundation studied the impact of the media on the lives of youth. Findings from its study, "*Generation M: Media in the Lives of 8-18 Year-olds*" (Roberts, Foehr, & Rideout, 2005), demonstrate that baseball must fit into the lives of kids, which isn't easy to do.

Box 7
Time Spent With Media and Selected Non-Media Activities In a Typical Day

Activity	Time
Watching TV	3:04
Hanging Out With Parents	2:17
Hanging Out With Friends	2:16
Listening to Music	1:44
Exercising, sports	1:25
Watching Movies, videos	1:11
Using a computer	1:02
Pursuing Hobbies, clubs, Etc.	1:00
Talking on the Phone	0:53
Doing Homework	0:50
Playing Video Games	0:49
Reading	0:43
Working on a job	0:35
Doing Chores	0:32

Source: Kaiser Foundation's *Generation M: Media in the Lives of 8-18 Year-olds* (2005)

In Table 2, the Kaiser study also shows that the amount of time spent on the computer is also a significant factor in how youth spend their time.

Table 2: Average Time Spent on the Computer

Race	Average time on computer	Went online from school Yesterday	Went online from home	Went online from somewhere else	Go online from home most often
White	1:02	27%	54%	14%	22%
Black	0:52	30%	37%	24%	34%
Hispanic	0:54	32%	40%	13%	30%

Source: Kaiser Foundation's *Generation M: Media in the Lives of 8-18 Year-olds* (2005)

Given the amount of time young kids are spending on the Internet, it's not surprising that a number of young African American little leaguers from Baltimore have suggested that the coolest thing to them is not sports but the Internet:

> "The Internet is cool because we can look up things. It helps us do homework, and we can play games and chat with friends online."

Before kids can get to the baseball field, they have to get out of the house and away from video games.

In an era of bold glaring colors, explosive sounds, lights, cameras, and action, kids grow up watching and being influenced by the boldness of video games. Consequently, they don't understand or appreciate subtlety. They need for the technique of the games they play to be aggressive and obvious, not hidden. The problem with baseball to this generation is that its greatness—its skillful strategy—is hidden in plain view. You can see the impact of skill applied, but not its actual application, which happens in the blink of an eye.

Kids that have grown up watching video games have become accustomed to their images being in a "parallel universe" form. They are "into" Avatars, not real people. Similarly, they are "into" simulated games, not real ones.

It is interesting that in this year's MTV (2007) awards a new award category was introduced for the best "Internet-based video" song. A British group won the award, and performed live for the first time what is depicted on their video clip. Their performance consisted of three or four guys in very loud clashing, multiple colored mismatched outfits on skateboards, jumping on and off moving conveyor belts at different times. While music was playing, it was not the focus. The real focus was the visual imagery being created. The music was merely background noise. It was an "in your face" music video. No subtlety there; the video endeavored to and succeeded in capturing as much sensory perception as possible and holding it captive for as long as possible.

As if a firecracker going off at the fourth of July, the video had all of the colors of the rainbow at once with sound blaring at the loudest decibels possible, just short of deafening the eardrums.

This is the age we are living in. One strike against America's pastime is the sheer pace and "pitch" of today's society.

There is no question that some young African Americans think baseball is boring. They are the ones that prefer "in your face" victories. When a basketball player dunks a ball, it's an "in your face" show of superior talent. When a football player dances at the goal line, it is an "in your face" boastful, playful, exclamation point to the victory. Importantly, they present a standout moment for the individual in the game.

The challenge baseball faces is how to communicate its unique brand of fun to video-reared youth and adults. The audience needs help in understanding how to see that which is not obvious.

The foregoing presents a brief glimpse of some of the issues that have a bearing on the distancing of African Americans from baseball, but there's more to the story.

There's one thing about a perfect storm, it refers to the simultaneous occurrence of events which, taken individually, would be far less powerful than the result of them combined. This is the case for Blacks and baseball. The factors that have combined to

diminish the interest and participation of African Americans in baseball have created the perfect storm.

This book is about getting to the rainbow, however.

We will know when we have gotten there when African American youths once again consider it "cool" to play baseball.

Understanding how and why something gets to be considered cool is an important issue and a prerequisite for developing effective marketing and "reach in" campaigns to win back the African American audience. Accordingly, the next chapter, *Decoding Cool: How To Love Baseball From The Inside Out*, takes a deeper look into the issue.

Decoding *Cool*: Loving Baseball From The Inside Out

Decoding *Cool*: Loving Baseball From The Inside Out

"Baseball is not cool; it's not in the soul of Black folk these days."

This is one commonly cited explanation of the declining participation of African Americans in baseball, but the question is: W*hy and how* does anything get to be designated as cool?

If you want to know what cool is, ask some kids. Their responses underescore that "cool" is often defined in terms of what they think about their heroes. The following composite view captures the sentiments of young people from Baltimore who were interviewed for this book.

> "My hero is like me. My hero is doing something that I could do if given a chance because it is fundamentally within me to be able to do it. My hero makes everyone else envious of the special abilities that are associated with being able to do it. My hero is winning at something that everyone 'in my world' is focused on; therefore, my hero is cool." Sadly, some claim: "I have no heroes. My life is the Internet." While others claim, "Hip-Hop is the essence of cool and everything we consider to be cool must be channeled through the Hip-Hop prism."

The foregoing imparts a wealth of information about how young people feel. A closer look at what's behind these sentiments helps provide deeper insights into their meaning.

"My Hero Is Like Me"— Who Am I?

> "I am a Black inner city boy. Our household income is less than $21,000, which is similar to that of my other friends. Like them, my mother raised me with the assistance of my grandmother; I see my father infrequently. I grew up in Baltimore, which is one of ten American cities with a population of over 250,000. As of 2005, it had one of the lowest medium incomes of less than $32,500. The population is over 50 percent African American, the poverty rate is over 20 percent. The unemployment rate is over 7 percent. To be cool and to fit in with my peers, I recently got some tattoos, a gold tooth, and I shaved off all of my hair. I have dark skin and am proud of it."

> There are 21 million people residing in the inner cities of America. Compared to residents living in the surrounding metropolitan areas, inner city residents today are more likely to be of color (80 percent compared to 31 percent in the nation), foreign-born (23 percent compared to 11 percent in the U.S.), younger (42 percent under 25 years old compared to 35 percent), and have larger households (2.9 members compared to 2.1 members). Inner cities are more economically disadvantaged; unemployment is three times the level of the rest of the MSAs, college attainment lags significantly behind MSA rates, and inner city median household incomes are less than half those of surrounding areas.

My belief that "my hero is like me" is based on two things: That which is known, and that which is assumed based on the appearance of things.

During the Negro League era in baseball, Black heroes were known. They lived in the community, and their lives were an open book. There weren't many secrets about Josh Gibson, Satchel Paige, Cool Papa Bell, and Jackie Robinson, for instance. Even the casual Black observer knew what these heroes did on and off the field. One only had to pick up the weekly *Jet Magazine*, *Ebony Magazine*, the *Chicago Defender*, or the *Pittsburgh Courier*. Their lives were shared in the Black community of which they were an integral part.

By contrast, today, a lot of assumptions are made. The Black professional baseball player, given the rigors associated with mastering the game at the highest levels, are not in the community—they go off to camps, they play long seasons, they are engaged in intensive life-long-out-of-the-community training, and consequently, they are not known in the community.

June 18, 2004

WORLD NEWS

Ethnic Diversity
Doesn't Blend
In Kids' Lives

By MIRIAM JORDAN
Staff Reporter of THE WALL STREET JOURNAL
June 18, 2004; Page B1

Despite sharing a pop culture infused with a variety of ethnic influences, the most ethnically diverse generation of American kids ever is growing up in predominantly segregated environments.

That's the main conclusion of a new comparative study to be released by **Viacom** Inc.'s Nickelodeon, which taps into the lifestyle, attitudes and mind-sets of African-American, Asian, Hispanic and white children between the ages of six and 14. The study, by Viacom's Network and Cultural Access Group, a Los Angeles-based research firm, found that children growing up in the U.S. lead similar lives independent of their ethnicity: They are consumers of the Internet, radio and television. They value their family most -- their hero tends to be a parent, not a celebrity. Individually, they like the way they look.

Conversely, Blacks know a lot about Allen Iverson and Michael Jordan. What they know is that these heroes are "like them." They hail from similar backgrounds, and they wear the symbols of the "hood." In a word, they are "cool."

Blacks kids are "into" sports and sports teams, according to Nickelodeon's 2005 study on multicultural kids, but the trick is to focus their gaze on baseball.

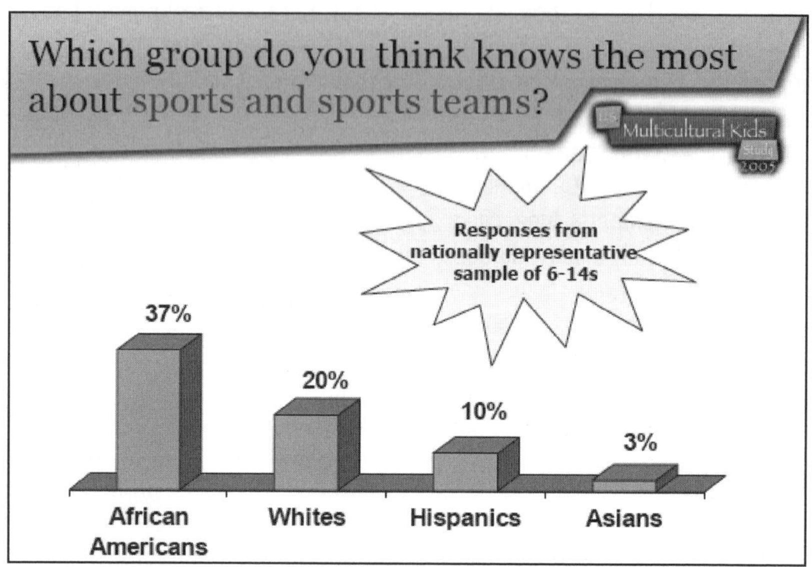

Cool and authentic are two inextricably linked concepts, and the desire to be cool, above all else, is a cultural value.

Values, attitudes, beliefs, mindsets, central tendencies, and orientations, are what culture is all about.

Confidence, grace, and the economy of movement and speech are its form, and its *raison d'etre* is the need for recognition.

What is vital to cool is authenticity—a whiff of falseness or visible exertion chases it away.

Culture and authenticity are inextricably linked. Culture is emotionally held and incorporates community-specific ideas about what is true, good, beautiful, and efficient. To be "cultural," those ideas about truth, goodness, beauty, and efficiency must be socially transmitted. Culture, thus, is what one knows to be effective in one's own environment; it is transmitted by family and peers, and is increasingly influenced by the media.

Culture embraces a value system of deeply ingrained assumptions, generalizations, pictures and images that influence how we understand the world and how we take action.

When African Americans embraced baseball in the late nineteenth century and well into the first half of the twentieth century, assimilation was an important cultural value. Today, as many African American urban youths wear they their hats on backwards, their pants half way on, and speak in their own special code language, the last thing they want to do is to fit in. For them the culture of "dis-assimilation" is the order of the day. In other words, "*it ain't cool to fit it.*"

> Though its star has faded in recent decades, baseball has historically played a dominant role in America's national imagination and lexicon. Baseball was not only a major topic of everyday conversation; it influenced the way we talked. Language has always had multiple dialects, but in America, from about the 1880s to the end of the 1950s, the dominant metaphor was baseball.

According to Harris pollsters, African-Americans are the least likely group to claim baseball as their favorite sport. Ironically, one explanation for this falling interest is that Major League Baseball so adeptly markets the game's connection to America's history. "Nostalgia for the American past doesn't sell well to the African-American community.

Gradually, as the disconnection of millions of African American youths from the mainstream has widened, the focus among many inner city African American youths has shifted from how to assimilate to how to express anti-authoritarianism, anti-establishment, and individualism. In the process, baseball has been all but struck out of the hearts, minds, and aspirations of young African American males, as it is no longer resonates as cool.

Viacom's Nickelodeon's study of Black "tweens" provides further insights into how they feel:

> Black tweens, ages nine to 14, were significantly more likely than others the same age to believe that they make people laugh, that peers pay attention when they talk, and that others try to be like them. White girls are less happy with their looks. Significantly, more white girls -- 44% compared with 16% of Asians and 28% of African-Americans -- reported they have tried to lose weight.
>
> Roughly two-thirds of Hispanic families, more than any other group, speak more than one language at home. That is a source of pride, not shame. The study found that Hispanic children are most likely to celebrate their culture, a likely reflection of their recognition that the Latino community is growing in numbers and influence. "What do I love most about being Latina? The food! Everybody loves our food," declared one 10-year-old girl.
>
> "There is a cultural comfort level when you're surrounded by people just like you," says Wanla Cheng, president of Asian Link Consulting Group in New York. Indeed, black children who live in mainly black communities reported feeling more secure than African-American children who live in ethnically mixed environments.
>
> It is possible to deduce from the study that the U.S. remains generations away from abandoning old prejudices and fully embracing diversity. But virtually none of the children used skin color, hair type or accent when told to describe differences between themselves and kids of other ethnicities.

Cool is possibly the most important force in the life of African American males in America today. What is cool exactly? In fact, it is not exact. Because of the varied and changing connotations of cool, as well as its subjective nature, the word has no single meaning. It entails, however, an aesthetic of attitude, behavior, comportment, appearance, and style, and is associated with composure and self-control. It is often used as an expression of admiration or approval. It is the latter portion of the definition that has long term implications for baseball.

Understanding the Culture of Cool

Marlene Kim Connor connects cool and the post-war African-American experience in her book, *What is Cool?: Understanding Black Manhood in America*. Connor suggests that "cool is the silent and knowing rejection of racist oppression and a self-dignified expression of masculinity developed by Black men denied mainstream expressions of manhood."

Duke University Professor Mark Anthony Neal explains, "During slavery, the only thing Black people could claim as their own was their style. What else could they uniquely bring to the world?" Cool was all that they had.

Neal explains that expressing cool during slavery times was tricky because putting a personal stamp on a slave's dangerously circumscribed world showed a display of insubordination and rebelllion that was severely punishable. Therefore, Neal suggests, "Black men learned to master the art of combining the hidden with the flamboyant."

Interestingly, this is an art that has its roots in feudal times. Cool had a purpose. It was anchored in rebellion and social consciousness. Its linguistic art form is *double entendre*, something that has two meanings. It's art is to openly express a word that when stated with one tone means one thing, but when stated in another tone means another thing. The Mandarin Chinese language, for instance, has four tones, which means that there are four opportunities to mask the true meaning of what is being said.

The art of *double entredre* has also been mastered in the Ethiopian languages over the millenia. An interesting book written about it is entitled "*Wax and Gold*." The cool trick that the Ethiopians have mastered is the use of the word that can to the enlightened mean something other than the obvious. For instance, the word choice might be "wax," but to deeply understand the meaning of what is being conveyed by the word "wax," one has to look deeper to perceive its "true" meaning to find the "gold" in the wax.

Cool is like that. One has to be enlightened to understand its true meaning.

Cool, though an amorphous quality—more mystique than material—is a pervasive element in urban Black male culture. "It helps Black men counter stress caused by social oppression, rejection and racism," according to Majors and Billson (1992). It also furnishes Black males with a sense of control, strength, confidence and stability and helps them deal with the closed doors and negative messages of the "generalized

other." As University of Pennsylvania music historian Guthrie Ramsey notes, "cool is about control over something, whether it is the basketball court, a musical instrument or just your wardrobe."

The identity of African Americans is more steeped in the necessity of appearing cool, and in the expectation that they institictively bring coolness to the table more than any other group. That expectation is fueled by the outsize influence of African Americans on music, language, culture, and sports. For this reason, if African Americans no longer consider it cool to play baseball, it's a sentiment that could have a growing ripple effect throughout the society. Consider, for instance, that "brotherhood" cool took fashion's most boring garment, the basic white tee, inflated it, tossed it over baggy jeans, and the look was copied from Tulsa to Tokyo. Black people are influential in defining the meaning and expressions of cool. Nickelodeon's 2005 study of multicultural kids, for instance, underscores the connection between Black kids and cool fashions.

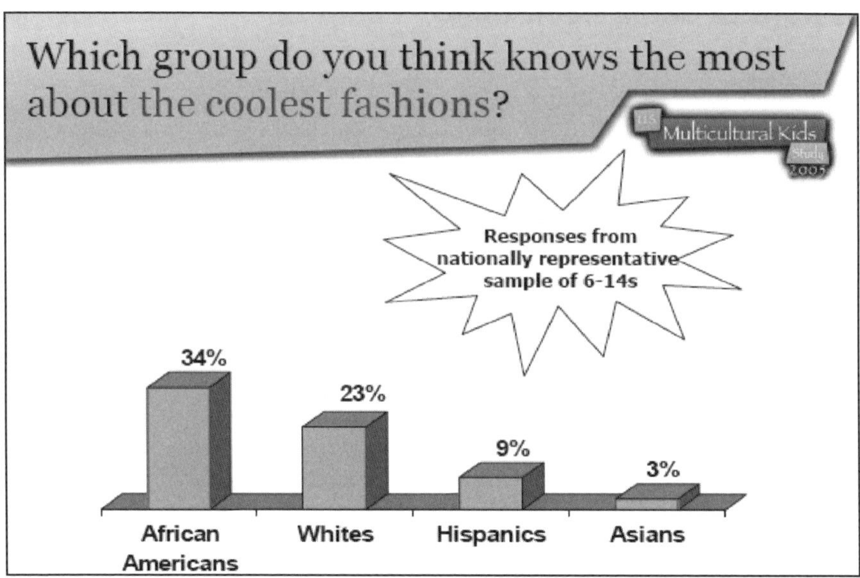

Cool is being on the cutting edge, whether it's politically, musically, or in sports. In this context, the emotional or cool barrier in reconnecting African Americans to baseball is the need to define a new cutting edge in baseball, and new ways for African Americans to express stand-out individualism in the game.

> "Part of the energy that makes cool is from the novelty of its newness, the fuel of creativity as people discover it, interact, and add to it. But somewhere at the root of the movement is need. There is something missing, a new thing comes along and addresses that need, and a movement arises..."

When rules were institutionalized in baseball, according to William C. Rhoden, to regulate Black athletic styles and to minimize the incidences of Black athletes acting as "hot dogs" and "showboats," some of the pizazz was also taken away.

Being able to express "cool" in every walk of life, including sports, is vitally important to young African American males. And while media and academics have on occasion demonized "cool" aspects of African American culture, at the same time, through their sustained fascination with Blacks as exotic others, many throughout the society have appropriated aspects of "cool pose" into the broader popular culture.

Interestingly, Viacom's Nickelodeon's 2005 study of multicultural kids found that African American children had the most positive sense of self, being more likely than any other racial group to see themselves as influential.

Social marketers and advertisers have caught on to the importance of "cool" in marketing. They realize that marketing sucessfully to youth is dependant upon being able to claim their products are cool. Especially for Black urban youth, whether marketing an article of clothing, music, or a sport, it's "gotta be cool."

"My Hero Is Doing Something I Could Do"

> "After school I go to my neighborhood basketball court to practice my dunk shot. My friends join me and sometimes we have a contest and bet against each other. Just about everybody can play, though we clearly have our share of 'phenoms.' I may not be so tall, but, hey, neither is Allen Iverson, and I can slam dunk with the best of them—*and that is cool*."

Marlon Brando said it best in the film *On the Waterfront*, "I cudda been a contenda."

To feel an inch away from greatness is a powerful motivator and draw. The fact is, many young Black people feel that they are just an inch away from being great basketball "phenoms" themselves. They think *if only they could be discovered*, or, if not themselves exactly, at least they have a neighbor, a "home boy," who has made it. This is the perception. The reality of how many Blacks make it to the NBA is another thing altogether.

The NCAA provides a reality check on the chances of making it in basketball, which shows that such chances are even slimmer than in baseball. Table 3 shows that as of 2007, the NCAA estimates of the probability of competing in athletics beyond high school for different sports.

Table 3: NCAA Estimated Probability of Competing in Athletics Beyond the High School Interscholastic Level						
Student Athletes	Men's Basketball	Women's Basketball	Football	Baseball	Men's Ice Hockey	Men's Soccer
Percent High School to Professional	**0.03%**	**0.02%**	**0.08%**	**0.45%**	**0.32%**	**0.07%**
Percent High School to NCAA	**3.0%**	**3.3%**	**5.7%**	**6.1%**	**11.0%**	**5.5%**
Percent NCAA to Professional	**1.2%**	**1.0%**	**1.8%**	**9.4%**	**3.7%**	**1.7%**
Percent High School to Professional	**0.03%**	**0.02%**	**0.08%**	**0.45%**	**0.32%**	**0.07%**

When a young Black man thinks that his hero is doing something that he himself could also possibly do, an operational definition of "self" is in play. Accordingly, "if my home boy makes it to the NBA, it's almost as if it were me." The next best thing to actually being the lucky one is to be able to say I grew up with LeBron or Allen and won some shots against them when we were playing on the corner in the "hood." Proximity to fame and greatness earns one lifelong street "cred" (credibility).

Baseball's development pipeline is long and takes Black players out of the "hood," if they were ever in it in the first place. Chances are, however, that today's Black baseball player didn't emerge from the "hood," but rather from the suburbs far and away from the maddening crowd.

Today, who knows Black famous baseball players? Who has a stake in them and who gets any street "cred" from any prior associations with them?

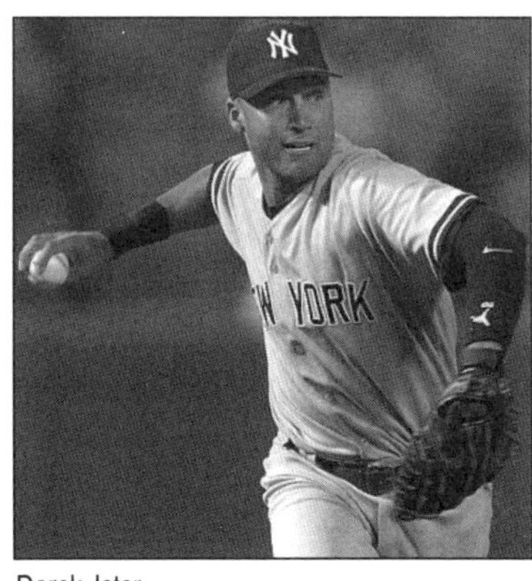

Derek Jeter

Is Derek Jeter like me, a typical inner city Black boy? Is Barry Bonds, whose father was a famous player, like me? Can I easily place myself in their shoes; could I honestly look at them and say to myself that "it cudda been me?" My father didn't raise me like their fathers raised them, and I have only a little league education in baseball. Frankly, I am down right afraid of the ball coming at my face at over 100 mph.

Basketball is a different story, however. Growing steadily since first introduced in 1892, it was originally a game played dominantly by Whites, but today, it's as if African Americans invented it.

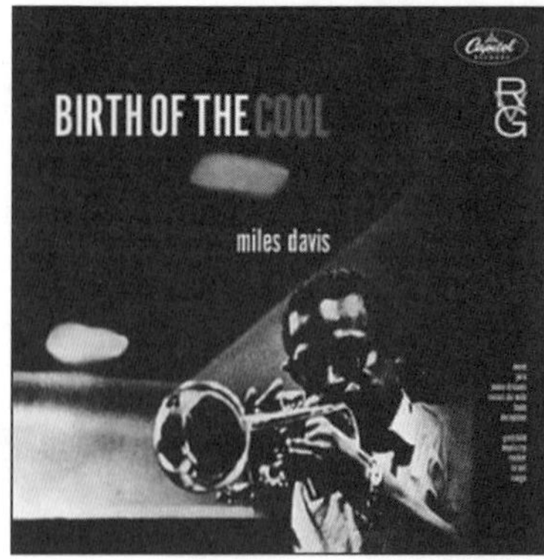

Basketball has become a reflection of Black culture, much in the form of how jazz and blues music have represented Black culture in the American past. Especially for inner city Blacks, basketball has become one of the most expressive modes of cultural expression, much like music, literature, and fashion. It has become a ritual of expression.

Some argue that for many inner city Blacks, basketball has become much more than a game: It has become a way of ritualizing racial achievement against social barriers to cultural performance.

The game played on the street is about more than winning and losing. It has become one of the greatest foundations of culture Blacks have, something they will fight for and something at which they will fight to be the best. Many coaches believe that it is the desire of inner city Black players that separates them from White players.

William Ellerbee, a basketball coach at Simon Gratz High School in Philadelphia, a national powerhouse in basketball, agrees with this hypothesis. He says: "Suburban kids tend to play for the fun of it ... but inner city kids look at basketball as a matter of life and death." The White basketball player often is simply not as hungry as the Black athlete; therefore, Black players often come out on top.

"It is this "life-or-death" style that defines what the game of basketball is known as today—"the Black brand of basketball." The Black aesthetic has not only changed basketball, it has been the catalytic force behind the sport's extraordinary growth in popularity and profitability. African-American inner city culture has brought a much more graceful, speed-oriented, physical, all-around skill aspect to basketball. Basketball is synonymous with cultural identity and cool.

In "*The Welcome Theory: An Explanation for the Decreasing Number of African Americans in Baseball* (2004)," Assistant Professor, David C. Ogden, School of Communication, University of Nebraska at Omaha, put forward an important perspective on explaining why African Americans are gravitating more towards basketball. Odgen explains:

> Feelings of belonging in a sports venue are, in and of themselves, powerful influences on self-identity in sport. Those who feel they do belong have acquired such an outlook because of exposure to and/or experience with those locales (Tarlgen, 2004). But for such a personal history to develop, individuals need access to such locales. Giddens' discussion (1979) ofstructuration theory can be instructive in how such access helps to form identity and subsequently

identification. An individual's resources and positioning within a particular set of social structures dictates how that person carries out social routines and activities. Those routines and activities, repeated often enough and endorsed by the subculture and significant others, provide what Giddens (1984) calls "ontological security," or a feeling of well being or comfort within a social structure. So, while interpersonal contacts and communication give initial direction to identity formation, ongoing routines (the nature of which are dictated by positioning within a social structure) serve to reinforce and somewhat stabilize behaviors. As applied to sports, this means that early and frequent exposure to an athletic activity can be instrumental in developing identification with that activity. But the individual's position within a social structure, which would include access to facilities and expertise and involvement by the subculture, will dictate whether that identification is sustained.

"My Heroes Make Everyone Envious Of The Special Abilities They Possess"

"Black people have exceptional athletic natural prowess."

> "Now, this is true, my truth, me, a little Black inner city boy. The sky is the limit for Blacks athletically. Imagine, we haven't won any medals for swimming, but we know if we put our minds to it, we could out swim anybody. It's like what we did with tennis. When we were ready to take it over, we conjured up the Williams sisters. When we were ready to take over golf, we conjured up Tiger Woods. The Black fathers of the Williams sisters and Tiger Woods seem familiar; if the Williams sisters and Tiger Woods can prevail as victors against all odds, so can we poor inner city Blacks—*now that is cool!*" "We have already shown the world that we could master baseball—been there, done that! Where's the new frontier?"

The subject of race is awkward—as anyone covering the early caucuses for the upcoming 2008 U.S. Presidential elections can attest. For instance, the code word referring to the "problem" of Barack Obama's race is "electability." No one wants to directly state that they believe that Barack Obama can't win merely because the color of his skin. Similarly, in the case of sports, there are many code words to mask the subject of race, but race is a factor and an issue that's never far from anyone's mind.

Addressing the subject head on, Jon Entine, a sportscaster from Philadelphia, provides the following insights on how the subject of race plays out in the minds of many:

> So here is what many of us assume about Allen Iverson: For starters, he owes his natural ability to the fact that he's black. Blacks can jump

> higher and dribble better than "most" whites, which is why 85 percent of the NBA is African-American. And for Iverson and other inner-city or rural blacks, basketball is seen as one of the only ways out of poverty. Isiah Thomas, the All-Star guard from the Detroit Pistons, used to say that he was sick of all the fawning over Larry Bird's brainy, hardworking play while he himself was praised for being so "naturally" athletic. "When whites perform well, it's due to [their] thinking and work habit," he commented. "It's not the case for blacks. All we do is run and jump. We never practice or give a thought to how we play. It's like I came dribbling out of my mother's womb."
>
> Many of us, white and black, don't say these things—especially if we're network sportscasters—but we certainly think them. We think them of Iverson, who escaped the inner city, as well as of Kobe Bryant, who grew up in affluent Lower Merion. "The growing black domination of the most popular American sports is twisted and offered a 'proof' that 'physically superior' blacks are less intelligent than whites," asserts Harry Edwards, a sociologist at the University of California at Berkely.

Entine acknowledges that race is an awkward topic, one that's difficult to discuss without drawing charges of racism. However, he suggests that the subject is provoking renewed interest for noble reasons. "The conventional wisdom of the past 30 years—that race is irrelevant to everything—is being overturned. The remarkable findings of the *Human Genome Project* are showing more ways in which our race affects our lives, from our susceptibility to certain diseases to our athletic abilities. Cultural stereotypes and socioeconomic conditions actually play far less of a role than they used to in determining who excels in particular sports. Indeed, athletics may have become the first true meritocracy in American life—and Blacks have risen to the top because they really are genetically better suited for running and jumping and the key skills required to play certain sports at the highest level."

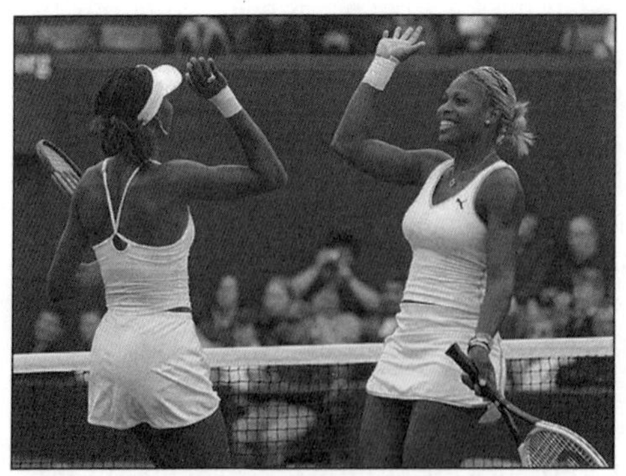

Many African Americans buy into the notion that they are athletically superior, especially African American youth, and when African American sports stars like the Williams sisters and Tiger Woods emerge as victors in sports that are not traditionally associated with Blacks, there are "high fives" all around the Black community.

The victories of the Williams sisters are particularly meaningful in the African American community because the sisters are not racially ambiguous and they are not from the suburbs; they are 100 percent pure, regular Black people with extraordinary athletic prowess, and they have succeeded against all odds—*now that is cool.*

A look at some of the companies that have signed Venus and Serena Williams to endorse their products and their reported annual income:

VENUS

Company	Product	Value
Reebok	Shoe, apparel	$8 million
Avon	Cosmetics	$1 million-plus*
Wrigley	Chewing gum	$1.1 million-plus
McDonald's	Fast food	$1 million-plus
Wilson's Leather	Clothing	$250,000-plus (sales based)

SERENA

Company	Product	Value
Puma	Shoe, apparel	$2.5 million-plus
Avon	Cosmetics	$1 million-plus*
Wrigley	Chewing gum	$1.1 million-plus
McDonald's	Fast food	$1 million-plus
Unilever	Close-Up toothpaste	$500,000*

* *Source: Los Angeles Times*

Outside observers may mistakenly assume that African American hero worship is simply about money and endorsements. Yes, these things matter and are associated with the outcome of being cool, but they are insufficient in making something cool.

Derek Jeter, a current top rated African American baseball player, is in the top ten moneymakers among all athletes, yet his name doesn't roll off the lips of inner city Black youths, and he is seldom cited as an example of a cool athlete. By contrast, ask any young Black urban youth who Shaquille O'Neal, Kobe Bryant, or LeBron James is and they will cite chapter and verse about their accomplishments.

Here's the subtle point: The embrace of the hero happens *organically* when the hero emerges directly from the "hood." When someone like LeBron James goes immediately to the NBA from high school, he is still young enough that a lot of people in the "hood" know him; the trail he left behind hasn't gone cold. There is still plenty of "barber shop" talk about him in the "hood." By contrast, Barry Bonds has been playing so long his trail among people in the "hood" has gone cold—few directly know him. Blacks know about him, but they don't identify with him. He may have blazed a trail, but few want to go down that road.

If a hero is *inorganic* (imposed on the society through media exposure), the marketing of that hero has to be intense. As many of today's African American baseball stars didn't emerge from the "hood," intense marketing programs are required to promote them to the Black community. Derek Jeter doesn't have a trail in the "hood," and he isn't identified physically as being African American, whereas many Hispanic players appear to be African American to the naked eye, such as Miguel Tejada, they also lack a trail in the "hood," and no one in "the hood" has a stake in their victories.

There are two strikes against baseball in terms of connecting with urban youth. The first is that the MLB doesn't market individual heroes; the other issue, which is equally important, is that many teams are considered losers, and have been on a losing steak for so long that there's hardly any hope for fans to hold onto. Take the Baltimore Orioles as an example. As of 2006, they experienced nine straight losing seasons and haven't won a world championship since 1983, and *"that's not cool."*

Things have gotten so bad that some Baltimore fans have suggested that the team should be sold to a new owner who can help the team win. In response, Orioles owner Peter Angelos sat down with PressBox publisher Stan "the Fan" Charles in September 2006 to answer the fan's questions have after the Orioles ninth straight losing season.

According to the *"2007 Fortune 50: Sports' Highest Paid Athletes,"* half the list is made up of NBA players, while only 12 baseball players and five football players made the cut. There were three NASCAR drivers and one woman, golfer Michelle Wie. Here is how the top 10 shook out:

1. Tiger Woods,
   golf, $111,941,827
2. Oscar De La Hoya,
   boxing, $55,000,000
3. Phil Mickelson,
   golf, $51,256,505
4. Shaquille O'Neal,
   NBA, $35,000,000
5. Kobe Bryant,
   NBA, $33,718,750
6. LeBron James,
   NBA, $30,828,089
7. Kevin Garnett,
   NBA, $29,000,000
8. Derek Jeter,
   MLB, $29,000,000
9. Alex Rodriguez,
   MLB, $28,000,000
10. Dale Ernhardt, Jr.
   auto racing, $27,111,735

Miguel Tejada

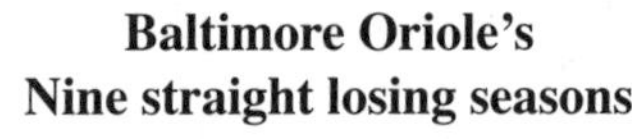

Baltimore Oriole's
Nine straight losing seasons

	Record	GB	Finish
2006	63-82	25.5	4th
2005	74-88	21	4th
2004	78-84	23	3rd
2003	71-91	30	4th
2002	67-95	36.5	4th
2001	63-98	32.5	4th
2000	74-88	13	4th
1999	78-84	20	4th
1998	79-83	35	4th

Stan "The Fan:" When you took over the team in 1993, you hit on the coattails of almost a perfect confluence of events. You had the new stadium, you had tremendous fan support built in and you had no NFL team here. All of those things are a little different now. There is an NFL team that has established some roots here; the stadium, while still fantastic, is not a novelty for the fans here in the area; and the team is coming off a run of nine consecutive losing seasons. How do you think you can turn that around to the point of people caring about the Orioles again, the way they used to?

Angelos: Well, the presence of the football team obviously results in some fans shifting loyalty from baseball, which is all they had, to the football schedule, which has great appeal. So we understood that was going to happen.

[In] the 12-13-year period you are talking about, many things have happened during that time, along with football coming back, which is fine. If the public wants [football], they ought to have access to it. If they want their own team, it's an old tradition here in Maryland. In fact, football got its real start here in Baltimore. Certainly, if the Baltimore metro area and the state of Maryland want a team, they ought to have it, and they do have it.

The World Series is the championship series of Major League Baseball and the culmination of the sport's postseason each October. It is played between the American League and National League, which currently includes 29 clubs based in the United States and 1 club from Canada. The modern World Series has been an annual event since 1903, with the exceptions of 1904 and 1994. The World Series championship is determined through a best-of-seven playoff. The New York Yankees, of the American League, have played in 39 of the 103 Series through 2007 and have won 26 World Series championships, which is far more than any other Major League franchise. For the National League, the Los Angeles Dodgers have appeared in the series the most at 18 times, but has only won the series 6 times. The St. Louis Cardinals have represented the National League 17 times and have won 10 championships, which is the most for any National League team. The Cardinals also hold a 3 Series to 2 edge against the Yankees in Series play, the only one of the "classic eight" National League teams to lead the Yankees overall.

[Regarding a new baseball team in Washington, DC]:

The presence of another team close to us is a problem. I do think that a baseball team in the nation's capital is positive for MLB. [By] not having a team for all those years, something was sort of missing for

MLB. Those who are great fans of baseball say that it's our national pastime. And there is a lot of truth in that. It's great tradition and having a team in Washington is a good thing.

We were concerned it would cause us severe economic problems . . . it already has caused us a certain loss of fan support. And we have lost fan support from the losing seasons. But we think we can restore that portion by way of investing more dollars in the club. We have a very low average ticket price. The Boston Red Sox tickets are over $45, ours $22. When [Fenway Park is] filled with 35,000 at $45 per and we are filled with 46,000 at $22, at the end of the day when the money is counted, that money is what ultimately determines how much one has [available] to spend on players. They are so far ahead of us, I can't do it in my head without writing on paper, but I would simplify it by saying in order for us to match what they take in [during a game] where they have a sell-out at 35,000 at $45 dollars [a ticket], we would have to have a ballpark that would hold 70,000 and sell that park out. They are doing this day in and day out. And they are selling out and have a rabid fan base. [The] strongest baseball fans are, I think, the Boston fans. And they went 80 years and didn't win a damned thing but they were supported and they are fortunate to have that kind of fan base. Our problem has been [an inability] to generate the kind of revenue that is needed to compete in the AL [American League] East.

Compounding the woes of the Orioles, one of its recent former star players, Miguel Tejada, was named in the "Mitchell Report" as one of the 88 MLB players who are alleged to have used steroids or drugs—*and that's not cool.*

The accusation against Miguel Tejada is particularly unfortunate because many young African Americans, especially in Baltimore, looked up to him, and considered him to be a role model as a "Black" player.

> The Report to the Commissioner of Baseball of an Independent Investigation into the Illegal Use of Steroids and Other Performance Enhancing Substances by Players in Major League Baseball, known as the "Mitchell Report", is the result of former United State Senator George J. Mitchell's investigation into the use of anabolic steroids and human growth hormone in Major League Baseball (MLB). The 409-page report, released on December 13, 2007, covers the history of the use of illegal performance-enhacing substances by players and the effectiveness of the MLB drug testing program. Mitchell also advances certain recommendations regarding the handling of past illegal drug use and future prevention practices. The report names 88 Major League Baseball players who are alleged to have used steroids or drugs.

What takes "em" out to the ball game? Hero worship takes 'em" out to the ball game, and the converse is also true.

In 2004, Philadelphia-based Journalist Mark Reynolds wrote an insightful article about Black youth and hero worship. In the summary below, he underscores that what sports heroes do—on and off the field— matters.

> For all of his achievements on the basketball court, the most famous thing Charles Barkley ever did during his playing days may have been a TV commercial. It was a stark, black-and-white spot for Nike in which he announced, "I am not a role model." Just because he could dunk a basketball, he soberly proclaimed, didn't mean that he could raise his audience's kids. The ad, which made ESPN's list of top 25 sports commercials, generated a lot of discussion about the role of star athletes, especially black ones, in the society at-large. What do these young, strapping millionaires owe their fans and their communities? What is their responsibility to boys who spend hours in playgrounds and parks practicing their moves, hoping to join their exalted ranks one day? Should these kids look up to athletes more than their teachers, more than their preachers, more than their parents?
>
> ...Years later, ...I got jolted back to my childhood for a moment, and I was reminded that the answer to Barkley's gauntlet isn't quite so cut-and-dried. At that very moment, on my TV screen, Barry Bonds was at the plate, with a chance to make baseball history.
>
> Like many a young American lad, my first love was baseball. Never mind that while growing up in Cleveland in the late '60s, I didn't see a lot of very good baseball. The Indians were in the midst of what would be a 41-year drought between first-place finishes, with the only serious pennant chase during that stretch coming in the year I was born, a tad too young to fully appreciate it. No matter: I was an Indians fan, and I soon fell into the inexorable rhythms of a season spent rooting for a losing team. The anticipation of the late winter's exhibition warm-ups would give way to the excitement of Opening Day and the season's start, followed by the initial disappointments, the flurry that suggested this might be that magical year, the realization that no such magic would be happening after all, and the futility of playing out the meaningless schedule, all wrapped up by the spark of a late-season call-up from the minor leagues that dangled the carrot of better days ahead all winter long.
>
> But while the Indians sucked, I had no shortage of stars to cheer for. They were displayed for me in the pages of Ebony magazine. For generations, no self-respecting, aspiring black household was without a subscription to Ebony. At a time when black faces in mass media were exceedingly rare, Ebony was both a template for achievement and a monthly dose of affirmation. It was published by a black-owned company; beautiful black men and women were featured on its covers, and its articles treated the stars, issues, and black life trends of the day with a level of class and respect not forthcoming anywhere else.

Every April, Ebony saluted the start of the baseball season with a photo spread of all the black ballplayers on major league rosters. Some teams, even a quarter-century after Jackie Robinson's breakthrough, would have only a handful, while others had close to a dozen (out of the 25-player squads). Every black ballplayer (and most of the Hispanic players), from the superstars to the benchwarmers, got a postage stamp-sized black-and-white headshot. That annual feature was the only thing in Ebony I recall reading passionately, studying the faces and memorizing the players and their positions. In 1971, I rooted for the Pittsburgh Pirates in the World Series, in part because that year they became the first team in major league history to field an all-black starting lineup for a game.

The years of my youth also happened to be the glory years for blacks in baseball. Some of the game's greatest black ballers —some of the game's all-time greats, period—were active and excelling. It was, looking back, an unequalled confluence of baseball generations: veterans of the last breaths of the Negro Leagues, like Willie Mays and Ernie Banks, acquitted themselves well during their final seasons against stars in their prime like Bob Gibson and Ferguson Jenkins, while young talents such as Dusty Baker and Reggie Jackson reaped the benefits of all that wisdom and experience.

I remember my first Willie Mays baseball card. It was late in the '71 season, and I had been collecting cards for about four years by then. I had acquired virtually every superstar of the era except Mays, and it was driving me crazy. None of my friends had extra Mays cards they were willing to trade me, so I was left to the luck of the draw in pack after pack. When the Mays card finally showed up, I swear that time seemed to stop and a choir materialized in my 12-year-old head, singing hosannas.

I also remember the time Frank Robinson inserted himself into the game for my beloved Indians. It was 1975, and the Indians still sucked, but it was a memorable moment, nonetheless. Robinson had been named manager that season, the first black manager in the big leagues (and a player-manager to boot!), and celebrated by hitting a home run in his first at-bat on Opening Day. Now it was July, the Indians had long since fallen out of contention, but it was late in a close game, and Robinson came to bat in a crucial situation. Hit a homer, Frank, I wished — and it came true! I don't remember if we won that game, but it doesn't matter. It was that moment, a moment when I wished upon a hero, which stands out through the years.

But the greatest of all the black stars back then was Henry Aaron, a slugging left-fielder who spent the bulk of his career piling up huge numbers for the Braves in Milwaukee and Atlanta. He didn't do it with the flair and flash of Mays; in fact, non-baseball aficionados probably didn't realize how good he was until he approached one of baseball's holiest grails. Aaron began the 1973 season 41 home runs shy of Babe Ruth's all-time career mark of 714.

As he slugged his way through the '73 season, the publicity mounted — and so did the hate mail. Aaron received sackfuls of venom and vitriol for even daring to come close to Ruth. It was only a game, but still there were plenty of folks who didn't want to see any black man break a white man's record. Black fans, needless to say, were cheering Aaron every step of the way, not to overturn a white icon as much as to finally become a black icon.

The moment finally came April 8, 1974—six years and a few days after Martin Luther King was assassinated. Aaron hit a fastball off the Dodgers' Al Downing (another black ballplayer of note) over the left field fence, and was congratulated on the way to third base by two white fans that just wanted to share the moment. I was on a cloud all that night, and I dare say every black baseball fan, and a lot of white ones too, were there with me.

Now, none of this hero worship made me a particularly decent baseball player (I also rooted for black football and basketball stars, but wasn't much better at those sports, either). And I didn't lack positive black men in my life, what with my dad, uncles and brother-in-law for starters. But watching Aaron, Mays, Robinson, and the others gave me people to root for, people in whom I could invest a personal interest. It wasn't (and isn't) that I couldn't appreciate the talents of white stars; I simply could glean more from the feats of the black ones. What they did meant more to me for the sole reason that they looked like me.

Were they role models? No, not in the hands-on sense, of course not. I never met them, they didn't help me with career advice, or encourage me to fight the neighborhood bully or my give me advice on how to cope with my first crush. But they were exemplars of success; they were people I could point to as proof that anything was possible for me. They left a mark on me that I cherish to this day...

Possible, but not likely. On the night I wrote this, Bonds stood at 699 home runs; only Aaron and Ruth are in this particular 700 club. ESPN and ESPN2 cut away from their regular broadcasts to show Bonds' at-bats, hoping to catch homer #700. I got up from the computer to watch, seeking a live shot of something memorable more than any sense of validation (alas, he didn't hit it that night). But even though baseball isn't as big a deal among blacks as it used to be, and black baseball stars seem to be far less plentiful nowadays, black stars are still black stars, and as long as black life in America remains the adventure in search of wholeness that it's been these last few hundred years, black kids will look up to their stars, for whatever reasons, whether or not Charles Barkley thinks that's a good thing. Somewhere in the 'hood, there's a kid that was rooting for Bonds just a bit more fervently than the rest of the fans.

"My Hero Is Winning At Something That Everyone 'In My World' Is Focused On"

> "I come home from school and play video games, watch television, listen to my favorite all-Black radio station. Sometimes, I go outside and play 'a pick up game' of basketball, like my other friends in the 'hood.' My world is largely defined by what I see and hear around me. During the day I receive many messages from the media, some subtle and some not so subtle, about what is cool and who is cool, and I must admit, these messages influence me.

One thing is clear about the messages Blacks receive: "Blacks belong in basketball; Blacks own basketball."

The following statement summarizes the view held by many Blacks about basketball.

> "Just as important to the Jordan icon as his amazing play and remarkable marketing skill is the game he played. Blacks began to play the game in the cities as a sport of their own in post-Civil War America. The original peach "baskets" on barns have turned into rusted metal rims with chain "nets" on courts covered with broken glass in the inner city ghettos. It is now this image that defines a game that truly has become an African-American game. Black Americans have "invented" basketball just as much, or more than, Naismith did. Basketball has become a reflection of black ghetto culture, much in the form of how jazz and blues music represented black culture in the American past. Especially to blacks in the inner cities of America, basketball has become one of the most expressive modes of cultural expression--much like music, literature and fashion in other forms. It has become a ritual of expression."

In other words, *basketball is cool.*

The media is also on the bandwagon promoting basketball as being cool, and when the media's power is marshaled in a given direction, influence happens.

The Kaiser Family Foundation's 2005, *Generation M: Media in the Lives of 8-18 Year Olds* study provides insights into the extent the impact of the media has on African American youth. Some of its key findings include:

> **Race/ethnicity.** African American kids are more likely than White kids to report bedroom televisions, DVRs, cable/satellite TV connections, subscriptions to premium TV channels, and video game consoles. In general, this pattern is consistent with results from earlier studies that indicate African Americans are particularly attracted to TV;

Socioeconomic status. The likelihood of a youngster having a VCR/DVD player or a video game console in the bedroom is negatively related to the level of parent education. That is, children whose parents have no more than a high school education are significantly more likely than those whose parents completed college to have a VCR or DVD in their bedroom and they are more likely than both those whose parents had some college and those whose parents completed college to have a video game console in their bedroom. The percentage of children with either of these kinds of media increased significantly from 1999 to 2004, but at a greater rate for those from the lowest parent education category. The only difference in bedroom media related to income emerges for TV. Young people from the lowest income group are significantly more likely than those from the middle or highest income groups to have their own TV.

Clearly, external voices are influencing the perception of children about what cool is and isn't; the more access youth have to external media, the more likely they are to be influenced by it.

Channeling Cool

Shoe manufacturer NIKE long ago mastered the sports marketing landscape and showed the world just how profitable it can be to harness and control perceptions of cool for marketing purposes.

NIKE understood that the key to effectively marketing something as being cool depended on its ability to capture and convey that the thing being marketed is different from other things.

> Michael Jordan was not only different; he was exceptional and his shoes removed any obstacles to the flow of his greatness.

Cool brands suggest that they have something others don't. They are marketed as being extremely observant and intuitive, as having their finger on the pulse of a given culture, and as not being afraid to challenge the norms. As a result, cool brands lead, pushing others into new ways of seeing things.

An essential attribute of cool is that it conveys that it has nothing to prove. In marketing terms, cool brands are led by people who are trying to bring something they love and appreciate–an experience, a product, an environment– to others. Cool is about standing up for one's beliefs, even when, or perhaps especially when, it doesn't appeal to the masses.

> Cool brands follow a set of convictions and a distinct sensibility to create an experience they feel personally passionate about.

As media images convey, part of the energy that makes cool is from the *novelty* of its newness, the fuel of creativity as people discover it, interact, and add to it. But somewhere at the root of the movement is need. There is something missing, a new thing comes along and addresses that need, and a movement arises.

One of the challenges baseball faces is that it lacks novelty and opportunities to be "added to" or transformed by individual styles. Currently, the "place holding" for baseball in the minds of many youth is that it is the game their parents played, and as such, is outside of their cool paradigm.

> By contrast, the Black aesthetic has not only changed basketball, it has been the catalytic force behind the sport's extraordinary growth in popularity and profitability ever since. African American inner city culture has brought a much more graceful, speed-oriented, physical, all-around skill aspect to basketball. Basketball is synonymous with cultural identity and cool.

Sound familiar? Twenty years ago, one might have been referring to baseball, but the fact of the matter is, baseball is no longer the sport *du jour* for Blacks.

Fathers and male role models used to be the ones who defined cool to their sons, but in their increasing absence from inner city African American households, others have stepped in to control the perception of what is cool and isn't.

Sometimes other youths step in to define cool. In fact, cool and the "boy code" are inseparable. Breaking through the "boy code" used to be a father's challenge. As William Pollack's (1998) *Real Boys* argues, a 'boy code' is developed and reinforced when boys observe the behavior of friends and characters in the media." If fathers are not around to mediate and help their sons interpret events, youths will simply emulate the behaviors of those around them and take on the values thrust upon them from television.

Pathways to Defining Cool

As cool can be learned, it can also be created. While researchers generally acknowledge that the cognitive development and behavior of youth are influenced by a wide range of institutions (schools, religion), social relationships (parents, peer groups), and economic factors (income), a key consideration in determining and transmitting what is cool in today's environment is the impact of the media.

Though cool is thought of as emanating from a person's innermost soul, according to sociologists it's in fact learned in many cases. Accordingly, there have been numerous studies undertaken to examine how cool is learned through the media. S. Craig Watkins, Associate Professor of Sociology and Radio-Television-Film at

the University of Texas at Austin, has undertaken important research in this regard. His work sheds light on the phenomenon and provides further clues in solving the mystery of the decline of African Americans in baseball.

Watkins notes that it is difficult to discern a substantive relationship between Black youth and the mass media prior to the 1960s. The initial exclusion of Blacks from popular media culture, he explains, was historically attributable to two main factors: a lack of discretionary income on the part of Black youths and their families, and racial exclusionary practices on the part of the culture industries.

Important economic and educational advances since the 1960s, however, sharply increased Black household and discretionary income (Farley & Allen, 1987) and also helped to establish a viable African American consumer culture. By the late 1960s and early 1970s, the film and television industries (Gray, 1995) began responding to the shifting sensibilities of Black youth culture by creating products that specifically targeted Black youth. It was also during this time that the wider distribution of television occurred, thus exposing Black youth to American consumer culture in ways unknown to previous generations (Nightingale, 1993).

> The challenge facing baseball is to figure out how to harness perceptions of cool and direct them toward baseball; baseball needs to partner with the media to send messages to African Americans that baseball is cool. New media strategies and new partners are needed to capture the attention and imagination of today's media savvy and saturated African American youth.

On their part, alternative sports are rising to the challenge. For instance, NASCAR is maneuvering to park itself inside every garage in America, even garages in urban America. NASCAR has also given more than a passing nod to minorities, an audience traditionally in short supply in stock car racing. Expanded minority initiatives were launched starting in 2000 and they continue to grow. In 2004, for instance, Earvin "Magic" Johnson was named as the co-chairman of the then newly-created Executive Steering Committee for Diversity. He assists NASCAR with creating grassroots programs such as "Drive for Diversity" that identify and develop African American, Hispanic and women drivers and crewmembers. He also helps NASCAR develop marketing programs to increase the sport's visibility in urban communities and raise awareness of career and competitive opportunities in motor sports. These kinds of initiatives are just one example that shows how alternative sports are being proactive in competing to engage African American participants.

NASCAR is not only staking a claim for African Americas, it's also actively pursuing the female market. Initiatives it has recently undertaken demonstrate creative and innovative approaches to building its female audience. The following *USAToday* newsclip (January 2006) demonstrates how NASCAR is strategizing to win over female audiences.

NASCAR–Harlequin Romance Partnership: "It's a partnership between two extremely brand-loyal groups," says Kerry Tharp of NASCAR. "We're trying to reach out and do more to appeal to our female fan base."

NASCAR fans buy $2 billion in licensed products annually. Harlequin devotees bought 130 million books last year. "It's a very good fit," agrees Marleah Stout of Harlequin, pointing out that women account for 40% of the sport's fan base.

"NASCAR very much portrays themselves as a family-oriented sport, and most romance fiction is about commitment and about the promise of happily-ever-after," says Gayle Wilson, president of the 9,500-member Romance Writers of America.

It's also about making money. Romance titles make up nearly 55% of all paperback fiction sales, generating more than $1 billion in sales each year. And, Tharp says, NASCAR research shows its female enthusiasts are 26% more apt to read romance novels than women who don't follow NASCAR.

In the Groove features down-on-his-luck NASCAR driver Lance Cooper and ex-kindergarten teacher Sarah Tingle. They meet when his car hits her. She gets a bump on the head. He's driven to distraction. When he looks at Sarah, Cooper it "feels like he has been shocked by a loose spark plug wire."

Britton, the author, drag-raced as a teenager and is a popular romance author with a half-million copies of her nine books in print. Dangerous Curves, published last year, also dealt with a racetrack romance. "NASCAR drivers are heroes," says Britton. "The books' appeal is that you can put yourself in the heroines' shoes."

NASCAR presents an example of not waiting to be discovered as cool; it is creating new pathways for defining cool, and for ensuring that its definition fits the NASCAR paradigm.

NASCAR is not a passenger; it is in the driver's seat, and this is what it takes to compete in today's market and to be considered cool.

Understanding the need to reach into—*and not just reach out to*—the Black community is key. Increasingly, those entities that want to reach the African American community are "reaching in."

January 9, 2007: The Nickelodeon network recently announced its new partnership with BET.

As part of their agreement, BET will broadcast two Nickelodeon series, "Romeo!" and "Just Jordan," which star rapper Lil' Romeo and comedian Lil' JJ (BET's "Coming to the Stage," *Beauty Shop*) respectively.

"This is a fantastic opportunity to broadcast and provide additional exposure to what we believe will become one of our newest live action shows, 'Just Jordan,' and the already established hit 'Romeo!' with the African-American audience to which BET caters," said Nickelodeon Vice President, Tom Ascheim. "We're very excited about building these kinds of synergistic opportunities with sister networks like BET, and look forward to future opportunities like this one."

Black Youth and Media Stereotyping

Not surprisingly, the widespread distribution and consumption of mass media continues to generate intense debate concerning the extent to which products like film, television, Internet, and music video affect youth behavior and social development. As Black youth have experienced greater access to the products and services manufactured by the mass media industry, additional questions have emerged, including that of the effect of mass media stereotyping on the self-esteem and cognitive development of Black youth.

For most of its history, according to S. Craig Watkins, the mass media industry has produced images that distort and misrepresent the complexities of the African American experience. Contemporary media representations of African Americans can be best described as paradoxical: Blacks are simultaneously under-represented

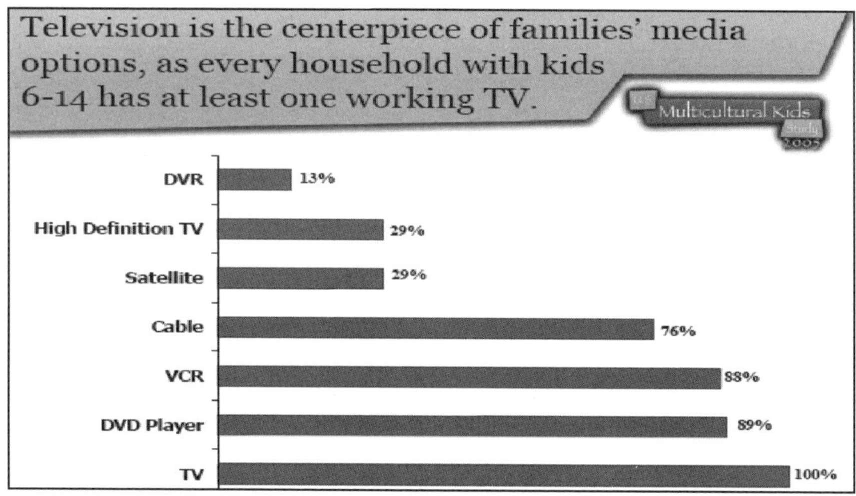

and over-represented in American media culture. For example, Blacks are most likely to appear in genre formats (i.e., situation comedies, variety shows) that are non-serious, light-hearted, and non-threatening. However, whereas Blacks are underrepresented in many areas of mass media, they are over-represented in television sports broadcasts. Hoberman (1997) maintains that the athleticization of the Black image reproduces and popularizes long-standing myths about biological and intellectual differences between Blacks and whites.

"*White Men Can't Jump*." More than a movie title from 1992, it is also a widely held perception of many young African Americans who "buy into" the athleticization of their images. Black youth want to be seen as superior athletes, which is an image that is part of the cool mystique.

The long-standing myths about athletic differences between Blacks and Whites described by Lee and Brown (1995), over a decade ago, still ring true today. Their early contention that Black youth might be especially influenced by television advertisements featuring Black athletes has been proven true, as has been their finding that poor youth pursue possession of compensatory status symbols (i.e., expensive sneakers, clothes, jewelry) in order to help them negotiate social stigma and economic marginalization.

Sports scholars have also found that television can be a means to enhance the self-concept of Black children, if parents and educators appropriately intervene to monitor and control viewing. According to the aforementioned Kaiser Family Foundation research (2005) on the lives of 8-18 year olds, Black parents are not intervening and monitoring enough.

Table 4: Average Daily Use of Each Screen Medium

Medium	**White**	**Black**	**Hispanic**
TV	2:45	4:05	3:23
Videos/ DVDs	0:45	1:00	0:44
Movies	0:17	0:48	0:29
All screen media	3:47	5:53	4:37
Proportion that used each screen medium the previous day			
Medium	**White**	**Black**	**Hispanic**
TV	79%	84%	83%
Videos/ DVDs	40%	51%	44%
Movies	10%	22%	16%
Proportion who Watched TV +1 and +5 hours the previous day			
Medium	**White**	**Black**	**Hispanic**
More than 1 hour	64%	74%	69%
More than 5 hours	17	31	23

Source: Kaiser Family Foundation (2005)

Sociologists suggest that high levels of television viewership tend to correspond with low economic status. Because poor and working class children are less likely to have access to non-school related extra-curricular activities, they spend more time at home, thus increasing their viewership of television. Also, because Black children are more likely to be reared in single parent households, they may not receive the same degree of parental supervision as White children. Consequently, Black youth may be more likely to use television for companionship.

Because of its accessibility and penetration of American domestic life, many researchers regard television as the most powerful form of media socialization, and one of the most powerful voices in determining what's cool. High levels of television viewership have important quality of life implications for youth. The repetitious depiction of Blacks in athletic roles creates a limited range of adult and professional role models for young Black males. Faced with few media images of successful African American men, young Black males are especially vulnerable to the widespread marketing and commodification of Black athletes.

It's all about marketing. The Boston Red Sox baseball team, for one, knows that, which is why it ranks as number 3 among top ten product placements in the first quarter of 2007, as shown in Table 5.

Table 5: Top 10 Brands: Product Placement Q1 (2007)

Brand	Total # Occurrences
Coca-Cola Soft Drinks	2,488
Pussycat Dolls Lounge Nightclub	376
Boston Red Sox Baseball Team	232
Nike Apparel	208
Dell Computer Systems	187
Chicago Bears Football Team	185
Cingular Wireless Telephone Services	
Wireless Text Messaging	164
Hewlett-Packard Computer Systems	159
Nike Sport Footwear	139
Under Armour Apparel	115
Total	4,253

*Source: Place*Views, Nielsen Product Placement Service*

> "I am into music and videos. I don't like to play sports. I'll go to the gym to stay "tight" but it takes too long, and too much effort to learn a sport."

According to Nickelodeon's 2005 study of the habits of multi-cultural kids, African American kids are not only spending a lot of time watching television, they are also spending a great deal of time listening to music.

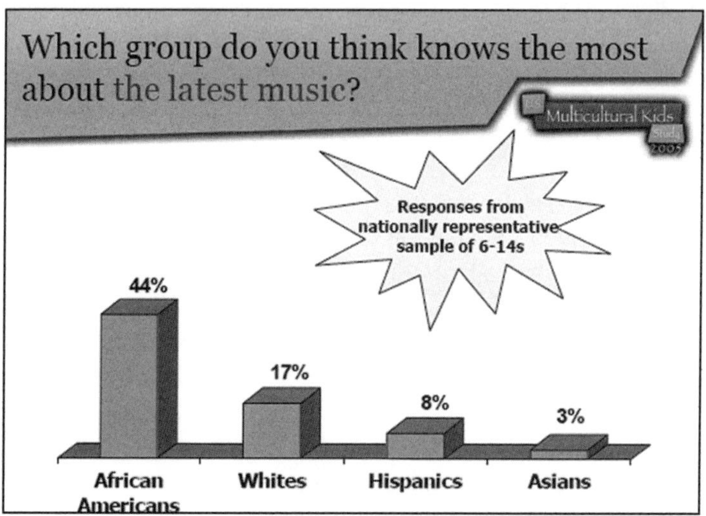

As explained in chapter one, baseball has to compete with attractions inside the house, and getting the child out of the house is no small feat, especially in today's world where videos rule. Videos not only keep the child in the house, they also influence the child's preference for entertainment outside of the house. The longer kids stay in the house the less fit they become and the less willing they are to exert themselves to play a sport of any kind.

Obesity is a "growing" problem in the African American community, especially among inner city youth and their parents.

According to The Institute of Medicine's *Preventing Childhood Obesity: Health in the Balance* (2005) study, obesity is enemy number one. It is a health concern that lowers the probability that those affected will play baseball or any sport. Findings from the study include:

> **U.S. Prevalence:** Over the past three decades, the childhood obesity rate has more than doubled for preschool children aged 2-5 years and adolescents

aged 12-19 years, and it has more than tripled for children aged 6-11 years. At present, approximately nine million children over 6 years of age are considered obese.

Causes of Childhood Obesity: The rise in childhood obesity is due to complex interactions across a number of relevant social, environmental, and policy contexts that influence eating and physical activity. Over decades, these have collectively created an adverse environment for maintaining a healthy weight. This environment is characterized by:

- Urban and suburban designs that discourage walking and other physical activities;
- Pressures on families to minimize food costs, acquisition and preparation time, resulting in frequent consumption of convenience foods that are high in calories and fat;
- Reduced access and affordability in some communities to fruits, vegetables, and other nutritious foods;
- Decreased opportunities for physical activity at and after school, and reduced walking or biking to and from school; and
- Outdoor leisure time competing with sedentary screen time, including watching television or playing computer and video games.

High-Risk Populations: There is evidence that certain ethnic minority populations, children in low socioeconomic status families, and children in the country's southern region tend to have higher rates of obesity than the rest of the population. The current increase is especially evident among African-American, Hispanic and American Indian adolescents. With both sexes combined, up to 24 percent of African-American and Hispanic children are above the 95th percentile. Among boys, the highest prevalence of obesity is observed in Hispanics and among girls the highest prevalence is observed in African-Americans.

The implication of the study for all sports is clear: Unless it is considered "un-cool" to be obese and to stay in the house playing indoor games, generations of potential future ball players—of any sport—will be forever lost.

"My Hero Is The Internet"

"My hero is the Internet; it's really cool. I live in a rough section of Baltimore. I am scared to leave the house, so I stay home and surf the Internet. My mom encourages me to play baseball because her

> father played, and she is a fan, but I don't really like it because it's not physical enough. I like contact sports.

There's a lot of hidden meaning in these words.

Those who espouse them have opted out of the whole cool paradigm. They don't feel they can compete, so they don't even try. They recognize that to be considered cool by their peers, they have to be bigger, stronger, faster, and perhaps even better looking than they are.

The reality is that some Black youths are institutionally, culturally, and interpersonally disconnected; they feel that there's "no place to be somebody," so they retreat into the virtual world.

But there's more to it.

The issue of Black masculinity is at the core of the matter. Increasingly, masculinity is represented in popular culture as being associated with demonstrating athletic prowess in basketball and football. Black male youths who are neither tall, nor big, nor athletically inclined therefore reject sports. According to T. Boyd, co-author with A. Baker of *Out of Bounds: Sports, Media, and the Politics of Identity* (Indiana University Press, 1997), the notion of masculinity is equally problematic for those who work to repress it, as it is a potential source of power for those who seek to exploit it.

With little resistance, African American males continue to be channeled in three venues, from mainstream institutions: athlete, entertainer, and criminal. Community uprising is needed at both the institutional and individual levels to interrupt this dominant paradigm, according to Boyd.

> Nike, Reebok, L.A. Gear and other athletic conglomerates have profited enormously from postindustrial decline. TV commercials and print ads romanticize the crumbling urban spaces in which African American youth must play, and in so doing they have created a vast market for overpriced sneakers. These televisual representations of "street ball" are quite remarkable; marked chain-link fences, concrete playgrounds, bent and rusted netless hoops, graffiti-scrawled walls and empty buildings, they have created a world where young black males do nothing *but* play.

"These words critically capture the "inner city" narrative, where sports ads are bombarded day and night by the mass media of urban communities, hopeless youth, and pick-up basketball games taking place 24 hours a day. The 'Be Like Mike' slogan, image, and narrative is a fixture in virtually all societies, portraying and valuing a sports dream versus an educational and/or scholar-athlete progression," according to Kelley (2005).

For some Black inner city youth who have chosen to opt out of the whole "cool" thing, "athletics are fleeting, but the mind endures" (Kelley, 2005). For them, the dilemma of athletics vs. education—as a pathway out of the ghetto—is at the heart of the professed love of the Internet. But loving to learn academically is not inconsistent with learning through sports. All learning is good; the challenge is to convey that it is not a matter of "either or," but one of "both and." Life's lessons can be taught in many ways, with each thread contributing to a rich tapestry of knowledge.

Baseball little leagues throughout America play a critical role in helping young people learn life's lessons through sports. With a little help, these little leagues can go further and deeper reaching into their communities to pull in those disaffected youth to give them a place of belonging in a cold cruel urban environment—*and that is very cool.*

Hip-Hop Is The Prism Through Which All "Cool" Must Flow

> "Hip-Hop rules my world. What its music conveys about Black life is truth; I love its style and form, and I love that it empowers ordinary Black people. Basketball players who wear tattoos, cornrows, and talk and look like me—and who embrace the symbols of the Hip-Hop world—are cool."

Hip-Hop is not a fad: I t's part of a social movement and its energy has been fused with basketball. In the stories of the multi-ethnic urban youth and the communities they live in, the lives of inner city African Americans take center stage. Hip-Hop is about inner city lower-class life. It's about trying to live out the American dream from the bottom up. It's about trying to make something out of nothing. Hip-Hop is about the youth culture taking over the world. It's about dance, art, expression, pain, love, racism, sexism, broken families, hard times, overcoming adversity, and even about the search for God. Anyone who looks at Hip-Hop and just sees rap music doesn't truly understand the history and the influence Hip-Hop has on youth culture.

Not surprisingly, Hip-Hop culture has received increasing attention from practitioners of cultural studies, as it underscores how dramatically the relationship between Black youth and the media culture industry has changed.

Hip-Hop youth culture developed in the context of profound social, economic, demographic, and spatial transformation, and its movement has developed into a fertile reservoir of youth culture and media production, with rap music being its most prominent expression.

Youth actively select from a varied field of media products and services in order to fashion their own distinct cultures and generational identities. Youth cultures commonly come into conflict with the presumed values, beliefs, and practices of mainstream society; thus they can mobilize distinct forms of cultural resistance. Many analysts argue that rap music enables Black youth to cultivate a complex body of ideas, worldviews, and representations that generate poignant expressions of social critique. Rap music is a multi-layered terrain of youth and media culture defined by various styles and sub-genres. Rap music is not exclusively the domain of African Americans. It has been embraced by youths of every race, as the data, shown in Table 6, from the Kaiser Family Foundation's 2005 study, *Generation M: Media in the Lives of 8-18 Year Olds*, shows.

Table 6: Among 7th to 12th Graders Who listened to Audio Recordings the Previous Day
Proportion Who Listened to Each Genre

	Total	White	Black	Hispanic
Alternative Rock	32%	38%	9%	16%
Classic Rock	16%	21%	6%	8%
Country	18%	26%	3%	6%
Gospel	11%	10%	19%	4%
Hard Rock	27%	33%	7%	20%
Jazz/Blues	8%	7%	13%	5%
Latin	8%	2%	2%	33%
Rap Hip Hop	**65%**	**60%**	**81%**	**70%**
Rave Techno	13%	12%	6%	8%
Reggae	14%	9%	24	17%
Rhythm/ Blues/ Soul	12%	5%	33%	11%
Punk	23%	29%	6%	14%
Soft Rock	12%	12%	6%	9%
Top 40	17%	18%	11%	13%

Source: Kaiser Family Foundation (2005)

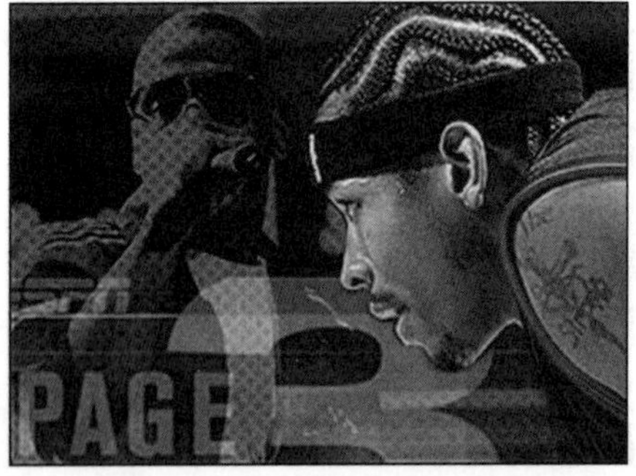

Although created by Black youth on the street, Hip-Hop's influence has become worldwide. Today, Approximately 75% of the rap and Hip-Hop audience is non-Black. It has gone from the fringes to the suburbs to the corporate boardrooms. Indeed, McDonald's, Coca Cola, Sprite, Nike, and other corporate giants have capitalized on this phenomenon. In the 1950s and 1960s, the "Beat Culture" challenged the status quo in ways that unified liberals and prompted change. In the same vein, the Hip-Hop culture has challenged the system in ways that have unified individuals (particularly youth) across a rich ethnic spectrum.

Dr. Todd Boyd, Professor of Critical Studies in the USC School of Cinema-Television, and author of "*Young Black Rich and Famous: The Rise of the NBA, the hip-hop Invasion, and the Transformation of American Culture*," wrote an article reported by *ESPN* that explains the connection between Black youth culture, Hip-Hop, and basketball. Key issues raised in the article are presented below.

Players like A.I. are the living embodiment of hip-hop in a basketball uniform.

> **By Dr. Todd Boyd:** ...When hip-hop pioneer Kurtis Blow released his single "Basketball" in 1984, he verbalized a connection between hip-hop and basketball that is more real now than even Blow himself could have imagined when he originally spit the lyrics to the song.
>
> Now, 20 years later, the combo of hip-hop and basketball is as common as Will Smith in a summer blockbuster, and the connection is only getting stronger.
>
> When Blow's record first came out, hip-hop was still in diapers, and basketball was a lot different, too. The year 1984 was not only the infamous year invoked by that George Orwell novel, but it marked the beginning of the modern era in the NBA. For the first time that year, Magic Johnson and Larry Bird faced each other in the NBA finals, while Michael Jordan and Charles Barkley were the 3rd and 5th picks in the draft that summer. All four of these figures helped, in their own way, transform the NBA from being perceived as a league of "overpaid black drug addicts" to its current status as a preeminent sport around the globe.
>
> In my mind, ...I have always said that hip-hop and basketball go together because they have so much in common. Both endeavors start off as solitary pursuits, be it writing in your book of rhymes or shooting jumpers on an empty court. In the beginning it's a solo endeavor. It's all about the individual and his craft. There is something like a spiritual connection here, a oneness even, between the artist and the art form, between the baller and ball, between the rapper and rap. The two become as one.
>
> When Michael Jordan arrived at the 1985 NBA All-Star Game as a rookie, he didn't rock the traditional Eastern conference warm-up suit, he wore his own Nike Air Jordan warm-up. At the time, Jordan was also fond of wearing gold chains. When he debuted his new Air Jordan sneakers, the league not only

fined him but they banned the shoe as well. Jordan, though, in defiance of the league continued to wear them. The notoriety surrounding the shoe, along with Jordan's funky fresh game, quickly propelled Jordan and his sneaks to legend status.

Jordan's defiance of convention early on in his career was not unlike what the trio Run-D.M.C. was doing in its music. The Air Jordans, along with the Adidas "Shell Toe" favored by D.M.C., went on to became staples of the hip-hop wardrobe. Jordan's shaved head and his long baggy shorts eventually became the style as well, both on and off the court. He was not only a trendsetter and style arbiter, but he was a young rebel intent on gettin' money and dominating the game. These things would become mantras in hip-hop, too, over time.

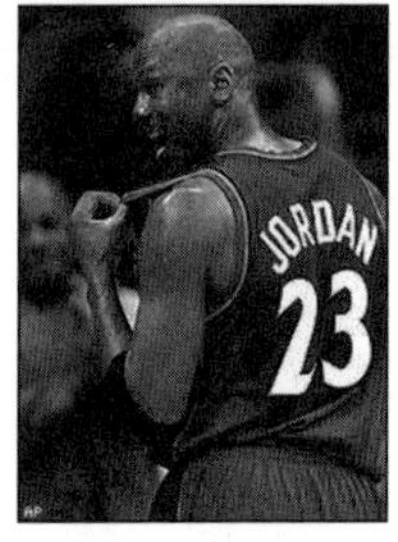

If Jordan set it off in terms of style, it was his boy, Sir Charles Barkley, who added the lyrics. Barkley's roughneck steez made him an instant favorite on the court with the hip-hop set. Chuck D immortalized Barkley when he said, "Simple and plain/give me the lane/I'll throw it down your throat like Barkley," on Public Enemy's classic, "Rebel Without a Pause."

Off the court, though, you could always count on Barkley to "keep it real." In the early '90s Barkley described himself as a "90s n----." Shortly thereafter, he did the Nike commercial that would make him a household name when he told the world that he was "not a role model," rejecting the cultural noose of control that many were still trying to tie around the neck of black athletes.

College basketball too had its moments in this evolution. The UNLV Runnin' Rebels of the late '80s to early '90s represented in basketball the gangsta ethos that rappers N.W.A. popularized in music. The Rebels played like "n----," displaying a defiant attitude. UNLV put the fear of God in their opponents and, like Mike Tyson in his prime, they were not content beating you, they wanted to destroy you. UNLV, like John Thompson's predominantly black Georgetown teams of the early-to-late '80s, which featured one of the game's original gangstas, Michael Graham, bought thug life to collegiate life in a real way.

Yet it was the University of Michigan Wolverines basketball team who really bought hip-hop and 'ball together like no other. Lead by two Detroiters, Chris Webber and Jalen Rose, the "Fab Five" enacted the takeover of college ball in 1991 when their coach Steve Fisher decided to start five freshmen. The five teenagers, with their shaved heads, extremely baggy shorts, black socks and overall swagger, were straight out of a hip-hop video. Because of the influence of the Fab Five, Michigan basketball jerseys and athletic gear in general started becoming quite common as the attire of a newly emergent hip-hop generation.

By the mid '90s hip-hop had overtaken all other forms of popular music and many of the newly minted NBA millionaires had grown up with hip-hop as the exclusive soundtrack of their lives. When Shaq was just an Orlando Magic rookie, he appeared on "The Arsenio Hall Show" and spit a verse with the rap group Fu-Schnickens. A connection that had only been suggested before had suddenly become the real deal.

Shaq would go on to record several hip-hop albums, and he would later be joined in the music game by several of his NBA colleagues, also aspiring rappers. At one point several ballers disguised as rappers even recorded an extremely wack compilation album called "The NBA's Best Kept Secrets," which featured an array of NBA players attempting to showcase their rap skills. This record served to underscore the fact that all of these ballers should keep their day jobs.

When the Philadelphia 76ers made Georgetown's Allen Iverson the first pick in the 1996 draft, the connection between hip-hop and 'ball entered a new more overtly dramatic phase. Iverson was the living embodiment of hip-hop in a basketball uniform. His own take on stylish penitentiary chic involved wearing his hair in cornrows and more tattoos than a Hell's Angel. He refused to bend over backwards to accommodate the tastes of the mainstream, traveling with a crew of friends from back in the day, and getting popped right after his rookie year with a gat and a bag of that sticky icky under the seat of his car. His unrepentant, "I don't give a f---" attitude provided hip-hop's "Answer" to a world of potential haters.

Iverson was considered so toxic by the establishment that the NBA airbrushed away his tattoos when he was on the cover of the league's official magazine, "Hoop," hoping to make him look more "acceptable." But in his own way, Iverson, like Jordan and Barkley before him, pioneered a way of behaving that set the tone for the league. The baggier-than-baggy shorts that he helped popularize even cost some players -- including superstars Shaq, Kobe Bryant, and Rasheed Wallace-- a little cash when the NBA fined them for wearing their shorts too long.

No one now doubts that hip-hop and hoops are blended, one large whole. What happens on the basketball court is often influenced by what happens in hip-hop, and vice versa. Much of what was once controversial has now become quite mainstream.

As new players come into the league now, like LeBron "Straight Outta High School" James, the league gets younger and younger, and hip-hop gets woven more tightly into the fabric of the game. Jay-Z made a career in hip-hop spittin' some of the dopest rhymes ever, often comparing himself to Michael Jordan in the process, and now he owns a portion of the New Jersey

Nets, who are scheduled to move to Jay's beloved Brooklyn in the near future. Black billionaire Robert Johnson parlayed his penchant for playing hip-hop videos on his Black Entertainment Television (BET) network and used the capital acquired from the sale of BET to purchase the expansion Charlotte Bobcats, becoming the first African-American to own a major sports franchise in America.

Though there may still be many haters out there among us, it doesn't matter. Hip-hop and hoops are as tight now as Halle Berry's catsuit, and that does not appear to be changing anytime soon. The connection between basketball and hip-hop may have started in the 'hood, but it has taken over the suburbs, and the style that comes from this merger also influences the many foreign players around the world now who aspire to be the next KG or the next Carmelo Anthony.

Meanwhile, young black men look to hip-hop and the NBA as their way out of impoverished circumstances, and as they travel "on the road to riches and diamond rings," as Jay-Z said, they recast the American Dream in the process. As Biz Markie once said, *"Damn it feels good to see people up on it!"*

The Negro Leagues and Hip-Hop: Economically Empowering the Black Community

The Negro Leagues and Hip-Hop have both provided a way for ordinary Black people to be "*up on it*," and in both endeavors Blacks were/are the ones at the helm controlling the conversation about cool.

The coolest thing about the Negro Leagues and Hip-Hop is that they have helped to economically empower ordinary African Americans. In fact, arguably not since the Negro Leagues have so many "ordinary" Blacks been economically empowered through a particular business endeavor as through Hip-Hop—*and that is "way cool."*

As an entrepreneurial endeavor, the Negro Leagues were a trailblazer, and where its trail ended, Hip-Hop entered and charted a new path. It has been suggested that Hip-Hop has created more African American millionaires in the past few decades than in all previous years combined. Notwithstanding its artistic and cultural value, Hip-Hop is here to stay because of its entrepreneurship.

Arguably, in order to connect with the young urban African American community, a pathway through Hip-Hop to "cool" has to be carved, and there's a price for it. The days of the three "Es" (**embrace, enhance, and extinguish**), as in the case of the demise of the Negro Leagues, are over. Today, the African American community wants a piece of the business action and *that's what's cool*.

Negro League business pioneer Rube Foster would no doubt be proud to see how Hip- Hop moguls, such as Russell Simmons (an original contributor to the rap music movement), are charting new entrepreneurial paths going beyond music into multiple

entrepreneurial endeavors that harness Black purchasing power, and direct it toward purchasing cool products and brands. The Simmon's venture with the *American Greetings Corporation*, which includes a Hip-Hop news service and Hip-Hop greeting cards, as well as polyphonic ringtones, mobile street games, and wallpaper, demonstrates how the knowledge of what African Americans care about is embodied in the design of products. Such an integration results in a win-win for everybody.

While it is cool to be cool, and while to be young, gifted and Black is cool, to be a millionaire is even cooler. "*Show me the money*."

As a baseball entrepreneur, Negro League founder Rube Foster was clear about the "money piece." When baseball was the coolest to African Americans was when it was creating wealth in the African American community. Even then it was about being more than just a game. At the end of the day, it is not just about music when we talk about Hip-Hop, as it wasn't just about sports during the Negro League era. It's also about Black economic empowerment.

When Major Baseball League broadly and loudly broadcasts the message to the African American community that it welcomes it not just as players and as spectators, but also as business partners, is the day that baseball will be considered cool again. When the MLB encourages its Black stars to reach back to Black communities to inspire and be role models to young Black African American males; when it reaches into the households of single Black mothers to help them formulate a vision about how baseball is a path out of the ghetto for their sons; and, when the MLB charges its franchises with coming up with creative ways to support Blacks in inner cities playing the game—*is when baseball will be not only cool again—it will be hot.*

So What Is Cool At the End of the Day?

Cool is—*what those with power and influence define it to be.*

As the power and influence of fathers in the lives of African American males has diminished, the media has stepped in to control the conversation about cool. "Media literacy," "media consolidation," and "media justice" are three issues that have a bearing on the messages that are conveyed to Black youth about what cool is and isn't.

It's up to Black parents to step back in and take charge. If they don't, cool will continue to be defined by others—*rather than being a cultural expression of the soul of Black folk* it will increasingly be relegated to mere media slogan status.

The next chapter, "*From Home to Home Plate*," explores what it takes for stakeholders in the Black community to step back in, take charge, and step up to the plate. It's only when they do, that youth can make it all the way from home to "home plate," and making it all the way from home to home plate is *way cool.*

Mayor Sheila Dixon with James Mosher Little League

From Home to Home Plate

From Home To Home Plate: "Growing" Black Inner City Baseball Players

As sports scholar David Ogden opines, "it takes a 'Pied Piper' to lead kids to baseball." "Pied Pipers" lead kids out of something and into something, and their job for baseball is clear: They are needed to get the kids out of the house and onto the baseball field.

Today, there are a lot of attractions for youths in the house, especially for Black youth who spend an inordinate amount of time watching television and playing video games. There are also many distractions around the house in inner cities like Baltimore, and many of them that are negative and are lurking just outside of the window on the doorstep in the "hood" are not positive. Getting kids out of the house—and away from around the house—is no small feat. It is the first challenge that must be overcome to get them to play any sport.

> "Youth baseball kept me out of trouble; it kept a lot of my friends out of trouble," said Gary Sheffield, a former first-round pick of the Brewers who plays for Atlanta. "When you don't have anything to do, you'll find something to do. And a majority of the time, it's going to be the wrong thing. You've got to have resources; you've got to have people committed to the programs, and the right people running them. Baseball has the resources."

This is a story about how to get young African American inner city kids out of the house and onto the baseball diamond at a time when the diamond is not glittering in their sights.

Baltimore's story is representative of what's involved in "growing" Black baseball players in predominantly African American, poverty stricken inner cities. Baltimore's case was chosen for many reasons. The most important being that Baltimore and baseball are virtually synonymous.

Known as the hometown of baseball legend Babe Ruth, a lot is expected from Baltimore's baseball teams. When the Baltimore Oriole's Frank Robinson was chosen as Major League Baseball's first Most Valuable Player (MVP), that was to be expected. When Baltimore had two great Negro League teams, the Baltimore Black Sox and the Elite Giants, that was also to be expected. But no one expected such a poor showing from the Orioles for so long, or for African Americans to be fading from the game in Baltimore. What happened in Baltimore and in other cities?

A lot has transpired in Baltimore's history since the days of Babe Ruth, the Black Sox and Elite Giants, and as has been the case for many other "older core" cities across America, it hasn't all been good. Many curve balls have been thrown at the city that have had an impact on baseball in general, and on Blacks in baseball, in particular. The brief economic history of Baltimore, provided in Box 8, sheds light on some of the critical factors that have had an impact on the city over the years.

The Baltimore Black Sox were a professional baseball team based in Baltimore. It was one of the original six teams to make up the Eastern Colored League in 1923. The Black Sox won over 70% of their games during the 1929 season and won the American Negro League Championship. **The Elite Giants** moved first to Washington, then to Baltimore in 1938. Among the stars that wore the uniform were Hall-Of-Famer Roy Campanella, Joe Black (1952 National League Rookie of the Year with the Brooklyn Dodgers) and Junior Gilliam (1953 National League Rookie of the Year, also a Dodger). The team captured two league titles: 1939 (Negro National League) and 1949 (Negro American League).

James Mosher Little League Sign Up

Box 8:
Naked City: Brief Economic History of Baltimore

Baltimore's beginnings looked unpromising. Ironically, the Indian name for its river, Patapsco, means a backwater. The first ray of light came when steel was brought to the city with the construction of a steel mill and shipyard by the Pennsylvania Steel Company in 1893. By 1916, steel began to dominate the local economy. Workers from rural Maryland, and of Welsh, Irish, German, Russian, Hungarian, and African-American descent, were attracted to the high pay of industrial employment, and many came to live in the company town. The steel company segregated residents by race and by rank, which determined the size and location of houses. Community high schools prepared steelworkers' sons for jobs at the mill, reserving training in skilled jobs for whites.

During World War II, the steel industry underwent a production boom. Bethlehem's mill at Sparrow Point, which built cargo and transport ships, expanded quickly and reached its peak employment in 1959, with 35,000 workers.

The latter part of the 20th Century saw a nationwide decline in the manufacturing sector, and Bethlehem Steel was no exception to this trend. In 1971, when Sparrows Point was the largest steel mill in the country, a surge in steel imports led to massive layoffs among domestic producers.

Baltimore lost over 100,000 manufacturing jobs between 1950 and 1995, and 75% of its industrial employment, including jobs with union representation. It is estimated that, today, less than 6% of all jobs in the city are in manufacturing. The collapse of industry led to a number of changes in the demographic makeup of the city and the surrounding region, contributing to a crisis in urban poverty that lingers today. As factories bled manufacturing jobs, Baltimore bled residents: nearly one-third of its population left between 1950 and 2000. Businesses fled the city, followed by workers, and Baltimore began to lose its stature as the economic hub of central Maryland.

The city's share of the region's manufacturing employment dropped from 75% in 1954 to 30% in 1995. As the city's population shrank to 657,000 by 1997, Baltimore's suburbs grew at the expense of the urban core. Once the population center of central Maryland, by the end of the century, Baltimore contained only a quarter of the region's total population. Contributing to the suburbanization of the central Maryland region were changes in the racial makeup of the City's population and the phenomenon of "white flight." As a result, by 1997, Baltimore went from less than one-quarter to nearly two-thirds Black.

Exacerbating conditions was the subsequent flight from the city of middle-class African-Americans. Increasingly, Baltimore's Black middle class followed White Baltimoreans who had fled to the suburbs before them. Between 1990 and 2000, the number of African-Americans living in the city began to decline. Today, after decades of population drain, the characteristic that defines the city's polarization from the suburbs is not race, but economic class. With the decline of manufacturing, the service sector came to be the dominant base of employment for Baltimore City residents. Today, service-providing jobs account for over 90% of all jobs in Baltimore City. Such jobs have a heavily minority workforce; one study found that in 1990, 71% of low-wage service workers in Baltimore were African-American, though African-Americans represented only 59% of the City's population.

In many positions, such as in administrative support positions and personal services, the majority of workers are women, and many women who support a family are the sole source of income for that household. Service industries such as hospitals, nursing homes, and tourism have become the primary source of employment for poor and minority workers. Service jobs are largely characterized by low pay, high turnover rates, irregular or part-time schedules, lack of benefits, job insecurity, and lack of union representation. Few offer vocational training or skills-building opportunities for advancement. Low pay forces many service workers to work second jobs, and to increase weekly work hours to more than 60 in some cases. Also, many workplaces are located far from the neighborhoods where service workers live, adding to transportation and child- care costs for working families.

An increasingly poor and minority population, and the low-wage service sector has become the principal determinant of the economic status of Baltimore City residents. The growing concentration of urban poverty and the rise of low-wage service economy have at once reinforced one another and exacerbated poor living conditions for urban workers.

Source: Historical Society of Baltimore

Demographics of Inner City Residents

"Inner cities are defined as places of economic distress." The 21 million people (2006) residing in the inner cities of America's largest 100 cities represent a population the size of Texas. Compared to residents living in the surrounding metropolitan areas, inner city residents today are more likely to be of color (80 percent compared to 31 percent in the nation), foreign-born (23 percent compared to 11 percent in the U.S.), younger (42 percent under 25 years old compared to 35 percent), and have larger households (2.9 members compared to 2.1 members). Census data also confirmed that inner cities are more economically disadvantaged; unemployment is three times the level of the rest of the metropolitan area, college attainment lags significantly behind metropolitan area rates, and inner city median household incomes are less than half those of surrounding areas.

Far from a field of dreams, the Baltimore inner city landscape became a nightmare for many poor urban Blacks, especially during the "lost decades in the 1980s."

The highest poverty rate in Maryland, over 20 percent, is in Baltimore, where over 50 percent of the population is African American. Crime is an ever-present problem, single female-headed households are common, jobs are in short supply, and "weed warriors" (volunteers) are needed to help keep up the decaying baseball fields.

Amidst this, dedicated inner city little leagues throughout America are hanging in there trying to "grow" African American baseball players. The story of such a dedicated organization, the James Mosher little league program of Baltimore, one of the oldest inner city Black little leagues on the east coast, informs our story and provides a closer look at what it takes to stay in the game against all odds.

James Mosher: "Going To Bat With The Team They Have"

In 2009, James Mosher will enter its 50th year as one of the main baseball "Pied Pipers" for inner city Baltimore.

Every little league in America, no matter where it is located, or who its members are, is the first "Pied Piper" in the progression from "home to home plate." The only difference between the James Mosher little league program in inner city Baltimore, and its counterparts in the suburbs, is that its job as "Pied Piper" is exponentially more difficult. James Mosher, unlike in the fable of the "Pied Piper of Hamelin," is playing a tune whose music is drowned out by the noise of the urban ghetto.

> According to Dr. David Ogden, "There are two things seldom seen today on Little League and youth baseball diamonds...Black children... [and]... spontaneous play. What you find, typically, is highly organized play supervised by adults and undertaken by Caucasian boys. Despite the plethora of youth baseball programs, officials in those programs lament that boys are not experiencing the extemporaneous demands of pick-up ball; and, despite data showing the importance of sports to African-American youths and parents, those youths get little exposure to baseball, either formally or informally, according to officials and others.

Perhaps always knowing that it would be a battle to lead kids down the path of straight and narrow, and to baseball, the James Mosher little league program was formed, not only to "grow" baseball players, but also to grow fine young African American citizens.

According to *Baltimore Sun* writer Reginald Fields, "James Mosher took its name from the school field where it formed in 1959, when Eddie Watson and Archie Lewis, two area residents, wanted to organize summer activity for the boys playing in the playground." As one of the founders, Clifton Turner, who was 85 years old when Fields wrote the Baltimore Sun article about James Mosher, informed Fields: "Back then, it was so much bad stuff going on…we decided to do a "little league." But it wasn't to get them to become major league ball players, but to teach them something about life…how to be respectful and have good sportsmanship…to win with honor and to lose with grace."

The James Mosher little league program's constitution states that the purpose for which it was formed was:

- To elevate and advance the moral, intellectual and social conditions of the youth of the community, to combat juvenile delinquency…and to encourage and promote good sportsmanship, and to encourage citizenship through sponsoring, promoting, and supporting non-profit little league activities;

- To advise and assist in coordinating activities related to the operation of little league sports activities, and to stimulate public interest, support, and participation of the community with respect to such activities;

Its legions of volunteers recognize the potential of baseball not only for building interpersonal skills and relationships among youth, but also for issuing tickets out of the inner city ghetto for those few exceptional players who excel in the sport.

With one of the largest little league programs in the inner city, James Mosher has 22 teams with 15 members on each team. As Alan Meacham, Sr., one of the founders of the James Mosher little league program explains, "Up to the 1970s, everything was working just fine." There were ample available coaches, many of whom were educated teachers and professionals. Those in white-collar jobs had phones on their desks, which is key for being able to make contact with the parents. By contrast, many

In the United States, the term 'inner city' is commonly understood to mean poor, dysfunctional and Black. Nearly every large and mid-size American city has a core of neighborhoods where 40 per cent or more residents live below the federal poverty level. These concentrated poverty neighborhoods are characterized by abandoned and deteriorated properties, high crime, poorly performing schools, drug markets and family breakdown. Concentrated poverty neighborhoods also produce their own urban culture distinctive dress, music, speech patterns, and behavior that further isolate residents from the mainstream.

Frank Robinson (born August 31, 1935, in Beaumont, Texas), is a Hall of Fame former Major League Baseball player. He was an outfielder, most notably with the Cincinnati Reds and the Baltimore Orioles. During a 21-season career, he's the only player to win League MVP honors in both the National and American Leagues; he won the Triple Crown, was a member of two teams that won the World Series (the 1966 and 1970 Baltimore Orioles), and amassed the fourth-most career home runs at the time of his retirement (he is currently seventh). During the last two years of his playing career, he served as the first permanent African American manager in Major League history, managing the Cleveland Indians to a 186-189 record.

of today's service sector workers cannot access a phone during working hours.

Back then, according to Meachum, Sr., "there were plenty of talented and interested Black youth to play, most of who came to the little league with prior instruction from their fathers about how to play the game. Famous baseball players from the Baltimore Orioles were on hand, or just a phone call away; and, the annual pre-season James Mosher parade was the talk of the town." It was an exciting and hopeful time back then when Frank Robinson was the first baseball player to be named MVP (Most Valuable Player) in both leagues, and when the Baltimore Orioles won the World Series in four games.

The good times didn't last. As prospects for inner city Baltimore dimmed, so did those for the James Mosher little league program. Gone were the days when there were ample coaches and Black youth were enthusiastic about the game. Most of them now come from single female-headed households, reared by women who cannot teach them how to hold a bat, nor how or when to swing it, nor explain why they should try. Gone are the days when one can simply pick up the phone and call an MLB player to come on over and show the kids a thing or two—now, one has to go through a retinue of agents and handlers.

Despite growing inner city turbulence, James Mosher carries on as "Pied Piper" leading inner city Black children onto the baseball fields. Rounding up the kids at the shopping malls, calling on the church for help, placing ads in the newspapers, going on local radio shows, knocking on doors, James Mosher, as "Pied Piper," continues to play a Beethoven symphony in a world that only listens to Hip-Hop.

The Baseball Round Up Begins

Mike Singletary

"Baseball may be failing in terms of its popularity as a sport, but its humanity is not failing"

President
James Mosher
September 23, 2007

Mike Singletary has been the President of James Mosher since 2003, and one of its members for 17 years. He also played in the little league program from 1973 to 1978; "it was a transformative experience," he says. Like too many inner city kids in Baltimore, his parents didn't raise him; his grandmother did, and she raised four of his siblings as well. She signed Mike and his brother up for baseball, vowing, "Son, you're going to play baseball son, if it's the last thing you do." She had to search around for a league and found James Mosher.

Singletary knows how important baseball was for him, and how important it is for many other little kids who were raised in circumstances like his, without an intact family. "Baseball taught me to become a family man," Singletary said, "because the guys that taught baseball back then were family men, they took you to their homes, where we could observe how they lived. They helped us become who we are today."

Singletary underscores, "In order to be a man, you have to see a man."

Back then, according to Singletary, "the coaches and volunteers were excellent role models. They were professionals and mostly educators in the school system. They viewed the little league program as a continuing education program."

In contrast to the family men of yesteryear, "a lot of Black men today are fathers, but they are not "Dads," according to Singletary. The term "Dad," Singletary explains, is an affectionate term reserved for those who earn it through being involvedwith their children. Singletary is proud that his two daughters call him "Dad." He adds, "Fathers, on the other hand, come and go, and aren't available most of the time; they aren't responsible for their children, and they are not involved in the whole lives of their children."

Singletary understands the role of the "Pied Piper" from firsthand knowledge. He also knows what happens to those who don't pay attention to the music. He sometimes meets James Mosher "drop outs" in the prison system where he teaches carpentry. They invariably say, "Hey coach, I should have listened to you."

Having attended Carver Vocational Technical High School in Baltimore, Singletary is a journeyman cabinetmaker today, but in addition to building cabinets, he's all about building the character of little kids in the inner city.

In today's times, to understand what it takes to be a "Pied Piper" in leading Black inner city youth into baseball days, it's informative to walk a mile in James Mosher's cleats.

James Mosher has trained over 20,000 youths since it opened its doors. Its program involves a minimum of 22 managers, one for each team, and a minimum of 44 coaches to train the 330 kids in the program each year.

A 2003 article entitled, *"Diamonds in the Rough,"* by *Baltimore Sun* writer Reginald Fields, captures the essence of what James Mosher's program is about:

> "[It is] a baseball program for inner city youngsters [that] offers some invaluable lessons on teamwork, respect—and how to turn a double play.'

In fact, things are not much different today from when *Baltimore Sun* reporter Fields wrote about the league in 2003:

> "Practice starts with seven boys, not quite enough to field a baseball team, but that's why they are here, to prepare for a little league all-star tournament no one expects them to win. About 30 minutes later, two more youngsters ride in on bikes with an excuse: They went to the wrong practice field. Then two more arrive, and finally a coach finds the star outfielder on a basketball court and hauls him to the baseball diamond. Such is life for James Mosher baseball, a youth program trying to save lives in West Baltimore's mean streets by teaching boys a game…"

Each year it gets a little bit harder.

James Mosher officials

JANUARY · FEBRUARY · MARCH · APRIL · MAY · JUNE · JULY · AUGUST

As Singletary explains, the first task year after year, before the season begins, is for senior James Mosher officials to meet and decide how to round up the kids this time around. It gets harder and harder each year. Many would be players are already lost to the mean streets by the time they are 8 years old. The James Mosher little league program wants the kids from ages 4 to 15. To get them by 9 years old is already too late, according to Singletary.

It's always a question of how to get the kids each year. To do so, the recruitment team reviews what's working and what's not from the previous year. Currently, what appears to be working best is rounding up the kids from elementary schools. A team of coaches, league officials, managers, and players is dispatched to the elementary schools to "pitch' to the parents to make the case for why their kids should play baseball.

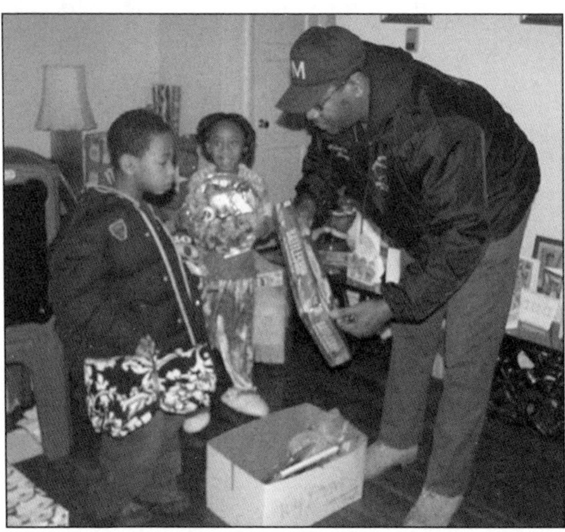

Mike Singletary at Christmas

The "pitch" doesn't just start during the baseball season: it's a continuous year-round effort. James Mosher is part of the community, and gives back to it in many ways year round. For instance, it has "back-to-school supply drives and Christmas gift drives, among other special events."

In rounding up the kids for the season, James Mosher draws on its goodwill, by advertising on Black radio stations, going to the shopping malls on Saturdays to physically interfacing with parents and kids, recruiting at churches, and hanging James Mosher banners at elementary schools.

Some team managers note that, unfortunately, despite all of their efforts, they typically only meet 45 to 50 percent of the parents. "Too many children come to the little league by themselves to sign up, bringing their own birth certificates."

When it's known where children live, James Mosher staff go the home to meet parents to encourage them to enter their kids in the little league program. This becomes necessary when bad weather prevents parents from going to the mall or getting out of the house to attend other "meet and greet" functions. Transportation is a problem for many of the parents, especially for low-income single parents.

The biggest problem, however, is for many of the parents to pay the $35 enrollment fee for their children to join the little league program. At $35, James Mosher's is possibly the lowest fee of any little league program in America. Still, many parents can't afford to pay it all at once, so they pay $15 down; the challenge is to get them to pay the balance. "Frankly, it is necessary to look the other way sometimes just to get the kid," says Singletary. Typically, kids in James Mosher's program have single mothers between the ages of 17 and 22 who are in the social service system. Sometimes the male parent is also in the social service system, and unfortunately, all too often, they are incarcerated.

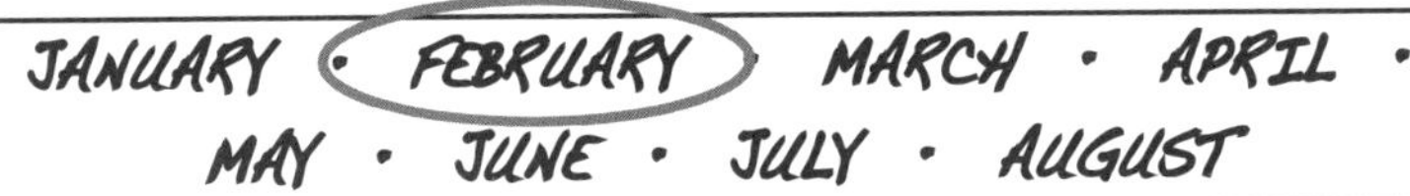

The "Pied Piper" must continue playing the music to draw the child out of the house and onto the fields. New challenges appear. After having registered youths week after week at the malls and at the schools to ensure that the roster is full, it turns out that the addresses for many of the households are not good. A percentage of the mail is *"returned to sender."* Apparently, some of the parents haven't paid their rent and have slipped out in the middle of the night; some change residences from night to night. The only recourse is to find kids at school who know the current whereabouts of the missing families. These families must be found so that they can pay the balance of the $35 they owe to complete the child's enrollment, but if they absolutely cannot pay, they still must fill out the registration card, Singletary explains.

All stops are pulled out during this month in order to get a full line up to play the game. For those households with a phone, and many don't have one, there is house-to-house calling, but too often voice messages must be left. When phone connections can't be made, more house-to-house visitation is required. Sometimes a note is left requesting the parent(s) to meet on the field, but many of them don't own their own transportation, so they swing by the field in a taxi, with the meter running, to grab the registration form, sign it, pay up, and then rush back to work.

Filling out the registration form is key, and filling it out properly, is vitally important. If a child is on medication, the league needs to know about it because the medication can affect the child's behavior and ability to play ball. Sometimes parents don't want to divulge this information because they are so eager to get the child out of the house and into the little league—as much to keep the child out of harm's way as to play baseball—that they don't want to provide any information that might prevent the child from being accepted into the league.

Uniforms have to be ordered in this month, and the sizes of children are changing dramatically. Parents must get involved; they must provide information about the sizes of their children, and they must pay the little league fee. While the fee helps defray the cost of uniforms and equipment such as bats, helmets, and baseballs, parents must buy the baseball gloves. Sometimes it's hard for parents to scrape the money together

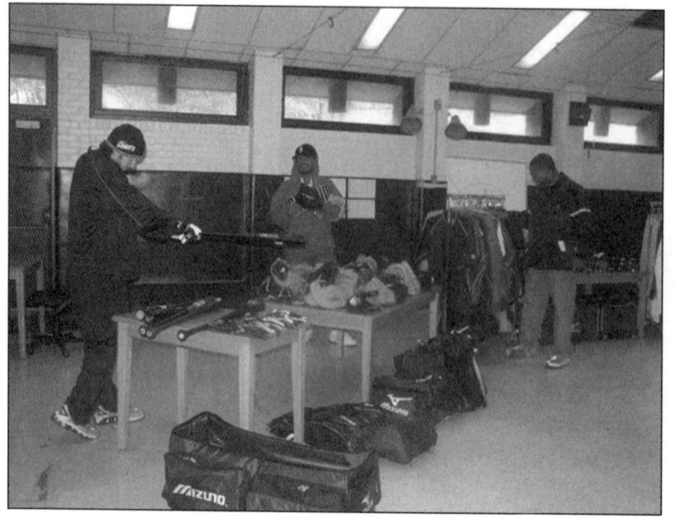

to buy them however. It's especially hard for parents with a number of children playing sports. James Mosher officials often step in to request donations of used gloves, and other supplies to ensure that no potential little leaguer is turned away.

JANUARY • FEBRUARY • MARCH • APRIL •
MAY • JUNE • JULY • AUGUST

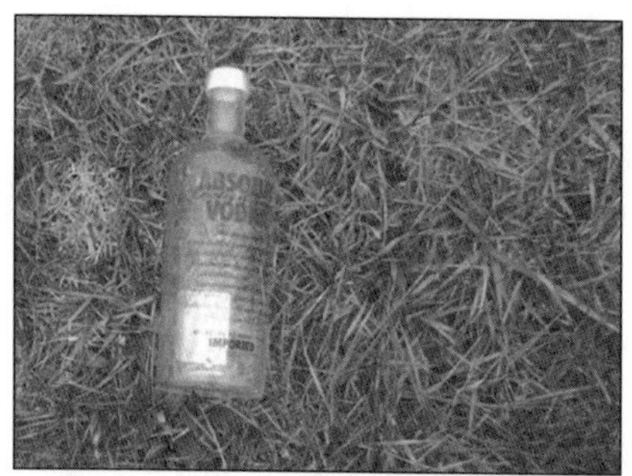

"March madness begins." The numbers are down for registration. It's time to hit the pavement hard.

Coaches must be recruited, which is becoming increasingly difficult for a number of reasons. One problem is that many of the volunteer coaches are as young as the parents, and many young single female parents aren't accustomed to taking orders from males in their same age cohort. Complicating the problem is that some children come from homes where there are multiple people in charge of the child's upbringing, such as boyfriends, girlfriends, and grandparents. In such cases, coaches may not know who is in charge of the child, given that multiple people might show up at a game claiming to be responsible for the child. The situation is exacerbated when the adults involved don't get along. Conflicts arise during practice and at games, when the parents act as undisciplined as their children. For this reason, the little league insists that parents sign contracts that set standards for behavior and codes of conduct. Such codes, in the case of the James Mosher little league program, for instance, stipulate no profanity, no fighting, no disrespect, no smoking and drinking, and no drug use on the field.

Behavioral problems are not the only problems and/or reasons why coaches may discontinue volunteering with the little league. When their children switch to other sports, so do they.

In the *"Economic Mobility of Black and White Families"* (2007) Brookings Institute researcher Julia B. Isaacs wrote: "While much of the racial disparity in family income and poverty rates is a result of lower earnings and incomes of blacks, particularly black men, large differences in family structure also contribute to differences in family economic well being. Blacks are less likely than whites to be in married couple families, and both races have seen a decline in marriage across the generations. Low marriage rates undoubtedly contribute to low family incomes; high percentages of blacks in their 30s are single parents with children or single men and women, and so are largely reliant on income from only one adult in the family."

All too often the baseball music stops playing for the African American child in baseball at 15 years old when "Pied Pipers" playing the tune of other sports take over. When this happens, coaches are lost, which poses a problem because "a league needs stability," Singletary informs.

The "music" that the parents and their children want to hear is the tune of "how to make money fast—*show me the money."* Going directly into the NBA or the NFL is "now" money; the minor leagues, by contrast, don't provide "now money." The prospect of languishing in the minors in relative obscurity, for long periods of time without any endorsement contracts, is not a welcome one.

Many James Mosher coaches have been with the organization for many years. They don't want to retire because they fear that there's no one to replace them. The older coaches are hanging on, just as the little league program itself is hanging on. But as they hang on, the "disconnect" between they way they did things in the past and the way things are done today looms large. The way children relate to coaches, and the way skills are taught, has also changed, and older coaches resist change. The coaching "disconnect" is often a matter of leadership style and of differing objectives. Some coaches are focused on winning while others are more focused on character building. Some believe that the measure of their success as a coach or team manager is how much knowledge they impart to the kids about the game, while others believe that the measure is how often the team wins.

Few are focused on whether the kids progress up the ladder in baseball to make it to "The Show" (Major League Baseball). Those who do care about this, however, are typically male parent coaches. For them, their time and effort as volunteers can only be justified if their male children are growing and developing in the sport, and progressing toward a future in baseball. But even the parents can't block out the music of basketball and football "Pied Pipers" that take over in the youth's adolescent years, drowning out baseball hopes and dreams.

For those who stick with the league, Singletary notes, "The league remains a refuge from sinister surroundings during the dead of summer, when school is closed, and there is little else for the kids to do."

James Mosher officials

JANUARY • FEBRUARY • MARCH • APRIL •
MAY • JUNE • JULY • AUGUST

It's the first day of April, and the first day of practice. It's time to play ball. "Let's see what we are working with." This is the first time the coaches are seeing many of the children. "Originally, it wasn't part of James Mosher's plan to include Tee-Ball (4 to 6), and the Instructional League (7 to 8), but parents demanded it about five years ago because they needed something constructive and positive for their children to do," according to Singletary.

Ideally, James Mosher coaches would like to have a roster full of athletically talented youths with knowledge of the fundamentals of baseball. There's a strike out on both counts, however. "Children are showing up who are overweight, who have never played a sport other than a video game, and who don't know the first thing about baseball." Many don't have fathers to teach them the fundamentals of the game to give them a head start. As time goes on, with fewer Blacks playing baseball, the probability of having a network of male parent coaches who can pass down the game down to their children also diminishes.

Unfortunately, the economic position of many parents places private instruction out of reach, and without a network of family and friends to pass the game down, many children come to little league with little prior exposure to and knowledge of the sport. Because of the dwindling number of African Americans with knowledge of the game, spontaneous baseball pick up games are also a rarity these days in the inner city.

While incomes have grown for both white and black families since the early 1970s, white families still have considerably higher incomes than black families. Some of the differences in economic outcomes reflect the persistent effect of income differences from the early 1970s, passed down from parents to children. In addition, even within income groups, white children have better economic outcomes than black children. In terms of absolute, relative, and integrated mobility measures, white children have substantially more upward mobility than black children of comparable incomes. Black children who are born into the bottom fifth of the income distribution have a hard time escaping upward, and a harder time than poor white children

Part of the precious and limited practice time has to be devoted to learning about the kids; not much is known about many of them beforehand.

Mothers who bring their sons to baseball practice tell the coaches, "Coach, from now on, my child is yours." According to Singletary, you hear this a lot. "Parents bring their children to the little league not only for baseball, but to get structure, to be around positive male influences, and sometimes, simply to have an adult male put his arms around a young boy and call that boy 'son.'"

Some of the male parent coaches are really frustrated by this and underscore, "we're not babysitters. We're baseball coaches."

When low-income parents have multiple children, they have to make tough choices about what to do with their kids to keep them off the streets and to get them engaged in something productive. One child may go to basketball, another to football. Often, the young ones are fielded to little leagues, as much as for babysitting as for sports development. Sometimes mothers say, "Hey coach, you pick him up."

Some of the kids, perhaps most, don't want to be there, especially in the beginning, but their parents make them join. They come to baseball with bad attitudes, complain about the weather, and worse yet, they don't like to exert themselves, and aren't used to doing so.

It's clear that baseball "tools" must be learned, but more importantly, it's also evident that life skills must be learned.

Arguably, as between teaching baseball "tools" and life skills, the latter poses the greatest challenge. Teaching basic "tools" for life begins with teaching kids how to address the coach. "The coach is not to be referred to as 'Yo,' 'Slim,' "Dog,' or 'Homey.'" Coaches must be referred to as "Coach Lee, Coach Neal, Coach Evans, Coach Cager, etc.."

Coaches also have to teach boys how to be boys; how not to cry at the drop of a hat, how to resolve conflicts without resorting to swearing or fighting, and how to treat others with respect. It's evident that this wasn't learned beforehand, in many cases. In effect, the coach isn't only a baseball coach; he's a life coach, and sometimes not only for the child, but for the child's parents and/or caretakers as well. As Singletary puts

Baseball "Tools:" The ideal position player (non-pitcher); an athlete who excels at hitting for both high average and power, possesses good footspeed and base-running skills, has a strong and accurate throwing arm, and plays above-average defense. Major league scouts and instructors observe and evaluate the development of these "tools" in their "prospects" (aspiring Major League ballplayers). Some well-known "five-tool" players are Willie Mays, Roberto Clemente, Torii Hunter, Barry bonds, Alex Rodriguez, and Ken Griffey, Jr.

it, "The parents learn right along with the child, and as the child grows, so do the parents."

Clearly, there's a lot to learn. In addition to learning the "tools" of the game kids have to learn how to relate to each other civilly, how to conduct themselves while they are on the bench, how to lose gracefully, as well as how to win gracefully. They must learn discipline and how not to swear in the dugouts; they must learn how to leave their electronic media at home, and how to pay attention to the game. Most importantly, they must learn how to learn.

Watching, listening, and paying attention are prerequisites for learning, but having the will to learn must come first. This is where good coaches come in; by inspiring the kids and helping them understand why they should strive to be better. Good coaches are able to impart skills, wisdom, and enthusiasm, but often it's an up hill battle. The kids bring bad habits with them to baseball, and it's not just the kids. Too often, they get their bad habits from their parents.

Coach Nottingham explains, "The desire to excel in the sport is a matter of possibility thinking. Both the child and the parents must believe that paying attention and learning leads to positive outcomes in baseball. Some lack the life experiences and outlook on life to believe that things really can work out. They can't imagine how paying attention and dedicating themselves to learning can help them make it to greater heights in baseball. Some see the competition they're up against, especially when they go to the suburbs and see all of the equipment, resources, and beautifully manicured fields, and become disheartened when they contrast what they are working with in the inner city. They just give up," according to Nottingham.

It's hard for many youths to pay attention, and not just because they don't want to, many have been diagnosed with attention deficit and hyperactivity disorders, and they just can't sit still or pay attention.

There's not a lot of time left to teach kids—some of whom are not always paying attention—all that must be taught during the month of April. Astonishingly,

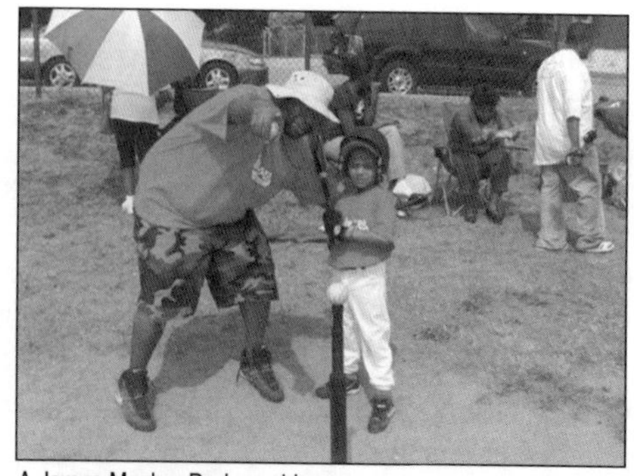

A James Mosher Dad coaching

A James Mosher Team

> In the United States, ADHD is diagnosed in approximately 8%-10% of the school-age population. Boys are more often diagnosed with ADHD than girls. Children with ADHD have difficulty attending to most tasks for extended periods of time. But they can concentrate on things that are interesting and stimulating, such as computer games. Stimulant medications help about 70% of those with ADHD improve many of the symptoms of ADHD by helping them increase focus and ability to control their own behavior. About 30%-80% of children with the disorder will continue to have ADHD symptoms into adolescence.

for all the years that James Mosher has been up at bat with the little kids of Baltimore, they have successfully pulled it out time after time, and there have been many home runs, but not necessarily on the field. Only two alumni made it to "The Show," Kevin Davis who played for the Pittsburgh Pirates, and Lloyd Jackson, who played for the San Francisco Giants. "James Mosher is most noted for helping to groom major players in the game of life. In this regard, there have been many home runs. For instance, former Baltimore Mayor Kurt Schmoke is an alumnus," according to Alan Meacham, Sr.

At the end of April, the James Mosher parade marches on. The annual parade makes efforts during the season worthwhile. The parade has been an important tradition in the inner city since 1959 and everyone looks forward to it. It's a big deal for the marching bands involved, for the concessionaires, for the motorcycle clubs, and for everyone involved. It's like the old days when baseball was king. Grandparents sit out on the front steps as the parade marches through the neighborhood. Thousands are in attendance and many are involved behind the scenes. The local fire department, local sponsors, and the whole community get in the game. It provides the inspiration that is needed to carry on next year. Having a church service at the "Church of the Holy Trinity" the next day is also an important part of the program. It brings the whole community together.

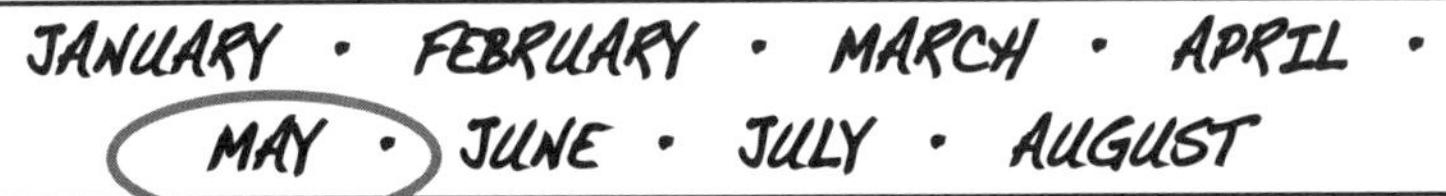

Games are played six days a week, from 6pm to 8pm, depending on the amount of natural light that's available, because unlike in the suburbs, James Mosher doesn't have access to baseball fields with flood lights. Parents or guardians have to arrive by 5:30pm to enable the kids to warm up for the games. Many parents can't make it on time, so little league staff have to scurry around and find transportation for the missing kids, otherwise games will have to be forfeited. There are other challenges. "It's 6:15pm and the catcher hasn't shown up either; if it's not one thing it's another, and it's always a scramble."

It's even a scramble to get a field to accommodate all of the teams. As a result, the teams often have to rotate, but one way or the other, they work it out, year after year. Having access to groomed fields upon which to play is also a problem.

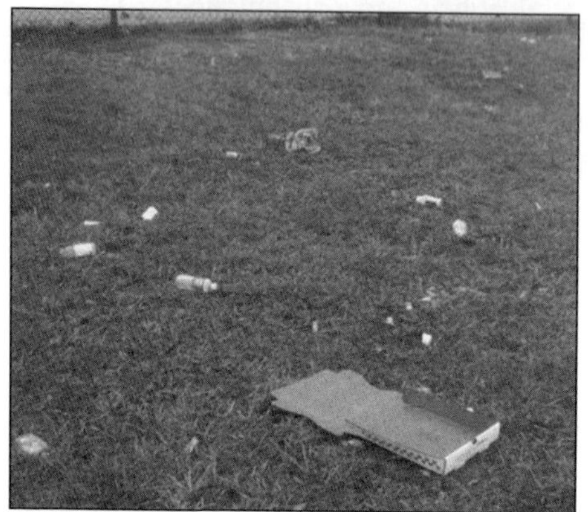
Unkept baseball field

In contrast to the James Mosher little league program, the Northwood Little League, which is within a stone throw's distance of Morgan State University, is lucky when it comes to having access to manicured fields. Morgan State allows Northwood to use its new baseball field, which was constructed for its women's softball team, which makes a difference.

Lessons learned in April have to be re-learned. Boys have to be reminded how not to be "mama's boys, and how not to cry when they don't get their way. All toys, games, and other distractions brought to the dugout have to be confiscated, and the kids have to be constantly reminded to "keep their eyes on the ball."

> Danger is one reason why there are so many "mama's boys." Because of the danger of the mean streets, mothers, particularly single mothers, are overly protective of their children and are reluctant to let them walk outside alone. Some insist that their boys, though perhaps 12 years old, be escorted to the baseball field that is only five blocks away. The mothers are scared and the boys are too, and for good reason. Gangs are a problem and the lines of the streets they control are strictly imposed. Kids who may live on one street, which is on the dividing line between two gangs, have to get "permission" to play on the other side; they may even need "a protector" during the practice. "The permission" they are granted to play on the other side is time limited. They must play and get back on the other side immediately after the game, or there will be consequences to pay.

No one can substitute for the parents. They're not only needed for protection, they are needed more for their love and support. Unfortunately, mothers, don't always understand the importance of attending games and cheering their children on. They have many excuses for avoiding the games, including "it's too hot; they just got their hair done; they just got their nails done; they have to go shopping. They use anything to get out of watching the game," according to Singletary.

The fact of the matter is that many young Black mothers didn't grow up with connections to or affinity for baseball. Now that they have children, they see baseball as a community development tool, and as a positive activity for their children, but they didn't necessarily grow up loving the game or being involved with it through family or friends. As Joe Durham (a former Negro League and Baltimore Orioles player) said, "If a young man today said to his girlfriend, 'honey let's go to a baseball game,' she would smack him." But if that same suitor suggests that they go to a basketball game that would be different and welcomed.

The excitement about baseball has to come from somewhere and it must to be nurtured. The problem, for many Blacks little leaguers in inner city Baltimore, is that they tend to come from single female-headed households with young mothers who have no family connections to baseball.

Ultimately, however, to get to sons and daughters, one has to get to their mothers. Young Black mothers understand the value of little leagues, but they don't necessarily have a larger vision about baseball in the futures of their children. Baseball hasn't effectively marketed itself to them, and as a result, many believe that the only sports options for their children are basketball and football.

Make no mistake, Black mothers and fathers are searching for ways out of the ghetto for their children, and sports scholarships can offer one option, but they prefer a faster road into the big leagues for their children than baseball provides. "The straight from high school to the big leagues" route, the LeBron James model, is definitely preferred.

JANUARY • FEBRUARY • MARCH • APRIL •
MAY • JUNE • JULY • AUGUST

It's getting hotter and harder to keep everyone focused. The teams are playing full innings now and more is at stake. If the team is doing well, it's easier to keep the kids in the game, but if the team isn't doing well, the kids start doing a *"Houdini Disappearing Act,"* according to James Mosher team managers. Basketball also starts drawing the kids into summer camps, and away from baseball. The basketball camps are "cooler" than baseball because they give the kids a chance to travel and to interact with the pro players.

James Mosher winners

With baseball having over 160 games, and a very long season, its pros are rarely available to meet kids during the summer. By contrast, pros in football and basketball have time off in the summer, which enables them to return to their hometowns and engage in activities with inner city kids.

Coach Cager in sunglasses

By contrast, there's very little "buzz" associated with baseball but one little light at the end of the tunnel for the kids that stay with baseball is the James Mosher "All Star Game." Everyone gets involved and everybody comes out a winner.

Coach Lawrence (Chris) Cager, whose son also plays with James Mosher, underscores the importance of awarding trophies. For instance, he says, his son has a room full of trophies, "but unless he can get the next one up on the ladder, he loses interest." But it's not just the trophies, it's the child's own understanding of whether there is effective competition, and whether their wins are meaningful. The level of the competition is important, and being prepared to excel in the face of stiff competition from boys trained in the suburbs is a challenge.

> Lawrence Cager, III clarifies, "it's not just the trophy that matters. It's what happens in the game, and what the trophy stands for, that matters most. When a lot's at stake and the team wins against all odds, this is what matters." He remembers his team losing against older age boys and he understood the loss—they lost because they played against a team of kids from the suburbs with more experience in using pitching machines; because Cager's team had never used one, they were at a disadvantage. A team sponsor subsequently donated pitching machines, and the Cal Ripken Sr. Foundation donated additional equipment. Subsequent victories were highly valued. "Trophies also matter when his team wins in the closing hours of a game, when a lot was at stake, and his team has made all the right moves."

As a coach in the James Mosher program, Lawrence Cager III is one of the lucky ones. His "Dad" is not only a fulltime "Dad," he has knowledge of the game, which he passes down to his son, and to other boys. "Dad knows what it takes to 'grow' a good baseball player:"

> "It's not just about having talent; it's about practicing enough to be able to spot different scenarios that might arise. What should you do if

you have a man on third and one on second? What should you do when the bases are loaded, etc? Kids from the suburbs, in contrast to those from the inner city, are getting enough practice time on good fields with good coaches to know how to spot scenarios. This knowledge is ingrained in them and helps them make the right decisions in given circumstances, without having to hesitate to ponder what to do.

JANUARY • FEBRUARY • MARCH • APRIL • MAY • JUNE • JULY • AUGUST

This is the final month, and it's the hottest, and the heat is not just coming from the sun: it's coming from the competition from football. James Mosher loses at least 20 to 30 percent of its kids to football during this month. The baseball rosters go down from 15 strong to about 10 or 11. The coaches commit to transporting the kids to ensure that they retain at least nine kids to play. It's a "touch and go situation" each year, especially for teams that are losing.

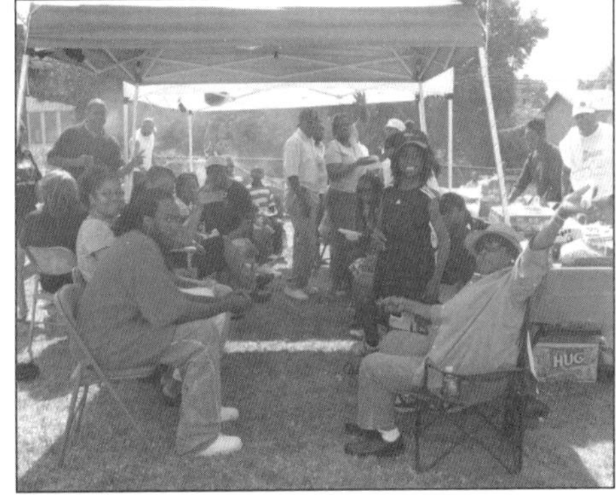
James Mosher Family Day

A lot is at stake. It's the month for the division titles, and for the final community-oriented event, which is "Family Day." At least 22 tents are set up to accommodate each of the 22 teams. With each team having 15 members, and each family having a host of friends, a lot of people attend the parade.

Kids don't play on this day, their parents do. In addition, the event is attended by a broad range of community stakeholders, including politicians, sponsors, and others. The parade is a reminder that baseball is an important part of the tradition of the community, but it's always a cliffhanger to get to this point. Along the way, there are many mis-steps, mis-haps, and missing kids, parents, and volunteers, but somehow through it all, James Mosher survived another year of "pied piping" inner city Black kids into baseball.

JANUARY • FEBRUARY • MARCH • APRIL • MAY • JUNE • JULY • AUGUST

The season ends and it's time to start all over again. Can James Mosher pull it out for another year?

Here's the problem for many inner city little league organizations: It is hard to see the forest for the trees. It's such a struggle getting the kids, teaching the kids, and retaining the kids that everyone involved—*on a volunteer basis*—is too busy, and frankly too exhausted to secure the help they need. Consequently, there is a lack of focus on institutional development. Yes, the little league institution is alive, but it's on life support. What James Mosher needs is:

- **Training in proposal writing and business plan development:** Requests for assistance are typically episodic and impromptu and when first efforts fail, there generally isn't enough motivation, energy, and resources to double back and re-propose and try again;

- **Organizational Management:** Do the leagues avail themselves of free training? As businesses, little league organizations could avail themselves of a wide array of government programs, such as those offered by the U.S. Small Business Administration (SBA), the Minority Business Development Agency (MBDA), the Small Business Development Centers (SBDCs), and other government programs that provide organization and management training. As it stands, however, volunteers are typically so busy providing a direct service to the little leaguers that the needs of the organization fall by the wayside. Opportunities to access student interns from local universities and free advice from SBA SCORE counselors, for instance, are not always accessed. What is needed is a bigger vision of greatness. Though within their grasp, they must envision it first. As the famous baseball saying goes, "build it and they will come." Inner city little leagues need to envision greatness and strive toward achieving it, and it will come;

- **Research:** Instead of living in their own little worlds, little leagues need to get out of the city, and visit other little leagues throughout the urban core of America, so that they can learn from them. What do they do better or differently? What are the keys to their success,? What solutions have they found to training and retaining coaches? What strategies have they developed to encourage single mothers to get more involved, and so forth? These questions have gone unanswered;

- **Advocacy and Public Relations:** As perhaps one of the oldest little league programs in inner city America on the East Coast, James Mosher has a story to tell, but who has heard it? Which organizations have they called upon to help them tell their stories? Where are the online bulletin boards, where are the success stories, where are the role models? Where are the videos, etc.? There are many knowledgeable public relations professionals in Baltimore For instance, leagues could call on Coppin State University for advice. However, the world of inner city little leagues has become insular, with each organization existing on an island on its own. Linkages between institutions have been broken;

- **Skills Development:** What measures are taken to ensure that the skills of coaches and managers are shored up at all times? Resources are out there, but the knowledge of how to access them is limited, just as the time of the volunteers is limited. For instance, the Cal Ripken Sr. Foundation has just invested heavily in the RBI, but the question is to what extent will the resources trickle down to organizations like James Mosher? The answer is that they will probably trickle down in proportion to the advocacy of the little leagues attempting to access them;

- **Linkages:** There is a networking and linkage failure throughout the inner city feeder system for baseball in Baltimore. What happens to the child after little league? Who is calling whom to monitor the children's progress? How is a potential star groomed? In short, how is one baseball development program linked to another? To revitalize baseball in Baltimore, all of the broken linkages must be mended, from little league up through the chain to junior high, high school, the amateur leagues, the minor leagues, all the way up to the major leagues. They must all work hand in glove.

What happens to the Black inner city child after little league? In inner cities throughout America, there are few options other than the RBI program.

Next Base for Urban Blacks: RBI

In the absence of junior varsity in public schools in Baltimore City, one of the few available low cost options for Blacks to continue playing baseball is the RBI league. If the experience of the James Mosher little league program is typical of other Black inner city little leagues, however, few Black youths will probably continue on in baseball after little league. In fact, the remaining kids will probably switch over to football or basketball.

In baseball vernacular RBI stands for "Runs Batted In." In terms of MLB's outreach program, it stands for "Reviving Baseball in Inner Cities," a program to "go beyond the ballpark into the community."

Reviving Baseball in Inner Cities (RBI) is entering its 19th season in 2007. Since its inception in 1989, the RBI program has grown from a local program for boys in South Central Los Angeles to an international campaign encompassing more than 200 cities, and as many as 120,000 male and female participants a year.

The Baltimore Orioles launched its local RBI program in 1997, it is 100% funded by the Orioles organization at over $30,000 per year. One of its main aims is to fill a void for older youth who are too old for little league, in order to give them an opportunity to play baseball longer.

The Oriole's RBI League has two divisions: Junior (ages 13-15) and Senior (ages 16-18). Teams are signed up through the Baltimore City Recreation and Parks Department and the local Boys & Girls Clubs. Over 200 children participated in 2007.

RBI participants must demonstrate consistent scholastic effort and display good citizenship, both on and off the field. Specifically, the goals of the Orioles RBI program are:

- To motivate children to do well in school;
- To generate interest in major league baseball;
- To promote the development of self-esteem among inner city youth;
- To provide positive role models in both the educational and recreational aspects of students lives;
- To facilitate the development of skills, team work, and self-discipline.

The Baltimore Orioles provide an RBI coordinator staff member and all equipment for participants, including bats, balls, gloves, and uniforms (even including socks and stirrups). The Orioles also give each team the opportunity to play at Camden Yards at the end of their season. In addition, the Orioles hosts RBI players, coaches, and umpires for several Orioles games each year and provides them with game tickets, souvenirs, and concessions. The club holds a recognition ceremony prior to an Orioles game for the two top teams (Junior & Senior divisions), and an Orioles player presents team members with trophies. The club also sends two teams to the RBI Regional Tournament (providing bus transportation, overnight accommodations and meal money). The League grew by four teams in 2006.

It's not clear how many, if any, Black inner city players ascended to higher levels in baseball from the RBI. The Orioles own measure of success is that "more teams have entered the leagues over time," according to Orioles officials. Now that Orioles Scout **Dean Albany** has taken over the program, however, it's expected that a higher level of play within the RBI leagues will ensue. In the dual capacity as Manager of the Orioles amateur team, the *Youse's Maryland Orioles*, Albany is used to winning and is expected to bring his long years of knowledge and experience to reinvigorating the RBI program.

According to *The 2006 Racial and Gender Report Card: Major League Baseball* (Lapchick, Ekiyor, & Ruiz), the MLB has a number of initiatives, in addition to the RBI program, which endeavor to reconnect African American youths to the game of baseball. The following list, shown in Box 9, is from the "2006 Report Card." It's interesting to note that none of the James Mosher officials have heard of any of listed initiatives, except the Baseball Tomorrow Fund. There's no *"Academy"* in Baltimore, though reportedly one is soon coming to Washington, DC in association with the Washington Nationals.

Box 9
MLB's Urban Youth Initiatives

MLB's mission to grow its game entails:
1) Making meaningful contributions to the development of minority communities,
2) Providing safe and organized recreational activities for urban youth, and
3) Preparing minority high school players for college and professional baseball and softball programs.

One example of this commitment is ***Major League Baseball's Youth Baseball Academy*** located on the campus of Compton Community College in Los Angeles, California. The Academy is an actual brick and mortar presence in the community and is now officially open for business. The Academy is home to four fields: two regulation baseball fields, one softball field and one youth field. MLB will operate the facility and work with local youth organizations to identify the Academy's attendees. In addition to offering year-round baseball and softball instruction, MLB will provide academic support and career development through after-school study programs. Baseball's return on investment for this multi-million dollar facility is the marketplace strategy that eventually thousands will participate as members of the Academy and ultimately become players, baseball operation and business operations employees, franchise leaders and fans. The Academy opened on February 28, 2006 and has supported more than 2,000 youth through camps, clinics, tournaments and scout leagues.

"Breaking Barriers: In Sports, In Life" is a multi-curricular character education program developed by Major League Baseball, The Major League Baseball Player's Trust for Children, and Scholastic Inc. The program utilizes baseball-themed features, activities and lessons to teach children grades K-12 the values and traits they need to deal with the barriers and challenges in their lives. Using baseball as a metaphor for life, the curriculum is based on the nine values demonstrated by Jackie Robinson. The nine values are: Determination, Commitment, Persistence, Integrity, Justice, Courage, Teamwork, Citizenship and Excellence.

"The Baseball Tomorrow Fund" is a joint initiative between Major League Baseball and the Major League Baseball Player's Association. It is designed to promote and enhance the growth of the game throughout the world by funding programs, field improvements and equipment purchases to encourage and maintain youth participation in baseball and softball. Since its inception in 1999, BTF has awarded grants totaling more than $10 million and has benefited 120,000 youth participating in more than 200 baseball and softball programs across the US.

The "Civil Rights Game" will be staged by Major League Baseball on March 31, when the defending World Series champion St. Louis Cardinals play the Cleveland Indians in an exhibition game at AutoZone Park in Memphis, the home of the National Civil Rights Museum and the city where Rev. Martin Luther King Jr. was assassinated on April 4, 1968. The game is planned to culminate a day during which baseball will celebrate the nation's civil rights movement.

The job of reviving baseball in inner cities cannot be left to the MLB alone, however. As with everything in life, leadership matters, and in the case of baseball, it's important for leadership to come from the bottom up, as well as from the top down.

One well-known leader for baseball in Baltimore is Cal Ripken, Jr.. There's hardly a little league or baseball effort in the city that his foundation hasn't reached and contributed to in some way, including the James Mosher little league program.

Cal Ripken with James Mosher kids

The impact of the Ripken Foundation's recent contribution to the RBI program on inner city leagues like James Mosher will depend in part on the ability of such leagues to make a compelling case for assistance.

Box 10
"Headlines: Read all About It"

April 9, 2007: BALTIMORE -- Baltimore icon Cal Ripken Jr. joined forces with Major League Baseball on Monday in a joint press conference that emphasized their shared interest in reaching the youth of America.

Ripken announced that the Cal Ripken Sr. Foundation will donate nearly $1 million worth of cash and equipment to the Reviving Baseball in the Inner City (RBI) program, which is designed to increase interest in the game among inner-city children as well as teach them life lessons. The donations will take place over the next two years and may increase participation in the program by up to 30 percent.

"We all have a common vision to improve the game and to reach kids," Ripken said. "Sometimes, it's misunderstood. We're not necessarily reaching kids where the end result is a big-league baseball career. It's actually using baseball to help teach life lessons, and that's really what the Cal Ripken Sr. Foundation is all about. "A very small percentage of all kids will fulfill the dream of going on to be a big-league player, but baseball can impact positively the direction of their lives."

Ripken's foundation, named after his late father, stresses education and nutrition in addition to all the baseball lessons. The foundation's overriding mission is to "use baseball and softball to develop character and give disadvantaged youth opportunities to succeed." In that respect, its goal dovetails perfectly with the RBI program. "I have great admiration for Cal Ripken, Jr., and his family and am extremely pleased that Major League Baseball

and the Cal Ripken, Sr. Foundation will join forces to provide children with a program that will help them grow and build a better future," Major League Baseball Commissioner Allan H. (Bud) Selig said in a statement.

MLB has administered the initiative since 1991, and it's grown from 14 cities to more than 200 worldwide. The program embraces more than 100,000 kids each year and has donated more than $20 million in resources over the last 15 years. One hundred fifty players have been drafted from the ranks of RBI, and six of them have been first-round picks. Ripken, ...inducted into the National Baseball Hall of Fame... said it's important to use his fame to impact the game in a positive way.

Bob DuPuy, the president and chief operating officer of MLB, said he couldn't ask for a better partner than Ripken. "We're enormously honored to [have] one of the terrific ambassadors of the game," DuPuy said, "who played his entire career here in Baltimore and who is just revered throughout Major League baseball for his work ethic, for his sportsmanship and for the type of grace we'd like to see instilled in young people throughout the RBI program." When asked about the dwindling number of African-Americans taking part in today's game, DuPuy made a few societal points and addressed his hopes for the future. First and foremost, he said the league is concerned with keeping itself relevant in an ever-changing sea of sports culture.

"Our game is extraordinarily diverse, and it reflects the diversity of American society," he said. "But it's also true that we've lost kids to other sports over the last 25-30 years. We'd like to recapture those kids and those athletes and get them into Major League Baseball. ... I think we're doing better, but I think we've still got a long way to go."

 Next Base for Suburban Youth— Junior Varsity (JV)

This is where *"A Tale of Two Cities"* comes into sharp focus. The public school system of the City of Baltimore has had to take some funding hits. Apparently along the way, it has dropped the ball on baseball.

Exactly when junior league baseball was cut from public schools in the City of Baltimore is an open question; it was apparently so long along that no one remembers when it was, but one thing is clear: it's gone and there is nothing in its place except the RBI program for inner city adolescent youth.

Hours of competitive playing and top coaching are lost in the absence of junior varsity; as a result, opportunities to connect young African Americans to baseball are being lost. By the time Black inner city youths show back up in high school to play baseball, after their little league experience some years earlier, they are rusty and far behind their suburban counterparts in skill and knowledge of the game. Whereas inner city little leaguers might have shown promise early on, and may have natural ability, without constant learning and opportunities for high level competitive play, their ability diminishes.

There's no money for junior varsity, but money can be found under the right set of circumstances—and with the right amount of political pressure—for other baseball priorities. The financing of the baseball stadium in Baltimore provides a glimpse of what was involved, as discussed in Box 11.

Box 11
New Stadium: Baltimore

...The Orioles occupied Memorial Stadium since 1954. Originally constructed for football, Memorial was located in a residential neighborhood on the north side of Baltimore. With only 5,000 parking spaces in the neighborhood and the nearest freeway several miles away, big crowds meant even bigger traffic jams at the end of the game.

Although the Orioles periodically talked about the need for a new stadium, their pleas fell on deaf ears until March 29, 1984-- the day when a caravan of moving trucks hauled Baltimore's beloved Colts out of town in the middle of the night. With forty years of football history en route to Indianapolis, Baltimore Mayor William Donald Schaefer wouldn't risk the Orioles following suit.

...Schaefer sought advice from Hellmuth Obata Kassabaum (HOK), the nation's leading sports architecture firm. In August 1986, HOK recommended construction of a huge new multipurpose stadium, surrounded by parking lots, at Camden Yards.

That November Mayor Schaefer was elected Governor of Maryland. Soon after he took office, the state legislature established a new instant lottery and dedicated its proceeds to construction of new sports stadia. The Maryland Sports Authority would first build a new, baseball-only park at Camden Yards, then seek to lure a replacement NFL franchise with promises of a new football stadium.

Many legislators who had opposed the stadium were even angrier about the financing. The lottery drew most of its money from the poor, making it a spectacularly inappropriate vehicle for subsidizing a new stadium. Moreover, before earmarking lottery money for the stadium, **Maryland had rejected other attempts to dedicate proceeds from the lottery for education or other public purposes.**

At least the legislature had chosen the right location. Camden Yards was a short walk south of downtown Baltimore, close to both highways and mass transit. The site ... was even intimately tied to Baltimore's baseball tradition: Babe Ruth was born a few blocks away, and his father ran a saloon in what would become center field.

Since 1960, two basic stadium designs had evolved: isolated islands in an ocean of parking (Anaheim, Kansas City, Philadelphia, San Francisco), and downtown domes that overwhelmed the game (Minnesota, Seattle, Toronto, Houston). The Orioles demanded

something different -- a design as harmonious with its urban setting as the modern need for skyboxes and premium seats would allow.

Camden Yards is an esthetic success -- but is it also a financial success? That depends on your perspective.

For the State of Maryland, which built and paid for the facility, Camden Yards was a relative bargain. $99 million of its $205 million cost went to acquire the land and prepare the site. The stadium itself, originally budgeted for $78.4 million, cost $106.5 million after cost overruns and the Orioles' design changes. Camden Yards cost barely 1/3 as much as SkyDome, and just $38 million more than New Comiskey, which had been built at a much cheaper location with no apparent concern for esthetics.

For the Orioles, of course, the new park was a license to print money... Their 72 luxury boxes command premium prices.

A 1997 study found that the move from Memorial Stadium to Camden Yards brought the Orioles $25.5 million/year in added revenues, while rent and related expenses rose only $2.4 million. (The Maryland Stadium Authority deliberately charged the Orioles a sub-market rent to give the club more money to spend on players, and allowed the club to keep nearly all the revenue generated by premium seats, luxury boxes and in-stadium advertising.) Without investing a dime of their own to build Camden Yards, the Orioles received an annual windfall of more than $23 million.

Teams in other cities took notice. In 1995, Bud Selig declared that Camden Yards "changed stadium financing. Those clubs have revenue sources that people didn't have before. There are a million of them. Luxury boxes, concessions, a whole series of things, club seating. There are stores within the park, restaurants within it. It started with Camden Yards and went to Cleveland, Texas, Colorado. If you want your club to be competitive, you have to have it."

Unsurprisingly, Selig made this comment at a time when he was lobbying the government of Wisconsin to build him a new stadium. "We'll build another Camden Yards" became the rallying cry of stadium advocates across the country as they promised that their new park would "revitalize our downtown and pay for itself by attracting out-of-towners."

But even Camden Yards hasn't generated such economic benefits. In 1997, Johns Hopkins economists Bruce W. Hamilton and Peter Kahn assessed the economic impact of Camden Yards in Chapter 8 of *Sports, Jobs & Taxes* (see sidebar). Their conclusion:

"Taking account of all of the measurable benefits of the Camden Yards investment (that is, job creation and tax imports), we estimate that baseball at Camden Yards generates approximately $3 million in annual economic benefits to the Maryland economy, at an annual cost to the taxpayers of Maryland of approximately $14 million."

Even Camden Yards doesn't come close to "paying for itself."

Hamilton and Kahn spend 20 pages elaborating on this conclusion. On the expense side, they calculate that depreciation and interest cost the Maryland Stadium Authority about $14 million per year. The other major expense, maintaining Camden Yards, is covered by the Orioles' rent.

On the revenue side, the economists accept Oriole estimates that more than 70% of the increased attendance has come from out of state. However, they note that hotel occupancy rates did not rise after Camden Yards opened, which suggests that most of these out-of-towners went straight home without spending much more in Maryland.

Hamilton and Kahn conclude that more than half of the $3 million in extra revenue comes from admission and concession taxes at Camden Yards itself. Most of the remainder is attributable to additional spending in the surrounding area, with less than $500,000 derived from the creation of new jobs. All told, each dollar of extra revenue from the ballpark costs Maryland taxpayers almost $5 -- making Camden Yards one of the few investments worse than the lottery which financed it.

Baltimore's experience shows that regardless of what owners and city officials say, investing $200 million of public funds in even the best-designed ballpark is virtually impossible to justify on economic grounds.

Of course, that doesn't end the debate. Camden Yards' $11 million annual subsidy costs each household in Greater Baltimore less than $15. For hard-core Oriole fans, that's a small price to pay for turning the Orioles from a medium-revenue to a high-revenue team. (Most would probably pay even more to keep the Angelos family from wasting their money on aging mediocrities.) But there aren't enough hard-core fans to persuade a legislature to appropriate the funds or to win a referendum, so stadium proponents need the support of casual fans and civic leaders.

These people don't live and die with the local team, but they recognize that on one level, the presence of the Orioles confers "major league" status on Baltimore. From this perspective a baseball club is a community asset, like a zoo or library, which even those who don't go to ballgames can support.

To win their support, ballpark backers need to convince them that the team will move unless a new stadium is built.

That's why in city after city the new-stadium dance has begun with the owner of the local club solemnly announcing that the team simply cannot survive without a new park. It's also why MLB keeps the number of franchises slightly below the number of interested cities: no one will listen to the owner's laments unless he can credibly threaten that if his hometown won't meet his demands, Washington or Charlotte will.

But there's no money to fund junior varsity baseball for public schools in Baltimore. It's unfortunate because JV baseball is an important rung in the ladder up to "The Show." An excerpt from a suburban Maryland school's JV program underscores the importance of junior varsity.

Box 12
JUNIOR VARSITY PROGRAM PHILOSOPHY
(Manifesto Taken From a Typical Suburban Maryland School)

"The junior varsity level is intended for those who display the potential of continued development into productive varsity level performers. Team membership is usually dominated by 9th and 10th graders; 7th and 8th graders may also be included if they have satisfied all selection classification requirements. At this level, athletes are expected to commit themselves to the team, program, and continued self-development. Emphasis on physical conditioning, refinement of skills, elements and strategies of team play, in addition to emotional development, is increased. The junior varsity player must realize that practice sessions are important and vital if the program is to be successful. Meaningful contest participation will exist over the course of the season, but specified amounts of playing time are not guaranteed. While contests and practices are rarely held on holidays and Sundays, practices may be held during school vacations. With the goal of becoming a varsity athlete in sight, a high level of dedication and commitment is expected at the junior varsity level."

As there's no junior varsity for Baltimore inner city youths, no one will ever know how many of its kids *"cudda been contendas,"* and how many might have been able to develop baseball "tools" like Torii Hunter.

Torii Hunter Los Angeles Angels

 "Extra Innings"— *Select or Travel Team*

How many hours of top notch coaching and instruction go into the youth who is chosen to participate on a select or travel team? How much did it cost to prepare the youth who is good enough to play on such a team, and how much does it cost to actually play on the team? Ask **Dean Albany.** He is the first to tell you how expensive it is to be on a select team. While there are some African Americans on some select teams, he says, "they're usually from the suburbs or from families in higher income brackets," but good talent is recruited from everywhere for the team. In the past, many famous African American players, like Reggie Jackson, played for the team.

Many who have pondered the question of why the number of African Americans is declining in baseball cite the cost associated with playing on such teams. Indeed it is expensive to play on a travel team. However, the much bigger hurdle is being able to foot the overall bill that accrues from Tee-Ball through select team ball. But the biggest hurdle of all, bigger than the money, is to get African American parents to attend practice sessions so that they can also learn the lessons and reinforce them with kids at home. If they don't find ways to increase the learning opportunities and practice time of their kids, a lot more money is required to obtain the quality coaching that is necessary to increase the child's competitiveness.

> Black children grow up in families with much lower incomes than white children. Median family income for parents of black children was $27,100 in 1967–1971, compared to $61,100 for parents of white children, in inflation-adjusted dollars. The lower economic status into which black children are born is also evident in the fact that nearly two-thirds (62 percent) of black children were born to parents in the bottom fifth, or quintile, of the overall income distribution. Only 8 percent of black children were born to parents in the middle fifth of the income distribution, compared to 22 percent of white children.

Lack of disposable income doesn't explain all, however. In, *"Collective identity and basketball: An explanation for the decreasing number of African-Americans on America's baseball diamonds,"* Ogden, 2003 wrote:

"To what extent youth select teams serve as the pool of prospective or future college and Major League players is not known. Select teams, however, supposedly contain the best players of their age group in the community and provide more playing time than other types of youth ball teams. Players usually are chosen by select teams via open tryouts or are recruited because of previously demonstrated skills; and they get many opportunities to demonstrate those skills in "select" baseball... Brian Embery... said some select teams groom players for college competition. He said about one-third of his college players were on select teams as youngsters. Most good Division I schools are stockpiled with kids who have grown up playing competitive baseball," ...The kids have traveled a lot and played against the best teams in the country, and that's what I try to do with my group of kids (Embrey). But inner city youth baseball leagues don't offer nearly the amount or level of competition that select teams enjoy. Teams in inner city leagues, such as those sponsored by Boys' and Girls' Clubs and YMCA's, usually play 10 to 15 games per summer and against each other instead of out-of-town competition."

Next Base—From RBI To High School Varsity Baseball

It has been said that "tomorrow's collegiate student-athletes are today's grade-schoolers and high-schoolers." Is this true for poor Black inner city youth, and specifically, is it true for most Blacks from inner city Baltimore? Unforunately not.

In the absence of junior varsity in the City of Baltimore, youths are losing the opportunity to further develop the baseball skills they began to acquire from Tee-Ball onward. By the time the inner child re-enters the world of baseball in high school, hard won skills have to be re-learned.

The staff of *Baseball America* and the *National High School Baseball Coaches Association* ranked **Calvert Hall High School** as number 32 in the nation, with a perfect record of 33-0. It's the only "Top 50 Ranked" High School in the State of Maryland. Its Top 50 ranking demonstrates that very impressive baseball is being played in Baltimore, but in the county's higher income districts, not in the city.

There's a stark difference between Calvert Hall High School and the two predominantly Black High Schools interviewed for this book, inner city based **Carver Vocational High School**, and county based **Randallstown High School**. Important differences include the percentage of students that are eligble for the school's lunch program; the percentage of Black students; the average test scores for algebra, and English; the percentage that attend college; and, average expenditures for the baseball program. The odds favor Calvert Hall High School.

Baseball coaches in high schools with a predominantly African American population face many challenges. They have youths in whom the minimal baseball investment has been made as compared to their suburban counterparts, and youths for whom the high school curricula poses great difficulties. Moreover, institutionally, they are championing a sport that has lost popularity, and not just among African American youth.

According to a 2006 *Harris Interactive Poll* (Box 13), baseball is trending down, especially among today's youth and certain demographics.

Box 13:
Demographic Variations in Favorite Sports
"If you had to choose, which ONE of these sports would you say is your favorite?"
Base: All adults who follow more than one sport

Sport	All Adults	Highest		Lowest	
	%		%		%
Pro football	29	East	39	Less than $15,000	20
		$35,000-$49,999	39	West	21
		Gen Xers (30-41)	36	$25,000-$34,999	21
		African Americans	35	Matures	22
Baseball	14	Liberals	20	African American	7
		East	19	Conservatives	10
College Football	13	Post-graduate	23	East	6
		$25,000-$34,999	19	$35,000-$44,999	8
		South	19	African Americans	9
		$75,000+	18	Less than $15,000	9
		$25,000-$34,999	19	Post graduate	1
Auto Racing	9	High School or less	15	Liberals	4
		Gen Xers (30-41)	13	College Graduates	5

Source: http://www.harrisinteractive.com/harris_poll/index.asp?PID=719

Despite the foregoing, dedicated high school baseball coaches like **Reginald Smith** of Randallstown High and **Travis Chapman** of Carver High School never lose hope. Both are convinced that their coaching skills, enthusiasm, and determination to win will draw more Black youth into their respective high school baseball programs. According to Coach Chapman, "the word that Carver's baseball team means business has already spread, and as a result, more interested players are signing up."

Chapman knows he is fighting an uphill battle, and the battle is on all fronts. What happens with the baseball player before he enters high school has a bearing on what can happen with the player in high school. Ideally, he would like to have a roster of highly motivated players with "hunger" in their bellies for baseball, but instead what he gets are players who, in many cases, would rather be playing football. He has to constantly "sell" baseball to them. The "sell" wouldn't be necessary, according to Chapman, if the MLB did a better job of marketing the sport in the first place. Furthermore, he underscores, if the players came to him better prepared, his job wouldn't be so difficult. Ill-prepared, and badly trained baseball players are factors, Chapman notes. "Some have received their foundation training in baseball from bad little league programs, and most come from households that don't place a premium on baseball."

Chapman is on the front line leading a charge to revive baseball in the inner city, but he can't do it alone. He underscores the importance of having better coaches in little league programs, and suggests that there should be better skills training program for them, as well as background checks on the coaches. "It's not enough for the coaches to know baseball; they must also be exemplary in their personal behavior and comportment." He underscores, "Baseball, after all, is a civil sport, and everyone involved must conduct themselves civilly at all times, and this includes the coaches." He also knows that mothers are on the front line; they have to understand what's at stake, and do their parts. "The RBI program also needs to be upgraded and to provide more competitive playing and training opportunities." In short, "everybody has to get in the game. It takes a village."

On his part, he is trying to fill in the resource gap he faces in his own program. He has no access to indoor training facilities; the team can't start practicing until the beginning of February; many need tutoring; and he could use a few more coaches—he only has two. The list of needs is long, but his passion is great. This is only his second year at Carver, but the word is getting out that he means business. Last year, only 13 players signed up, but the following year, 15 presented themselves. What Coach Chapman is trying to do is to present them with an opportunity, and to prepare them for a bigger future in baseball, against all odds.

Enthusiasm notwithstanding, inner city coaches know they are fighting an uphill battle to keep the dream of baseball alive. As **Reginald Smith** explained, "baseball is an outlet for Blacks, but it's not a priority. Upon deep reflection and pondering the question of why baseball has trended down among Blacks, Smith explains:

> For many decades, economic and social discrimination prevented Black people from being able to fully embrace baseball, but such circumstances did not extinguish the hopes and dreams of little boys in the neighborhood who wanted to grow up to be Major League baseball players. The dream was at its height when Frank Robinson was the local hero in Baltimore in the 1960s. He was an icon who brought greatness to the city, and was an ideal role model. He set an example demonstrating how a 'no-nonsense' powerfully built Black man could excel; he won the "Most Valuable Player" in both leagues, and was the last player to win the 'Triple Crown' (leader in homeruns, RBIs, and batting average). During his time with the Baltimore Orioles, the team won three pennants and a World Series.
>
> On every playground in city schoolyards, baseball was the game being played. It was inexpensive, 18 people played at a time, and it was played from sun up to sun down. A major league glove was affordable, a bat cost less than $5, and rubber balls could be purchased from the corner store for $.15 cents. Games were competitive and fun. Kids were not privy to any formal training, nor were there any skills camps to attend; one learned by watching major league players on television, then going out into the street to practice what they saw on television.

Every neighborhood had baseball "hot shots." Street teams formed to play against other street teams, and neighborhood teams formed to compete against other neighborhood teams. Back then, the Recreation Department wasn't needed to organize the games the community did it. Large crowds came out to watch the games, and each team's captain was a hero. These heroes soon became leaders. Though we were poor, we didn't know how poor we were, because we were rich in spirit and aspirations. We felt good about ourselves, we felt good about baseball, and were confident in our ability to master the game.

Things changed with the introduction of Pell grants. Many colleges and universities across the nation benefited from these grants, which saved them financially. It wasn't long before such schools caught on to how to play the new game. The new game entailed recruiting "blue chip" Black athletes from inner cities, and designing a financial package for them that lured them into their schools. Up to 90 scholarships per school could be offered to play football, baseball could only offer 11.7 scholarships. It didn't take long before the best athletes began to change their allegiance from baseball to football. Exacerbating the problem for baseball was that pitchers were the ones that got the full scholarships, while the remaining scholarships were sliced up among five or six "impact players." As Black college students needed scholarships to attend, the lack of baseball scholarships became a major contributing factor to diminishing the attractiveness of baseball as a route to economic empowerment for Blacks.

Overtime, the major universities started putting a better athletic product on the football fields and basketball courts than baseball. The alumni, local businesses, and media all got behind the football and basketball teams. Inner city kids were increasingly recruited by better schools to play football and basketball, while baseball was left in the dust. As Black neighborhoods began to decline in the 1970s, Black kids wanted a way out. When they began to see their neighborhood friends on television become stars in the NFL and the NBA, gaining lucrative endorsements, they want to follow the same critical path out of the ghetto. By contrast, the path of the baseball "Pied Piper" entailed many narrow pathways, circuitous routes, dark alleyways, and the journey of a 1,000 miles. Why take a journey of a 1,000 miles when you can leap in a single bound directly into the NFL or the NBA?

The very definition of fun has changed. The NFL and the NBA figured out how to market their games, how to make half times fun, and how to have the best cheerleaders who danced to the hip-hop urban beats. The slam-dunk, and the goal line dance, made the games more exciting to watch, at the same time, the NFL and NBA were amenable to making rule changes that sped up the games, bringing them into alignment with the new realities of modern day living. Baseball leadership, by contrast, has not stepped up to the plate; it has failed to realize that it too must change to compete.

Next Base: From High School to Community College

For many, going directly to a university from high school isn't an option. For inner city youth in Baltimore who don't go directly to universities, if they are still interested in playing baseball, they have an option to play at Baltimore City Community College (BCCC).

Ruffin Bell is the Head Baseball Coach at BCCC. He knows baseball and has been involved with it in many capacities in Baltimore, where he grew up. He has been on the staff of the Cal Ripken Foundation, having served as a Program Coordinator in 2005. He attended Coppin State University, received a degree in English from it 1999, and played baseball there from 1994 to 1997. He earned a Master's Degree in Sports Administration from Grambling State in 2001, and was featured in the February 2004 *Coaching Management Magazine,* for starting *Black College Baseball.com,* a website that highlights HBCU baseball programs.

Today, his mission is to grow baseball at BCCC, but like others in the inner city trying to keep baseball alive, he faces many challenges.

Like other baseball "Pied Pipers" in Baltimore's inner city, Bell is doing his part, and he is pulling out all of the stops. He's recruiting from all over, and he knows where to look, even beyond his own backyard, in such places as Atlanta, Chicago, Alabama, Detroit, and Boston. He knows there are "diamonds in the rough" out there, and he has a plan to help them shine in his program. Having landed the position of Head Baseball Coach in August 2007, he's just getting started. But, he's hitting the ground running by studying what other Division II schools are doing and learning best-case practices from them. "Philadelphia's program, for instance, is a good model," according to Bell. He's encouraged that the NCAA scholarship program may soon change to allow more baseball scholarships. This will help, he says. The main thing though is that he's on the case, and his baseball program is part of the plan to revive baseball in inner cities.

Next Base: High School Baseball to Division I College Baseball

There aren't many Division I HBCUs left, and only seven (Bethune Cookman, Coppin State, Delaware State, Florida A & M, University of Maryland Eastern Shore, Norfolk State, and North Carolina A & T) are in the Mid-Eastern Athletic Conference (MEAC),

Courtesy of the Library of Congress

Morris Brown baseball team

which includes Coppin State University. There was a time, however, when baseball ruled in HBCUs, but that seems long ago.

Today, the limited pool of available scholarships upon which many urban Blacks depend, given their relatively marginalized economic position, is an important factor that has a bearing on the ability of Historically Black Colleges and Universities (HBCUs) to attract baseball talent. Another important factor is that in order to qualify for available scholarships, players have to maintain NCAA-mandated academic standards to play on college teams.

> The National Collegiate Athletic Association (NCAA) is a voluntary organization through which the nation's colleges and universities govern their athletics programs. It is comprised of institutions, conferences, organizations and individuals committed to the best interests, education and athletics participation of student-athletes.

The issue of limited available baseball scholarships is a very important clue in the mystery of why the participation of Blacks in baseball has been declining. Mo Johnson, a sports fan, wrote an article that sheds light on the issue.

By Mo Johnson: ... Title IX is the most obvious reason there are so few blacks in pro baseball. The way Title IX has been interpreted and implemented, it effectively restricts the number of baseball scholarships colleges and universities offer. In fact, most schools, even major schools like the University of Florida, do not offer any "full-ride" college baseball scholarships at all.

Obviously, without a scholarship, many young black athletes cannot afford to go to college and play college baseball or, later, professional baseball. Naturally, young black athletes will gravitate towards football and basketball, which are; sports that offer more scholarships. Over the past generation, this shift has become pronounced.

Title IX was enacted by the Congress in 1972. The law, itself, is not controversial...It simply states that "No person in the United States, shall, on the basis of sex, be excluded from participation in, be denied the benefits of, or be subjected to discrimination under any education program or activity receiving Federal financial assistance."

So, Title IX prohibits discrimination on the basis of sex... [and] applies to discrimination in athletics. So far, so good. The problem comes in the interpretation of the law.

In 1979, The U.S. Department of Heath, Education, and Welfare (this was before we had a separate "Department of Education") issued a policy interpreting Title IX. The policy provided that, in order to comply with Title IX, a college or university must pass one of three tests. The college or university must show that it:

1. Provides athletic opportunities substantially proportionate to student enrollment; or,

2. Demonstrates a continual expansion of athletic opportunities for the underrepresented gender; or,

3. Provides full and effective accommodation of the interest and ability of the underrepresented gender.

Many schools try to comply with Title IX by passing the third test. The problem is that this test is very subjective. How do you prove you are providing "full and effective accommodation of interest and ability?" You can take surveys to get some gauge of interest. But, in the end, if a school relies on the third test, it will be vulnerable to a lawsuit by someone who thinks it has not complied.

Some of the larger, financially strong, schools comply with Title IX by meeting the second test. They "demonstrate a continual expansion of athletic opportunities for the underrepresented gender" by adding a women's sports team. Every time a school does that, it is "good to go" for about five years. But, adding new sports is a money-losing proposition and smaller, less affluent, schools can't afford to do that—at least, not forever.

So, ultimately, all schools will want, or need, to comply with Title IX by meeting the first test. And, it is this first test that has really caused the problems.

If a school has a Division I football team, it can award up to 85 football scholarships (per NCAA rules). The school can also award up to 13 scholarships for its men's basketball team. Of course, to compete in these sports, at the Division I level, the school will have to award these 98 men's athletics scholarships.

Women now make up a whopping 58% of college enrollment. So, to pass the first test, and award scholarships "substantially proportionate" to student enrollment, the school has to award about 110 scholarships to women just to equal the scholarships provided for men's football and basketball.

And, when you add in other men's sports – it becomes impossible to meet the "substantially proportionate" test without severely cutting scholarships in other men's sports or dropping some sports altogether.

So, that's exactly what schools do. When you look at sports like tennis, golf, track and field/cross country, swimming/diving – there are more scholarships awarded to women than men in each of these sports. Even in basketball–men's college basketball teams get 13 scholarships; women's teams get 15.

Wrestling is one of the biggest sports at most high schools. There is a large base of college wrestling fans. But, thanks to Title IX, there are few college wrestling scholarships.

James Madison University ...announced that it will drop 10 sports; 7 men's teams; 3 women's teams in order to meet the "substantially proportionate" test of Title IX.

You might say: "well, they should just get rid of football." The problem with that idea is that football is the only college sport that makes money. Men's basketball about breaks even (if the school is lucky). No other college sport pays for itself.

This means the college will likely lose money on every other sports team it adds, including every woman's sports team. Football is the bill-payer for many of these sports at many schools. So, getting rid of football is not the answer.

So, what does all this have to do with Jackie Robinson and the lack of black professional baseball players today?

Here's what.

Because of the way Title IX has been interpreted and implemented, college baseball programs are only allowed 11.7 scholarships. Since about 30 players are on a college baseball team, normally, no one gets a full scholarship. So, baseball is becoming, increasingly, a sport for the relatively affluent. The reason is simple. You have to be able to afford to pay for college to play college baseball.

By contrast, in football and basketball, almost everyone on the team has a full scholarship. For a young, black athlete, football and basketball offer a much more likely scholarship opportunity. It's not surprising, then, that black athletes have gravitated toward football and basketball and away from baseball. It's common sense.

It's ironic that, Title IX, a law intended to limit sex discrimination in athletics has morphed into, perhaps, the most significant cause of sex, race and class discrimination in college athletics today.

Coppin State University's Head Baseball **Coach Harvey Lee** is feeling the pain. He has two problems: First, students who present themselves to play on the baseball team haven't always met the NCAA-imposed grade requirements. Coach Lee explains, "Many students present themselves for the baseball team claiming to have the requisite 2.0 grade point average, but "when you look behind the numbers, you might find that the 2.0 is based on having excelled in basket weaving, and other 'non-core' courses." This is where years of living in the urban ghetto, and coming from households that don't put a premium on education and discipline, comes back to haunt the "would-be" Black college baseball player. Suddenly, excellence is demanded on multiple fronts simultaneously, and many of the students are not prepared to meet the challenge. The other problem, of course, is the lack of full-ride baseball scholarships.

Coach Lee is motivated and maintains his enthusiasm no matter what. He's hungering to win and he's pulling out all the stops to make it happen. In the process, he is searching high and low in the city, and outside of the city, looking for Black baseball talent to recruit to the university. He is even reaching all the way down to little leagues in Baltimore to catch talent on the way up.

Though motivated, Coach Lee is also a realistic straight shooter. He's clear on the fact that an HBCU, like Coppin State University, can't attract elite athletes, so his goal is "to attract average talent and try to make them into elite athletes." The key to doing this he says, is first, to maintain standards. He is adamant in his refusal to play Division II or Division III teams: "Coppin State University is a Division I school, and it will play other Division I teams," Coach Lee says.

Lee was an outstanding player at Southern (La.) where he finished his career in 1984 as the school career, and single season, home run record holder. He earned All-Southwestern Athletic Conference honors three times and ranked 14th nationally in runs batted in 1983. He spent the next three years playing in the Yankee farm system and was also a replacement player for the Montreal Expos during spring training in 1995. Lee spent one season as a student assistant coach at his alma mater and also served as the head coach of a summer league team in Atlanta comprised of collegiate players throughout the state of Georgia. He also has coached at various high schools in Florida and also worked with the Bucky Dent Baseball School and the Manny Sanguillen Travel Baseball School.

Coach Harvey Lee

The other key for success, according to Coach Lee, is to build a strong team of like-minded assistant coaches; but it's not just the coaches that have to be on the same page, the players must also understand how they are being coached and why. To ensure that the players are clear about what their strengths and weaknesses are, he believes that one picture is worth a thousand words, Coach Lee videotapes them during practices and games to show them where they need improvement.

There's a lot that Coach Lee must teach his team, and some of it is about the facts of life. Life isn't always fair, and neither is baseball.

Lapchik's *2006 Racial and Gender Report Card: Major League Baseball* puts one of the issues, stacking, in the spotlight.

> **Stacking:** The Racial and Gender Report Cards previously examined the issue of stacking for the positions of pitcher, catcher, and third baseman filled by African-Americans. The question still remains, but now takes into account the three positions specifically identified by MLB as pitcher, catcher, and now "infielder." While the terminology has changed slightly, the concerns remain the same. These are baseball's primary "thinking positions." Only three percent of pitchers, and nine percent of infielders were African-American. Historically, there have been almost no African-American catchers

and that remains the same. It is worth noting that in 2004 when the Report Card looked at the isolated position of third baseman versus the entire infield, the percent of African-Americans was only five percent. The percentage of African-American pitchers is less than one half of what it was in 1983. Twenty-eight percent of outfielders, who rely on speed and reactive ability, were African-American during the 2006 MLB season. This was nearly three times the percentage of African-Americans in MLB.

The issue of the fairness of umpiring has also recently been in the spotlight.

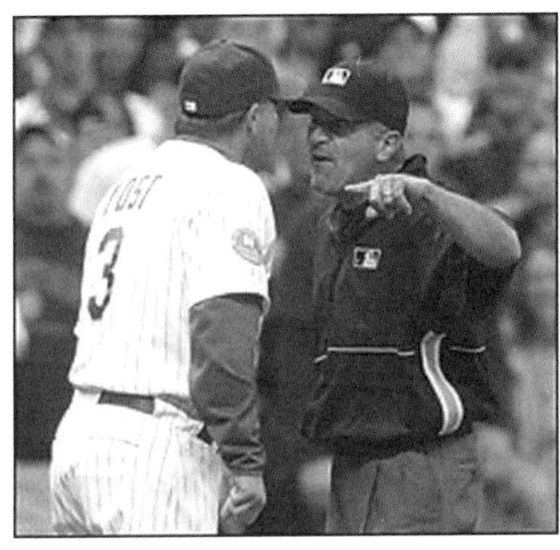

Milwaukee Brewers manager Ned Yost argues with umpire John Hirschbeck in this game in Milwaukee on Sept. 14, 2007. Umpires are livid that Major League Baseball has sent investigators to their hometowns, asking neighbors a series of questions that include whether the ump belongs to the Ku Klux Klan. (AP Photo/Morry Gash, FILE) (Morry Gash - Associated Press)

In the meantime, Coach Lee presses on. Beyond what he is doing in-house to build his team, he also keeps his eye on the larger field of what's going on around him in baseball. He knows that he needs to build strategic alliances and bridges, and is interested in breaking new ground in so doing. In a first for Coppin State, for instance, he has reached out to **James Mosher** to start a mentorship program that involves having regular sessions with kids as young as four years old to encourage them to attend Coppin's practices to mimic everything they see the Coppin team do. Coach Lee emphasizes the importance of getting kids young. He is also forming alliances with Baltimore City Community College (BCCC) sports officials, like Renard Smith, who although a basketball coach, has reached back to Coach Lee to share contacts and lend a helping hand. Coach Lee is also reaching out to the new RBI Director Dean Albany to form alliances, and to any others in the city or outside the city that can help him succeed in his mission.

Coach Lee loves baseball and wants parents to feel the same way. Answering the question of "what's in it for them, he reminds them that, "their son's baseball careers are a 401 K plan, but if they want to make withdrawals, they have to start making deposits now."

Despite his qualifications and enthusiasm for the job, Coach Lee is facing some very tough hurdles. His university's dismal performance, a function of years of dysfunction prior to his arrival, makes Coach Lee's job an uphill battle. Nevertheless, he remains undaunted in his enthusiasm and belief in his ability to turn the situation around. His job is definitely cut out for him, however.

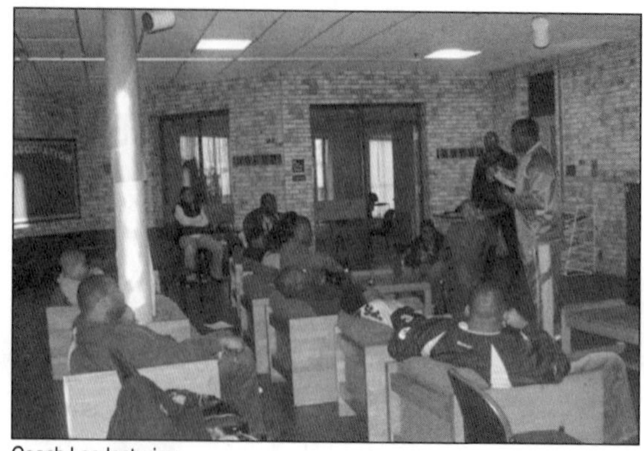

Coach Lee lecturing

The headlines in April 2007, soon after he arrived, read:

Coppin State: A baseball year lost
BALTIMORE: Apr 27, 2007 3:00 AM by Sean Welsh, The Examiner

Coppin State Head Baseball Coach Harvey Lee pauses for a painful moment earlier this year. The Eagles are 0-36.

"Due to recent occurrences within the athletic department I have decided to resign as baseball coach at Coppin." With that brief statement at the top of a letter last summer, Guy Robertson wrote off an entire season of Coppin State baseball. At least, that's what some associated with the program think.

"I feel like it was undermined," one Coppin State baseball parent said of the program. "If he made a commitment to the institution and the boys, he shouldn't leave."

That parent also questioned the mid-summer timing of Robertson's departure, blaming it on the struggles of this year's team, which remains winless. That parent, who also accused Robertson of sabotaging the team by getting players to leave the school when he did, provided The Examiner with a copy of a letter, dated July 3, 2006, in which Robertson told his players that he would be leaving to pursue a new job. Robertson is now the director of college recruiting for the Columbia-based Baseball Factory.

"I'm sorry that anyone feels that way," Robertson said. "Anybody who played for me, I think that they know I tried to keep the players' best interest in mind. I'm just sorry that they feel that way. I don't know what else to say other than that. It's probably difficult for them to speak. They never worked at Coppin. They don't know the circumstance."

This year's team, 0-36 heading into this weekend's home series against Florida A&M, carries just 11 players on its roster. While he feels for first-year coach Harvey Lee, Robertson had just 12 players in his first season in 2003, and only one played out his four-year eligibility for the Eagles.

The team's home field, Joe Cannon Stadium, is located 17 miles from campus. According to one source, the equipment budget in recent years made it difficult to buy baseballs, let alone catcher's equipment.

Coppin State administrator of athletics, Dr. Mary Wanza, whose department also oversees an 0-24 softball program, declined comment on the baseball team. An athletic department spokesperson relayed a message from herstating, "I really don't know much about baseball. I don't have much to say."

The team's new coach, Lee — a former New York Yankees farmhand — is doing his best. Not only is he filling out a lineup card of players in unfamiliar positions, he's also trying to build the program from the bottom up. When he was hired in late October, the team didn't have enough players to field a team.

"I respect Guy as a person, but — this is just me speaking — I don't respect him as a coach," Lee said. "If I'm the captain of a ship and my dying day is tomorrow, I'm going to jump off ship and tell everyone to come with me? That's not right."

While Robertson attached a letter of intent release form to his resignation letter to players, he said he did not ask anyone to leave with him.

"You can say what you want, but when kids that have been there for three years decide to go somewhere else for their senior season, you read between the lines," Robertson said. "It certainly has nothing to do with me."

What has happened to Historically Black Colleges and Universities (HBCUs) and baseball?

Kendrick Marshall wrote an insightful article on the subject in 2004 that still resonates today.

Box 14
Historically Black Colleges & Universities (HBCUs)

By Kendrick Marshall: Ping! That's the sound that vibrates through every college baseball diamond when a player's aluminum bat connects with a ball. That kind of vibration created Lou Brock, Dennis Boyd and Ricky Weeks, some of the best players in the history of black college baseball.

But to masses of African Americans, the appeal of what was once called "America's pastime" is fading, as such rival pursuits as football and basketball gain favor.

Experts have tossed around reasons for the decline of baseball among blacks. One sure bet is the leisurely pace of the game in a world where most things have speeded up. Even athletes who could play with astounding grace have said their attention wanders quickly when a game slows down.

You can already see the impact in the locker rooms at black colleges. There are more non-African Americans playing baseball at black universities. HBCU schools with rich traditions that fielded powerhouse all-black teams in the 1970s and 1980s now turn to whites and Hispanics for talent.

For example, Bethune-Cookman College, home to a great baseball dynasty for more than a quarter-century in the Mid-Eastern Athletic Conference, has nearly an all-Hispanic team. Mississippi Valley State University, an HBCU in the Southwestern Athletic Conference, has only four black players; the rest of the team is Caucasian.

Nearly all HBCU programs have at least one non-black player. Jackson State University, which has an all- black roster, is the exception.

Black colleges have to compete in a tough marketplace. Not only are HBCUs poorer, but their athletic programs aren't able to come up with the scholarship dollars that today's top-rated schools can offer. Many talented players no longer go to HBCUs because they are lured by promises of greater exposure at larger schools.

Would you believe that no HBCU has ever played in the College World Series since its inception in 1945?

Of course, the number of opportunities is limited. Baseball America magazine recently listed the top 15 college programs, and those schools had a total of 15 African American players.

And then there's the contrast with other sports.

Under NCAA rules, college football coaches have the luxury of filling 85 scholarship slots. College basketball teams can run to 10-12 players, but the coaches have 13 scholarships. But baseball gets only 11.5 scholarships, even though half the teams in the NCAA field 25-30 players on a roster.

College football and basketball are media darlings, televised nationally, and, in the case of football, in prime time. College baseball is televised nationally only during the College World Series.

A basketball player like Chris Duhon of Duke, picked by the Chicago Bulls June 24 in the second round of the NBA draft, will get more publicity than Ricky Weeks of Southern, who was the second overall pick in the entire 2003 Major League Baseball Draft.

The lure of making millions right after college -- or in some cases, after high school graduation -- has not helped baseball. Many young black athletes want to have $90 million shoe deals and aspire to go pro at 18 instead of 22 or 23, as major league baseball players do.

They wanted to be like Mike (Jordan), and now they want to be like Lebron (James) and Kobe (Bryant), who both made the jump from senior prom to the NBA.

Baseball tends not to hand out millions to teen stars. The normal salary for the No. 1 pick in the draft is $10 million-$17 million, and it might take three or four years before a talented athlete reaches the major leagues. With money being given out in the NBA and NFL faster than you can turn pancakes, many black players seem to feel that waiting for a baseball dream might take longer than they can bear.

Most important, though, baseball lags behind football and basketball because of how it is marketed. Rarely do you see top black players selling shoes, soda and the latest hip-hop gear. It isn't common to see a black player wearing a FUBU, Sean John or Ecko outfit during a news conference. Those popular brands are mainly seen in the thug-style culture of the NBA and NFL.

Nearly everyone knows Barry Bonds, Derek Jeter and Ken Griffey Jr. But they don't know underrated performers like Torii Hunter of the Minnesota Twins, Derrek Lee of the Chicago Cubs or Frank Thomas of the Chicago White Sox. These are some of the best all-around athletes in the world, but their talents are overlooked because they don't have the street credibility of football or basketball players.

...It looks as though the black community has forgotten that the game is rich in tradition and legend. Back in the 1940s and 1950s baseball was the most popular sport in the black community. You can go back and look at film of Willie Mays playing stickball in the streets of New York with black children. In those days, players like Mays and Robinson were bigger than any other black athletes.

Today, black players are dominating baseball even more than basketball and football. Bonds set the single-season home run record by hitting 73 in 2001. In 1999, Griffey was voted by the baseball writers of America as one of the all-stars of the 20th century. These are accomplishments worthy of the effort by any young black athlete who aspires to reach and exceed them.

Despite the increasing popularity of basketball and football for Black youth, what is the probability of being selected for the major leagues in either sport? The NCAA provides a reality check on the estimated probability of competing in athletics, beyond the high school level, shown in Table 7.

Table 7: Probability of Competing in Athletics Beyond the High School Interscholastic Level for Different Sports (2007)

Student Athletes	Men's Basketball	Women's Basketball	Football	Baseball	Men's Ice Hockey	Men's Soccer
High School Student Athletes	546,335	452,929	1,071,775	470,671	36,263	358,935
High School Senior Student Athletes	156,096	129,408	306,221	134,477	10,361	102,553
NCAA Student Athletes	16,571	15,096	61,252	28,767	3,973	19,793
NCAA Freshman Roster Positions	4,735	4,313	17,501	8,219	1,135	5,655
NCAA Senior Student Athletes	3,682	3,355	13,612	6,393	883	4,398
NCAA Student Athletes Drafted	44	32	250	600	33	76
Percent High School to NCAA	3.0%	3.3%	5.7%	6.1%	11.0%	5.5%
Percent NCAA to Professional	1.2%	1.0%	1.8%	9.4%	3.7%	1.7%
Percent High School to Professional	0.03%	0.02%	0.08%	0.45%	0.32%	0.07%

Source: http://www.ncaa.org/research/prob_of_competing/probability_of_competing2.html

Next Base: From College Baseball to the Minor Leagues

> "More than 41 million fans attended Minor League Baseball in 2006. It draws more fans than the NBA or NFL?"

The best-kept secret is: The Minor Leagues are not minor.

Even though Minor League players are paid considerably less than their major league counterparts, they are nevertheless paid for their services and are considered professional athletes. Baseball cards refer to "pro record" and "pro seasons" and include both major and minor leagues. For this reason, minor league players generally consider it an insult when someone asks, "when they're going to 'get to the pros.'" More accurately, a player's aim is to reach "The Show," or the "big leagues." A glimpse of how the Minor League system works is shown in Box 15.

Box 15
How The Minor League Works

Tryouts for a Minor League Baseball team? Tryouts are not held by our Minor League Baseball teams. Our teams are assigned players by their Major League Baseball affiliate. The Major League Scouting Bureau conducts tryout camps around the country.

Where will a player be assigned for this season? Players are employed by Major League Baseball and are then assigned to a Minor League Baseball club.

What do Minor League players earn? Minor League Baseball player contracts are handled by the Major League Baseball. The salary ranges are as follows:

- First contract season: $1,100/month maximum. After that, open to negotiation;
- Alien Salary Rates: Different for aliens on visas--mandated by INS (Immigration);
- Meal Money: $20 per day at all levels, while on the road.

How much is a Minor League Baseball team worth? Franchise values:

- Class AAA $10 million and up;
- Class AA $7.5 million and up;
- Class A $2.5 to $7 million;
- Short Season A $1.8 million and up;
- Rookie $650,000 to $1.1 million.

Many Black youth, along with their parents, believe that it is too difficult to make it to "The Show" from the minors. It's not only difficult, it's not certain that one will ever make it out of the minors. For the talented athlete, there are many options, and the best one, from the perspective of many Black youths, is not baseball. It takes too long to make it to "The Show." Compounding the problem is the robust competition from Latin American players.

The Minor League system, while providing professional playing opportunities, is considered a sidetrack. No one aspires to enter the Minor Leagues. The goal is the Major Leagues, "The Show."

There is another more positive perspective on the Minor Leagues, however, which is that it offers a "second chance" for those who can't make it directly into "The Show." Not everyone can be a sports phenomenon, but skills can be honed and developed in the Minor League system that will prepare a player for "The Show."

> **Glenn Harris,** a News Channel 8 sports anchor for 17 years, a sportscaster for 36 years, and a former Minor League baseball player, knows how important the Minor Leagues are. He agrees that, "The system provides a second chance opportunity, especially for those who aren't 'phenoms.'" It's definitely a tough circuit to play, he says, and some have languished in the minors for 15 years, but he still encourages African Americans to embrace the Minor Leagues, to pay their dues there, to grow there, and hopefully, to springboard out of there into "The Show." The bottom line, according to Harris is, "Hang in there, get seen, and get ahead, because making it to "The Show" is one of the greatest thrills on earth.

The Minor Leagues, as a "second chance opportunity," is neither widely understood nor appreciated in the Black community. Therefore, it's up to the MLB to do a better job in educating the Black community about the opportunity, and in marketing the relative benefits of the baseball system as a whole, especially to African American mothers who are in a position to influence their sons.

This is how the system works. Minor League players work at the lower end of major league pay scales and are covered by all rules and player agreements of the players association. This allows the other 15 players to play every day rather than sit on the bench. Minor league players not on the 40 Man Roster are under contract to their parent major league baseball club but have no union. They generally work for far less pay, starting at Rookie to Triple-A (highest). Many players have "signing bonuses," and other additional compensation that can run into the millions of dollars, although that is far more rare and is generally reserved for early round draft picks. Appendix 3 addresses information about the Minor League system, which is not widely known in the inner city.

Once African Americans make it to the Minor or Major Leagues, linkages they may have had to their inner city communities are broken, and the opportunity for their former community members to learn from them directly is lost. Furthermore, as baseball has lost its appeal in inner city America, unless a child is particularly talented, no one is keeping track of what happens to him as he progresses from Tee-Ball onward. Professional baseball team scouts are not reaching down to the little league level to assess the talent there, and even little leagues themselves aren't keeping track.

From the Minor Leagues to the Major Leagues— For the Lucky and Talented Few

Here is what's at stake:

> Only 25 of the players on the major league 40 Man Roster play for the major league baseball club, except from September 1 to the end of the regular season, when all major-league teams are allowed to expand their gameday rosters to 40 players. The remaining 15 players play at some level of the minor leagues, usually at the AAA or AA level (or are on the disabled list). Players on the 40 Man Roster are eligible for membership in the Major League Baseball Players Association.

How many African American Minor League players are there, and how many made it from the Minor Leagues into the Major Leagues—and how many of these came from inner cities in America? These are questions that are not easy to answer because no one is keeping track.

How many Black inner city kids have made it to "The Show" from Baltimore City in recent years? Once again, the trail has gone cold; no one knows, no one is keeping track, and no one cares. Consistent with this reality, it speaks volumes that the *Baseball Almanac's* last listing of *"Famous Black Firsts in Baseball"* stops in 1992.

Village Voices: Baltimore Baseball Stakeholders Speak Out

It takes a village to keep baseball alive, and there's one keeping it alive in Baltimore's inner city. Some of the voices from the village can be heard below. Their stories underscore that although each volunteer may come to baseball with his or her own goals, desires, and professional experiences, in the end, it's the baseball experience that transforms them, not the other way around. Despite the good, bad, and ugly of their respective experiences as volunteers, all would agree that baseball matters in inner cities, more than most people know.

Many of the "voices" heard below are of coaches who are alumni of James Mosher. Though that was a long time ago for many, their positive memories have never faded.

Volunteers understand what it means to poor fatherless African American boys to have someone call them "son." They know what it means to little boys when their coaches see that small light flickering in his eyes. They know what it means to boys to have that kernel of athletic talent in them grow to full acorn size under the loving tutelage of a caring coach.

Small victories matter, and of course, large ones do too. Everyone knows how great it is to have famous African American baseball players like **Torii Hunter, Gary Sheffield,** and **C.C. Sabathia** make it to "The Show" against all odds, and to reach back into the community to lend a helping hand.

It's equally meaningful, however, to have less famous, but loving African American neighborhood coaches, stick with the little "diamonds in the rough" day in and day out to help them shine all the way to home plate.

POLISHING THE DIAMONDS IN THE ROUGH

Lawrence (Chris) Cager, Jr.: ***James Mosher Coach***

Lawrence (Chris) Cager, Jr., a 1983 graduate of Carnegie-Mellon's Heinz School of Public Management and Policy, keeps his eye on the management ball. He's a coach in the James Mosher little league program, but he doesn't coach his son. He does, however, play a very active role in facilitating the development of his son's athleticism across a broad range of sports.

Cager & Son

As his son is athletically talented in multiple sports, Cager has had an "up close and personal" look at the management structure of the sports his son plays. His son plays baseball, basketball, soccer and football. His conclusion, based on firsthand comparisons, is that "baseball can't compete, particularly not with the management and marketing might of basketball."

Funny thing is, despite the national pastime status accorded to baseball, and the significant head start it has had against competitor sports, today, basketball has taken the ball and run with it, especially in inner cities.

Case in point, Cager says, "When my son was only 9 years old, two different AAU team scouts came to one of his basketball games on the same day to recruit him." They looked at him, liked him, but took a pass because he was going to turn 10 very soon and would therefore be ineligible for the 7 to 9 league for which they were scouting. They did offer to try him in two games to see if he could 'play up' (to the 10 to 12 level)."

"AAU basketball has set the 'gold standard' for recruiting today's young African American kids into basketball," according to Cager. "AAU basketball is far more organized and strategic than baseball in its recruitment and training approaches.

Whereas AAU scouts have every name in every zip code of every potential African American basketball player; by contrast, who is looking at the little league child in the inner city, Cager asks. "The AAU hears the sound of every basketball dunk, on every court in the ghetto. In short, "they're on it."

The whole AAU experience is a blast, according to Cager. "During a state or regional tournament, kids get to travel and stay in "cool" places like Las Vegas, and parents get to go as well. Companies like *Converse* often sponsor the tournaments, which lowers the cost to the parents. At the same time, AAU weekly camps during spring break are also fun and present another opportunity for scouts to see the kids and evaluate their potential." Cager explains, "for $125, the child gets to go to a basketball camp in the summer, and to interact with scouts, college players, and their friends from the neighborhood. Who wants to be stuck playing baseball in the summer when they can have so much fun at the basketball summer camp?"

"The hype, the buzz, the experience, and the opportunity to be with their peers, is what makes basketball 'cool.'" As a parent, you start to notice that all of your son's kids are the ones he attended *"Charm City Basketball Camp"* with, or are the ones with whom he did some other 'cool basketball.' You start to get the message just how cool basketball is in the eyes of kids."

"Baseball is operating on a 'catch as catch can basis,'" explains Cager. "Where, for instance, are the Baltimore Orioles scouts who are looking at a little league inner city kid, and for that matter, where are the sponsors for the travel teams, and how are the kids selected for the travel teams? Baseball's promotional structure can't compare with that of basketball, not by a long shot," Cager has observed.

Even with its shortcomings, as compared to basketball, baseball is still number one in the Cager household. "Dad" will not let the basketball scouts get to his son. He doesn't want his son to play basketball. He wants him to play baseball, for many reasons. According to Cager, there are more opportunities in baseball than in other sports. He says, "a player can be competent, as opposed to being a physical specimen; the playing life of a baseball player is longer, baseball players sustain fewer injuries, and the pay is good too." Additionally, Cager notes, "there is always opportunities to be 'specialty players,' which increases the longevity of players. Look at how long Cal Ripken, Jr. played baseball. Are there any football or basketball players in recent times that have had such longevity?"

Cager is a baseball fan, but he's the first to admit that baseball needs to be revamped in order to compete with the draw of basketball and football. "Baseball's leadership needs to figure out how to compete with basketball for the hearts, minds and *'soles'* of African Americans. Action is needed now."

William Neal: *James Mosher Manager*

William Neal, born in 1949, has been a Manager in the James Mosher program since 1978. He is a product of Baltimore through and through, and still lives in his old neighborhood, though it is infested with gangs. When he comes home from a day's work at the Post Office, where he has worked for over 35 years, gang members are sitting on his steps. But they give way, and they give him respect. They know him and they know that he cares; nobody bothers Mr. Neal.

Neal is in a battle with the gangs, because he is trying to claim the kids before the gangs claim them. The problem, as Neal explains, is that the gang members spot the weak kids, just like a hunting lion spots a gazelle. They see the weak ones and stalk them, and when they are down, they offer them five dollars a day to be a drug carrier. It's a job for the kid, but more than a job, the drug pusher is the only male in the child's life who is showing the child affection, false though it may be. Neal wants to help create alternatives for those children, and the best way he knows to do that is through baseball.

Through baseball, Neal wants to show the "gazelles" another way in life, another set of values, and he wants to instill hope in them, while helping them gain self-confidence through their triumphs in baseball.

It's not an easy job, but it's an important job, Neal underscores. It is a job that he has been committed to since he returned from Vietnam in 1971, where his experiences made him more committed than ever to lending a helping hand to those in need in his community. He chose to give back through baseball because baseball was meaningful to him in his life. Though he only played in the James Mosher little league program for one year, in 1963, it was a meaningful year for him, one that evokes positive memories, and one that he wants other kids in Baltimore to have as well.

Neal doesn't mind that he has to transport many of the kids to the games. He is also happy to spend his own money to take "his" kids to amusement parks and to other events to help give them some exposure, because he knows that if he doesn't do it, no one else will.

Neal firmly believes that one picture is worth a thousand words, and he is trying to create visions of success in their minds. He understands that many of his kids have no definition of success, and no examples of it within their own families. Through the James Mosher baseball program, he hopes to give them their first visions of success.

Thelphs Evans, Jr.: ***James Mosher Manager***

Coach Evans, son and grandsons

Evans is a graduate of Carnegie-Mellon's Heinz School of Public Management and Policy (previously named the School of Urban and Public Affairs (SUPA) in the early 1970s).

With academic training and professional experience in management, Evans runs a tight ship as a Manager in the James Mosher program. He has been with the organization in various positions for almost two decades now. In a departure from the norm, his son led him to baseball, not the other way around.

Evans didn't have a strong connection to baseball prior to his involvement with his son's little league. Although his own father had played a bit of baseball in high school, Evans was drawn to basketball, and played it in high school and in college.

When his son was young, he noticed that he appeared to have natural athletic talent. He had put a basketball hoop in his backyard, and his son, although only eight years old at the time, surprisingly could make some shots. Evans started to think about athletic options for his son, but before he knew it, his son at only eight years old, petitioned the neighborhood little league to accept him a year early into its league.

Evans attended each of his son's baseball games, but the more he watched, the more he realized that the instruction wasn't very good. He decided to learn how to be a coach himself, and he learned through every means possible, from reading books to watching videos to playing the game with the kids in the neighborhood. When he, a brand new coach, was able to coach his team to two consecutive championships, he knew that it was time to move on. After all, he was new to the game and if his team was winning something was wrong, Evans noted.

He remembered that there was a little league in the neighborhood where he grew up in inner city Baltimore. His parents still lived there. When visiting them one day, he decided to go over to the nearby field to watch a James Mosher little league game. His conclusion was—*and get this*—"the inner city team was much better than his son's suburban team." So, he took his son out of the suburbs, and took him into the city, "so he could really learn to play baseball."

As usual, Evans attended every game, but once again, he found that he wasn't happy with the coaching. He was compelled to put his coaching uniform back on. This time, he got involved more deeply. So far, his involvement has spanned two decades and counting.

After almost twenty years, however, it appears that it may be the end of the road for Evans and James Mosher because his son has decided to pull Evan's grandson from playing in the James Mosher league, as a result of two bad things that happened: First, a while ago, his son's car was car jacked with him in it in a dark alley near where James Mosher plays. The robbers also attempted to shoot him in the robbery, but fortunately, the gun misfired. Later, when a parent who was apparently "high" on something came to one of the games where Evan's grandson was playing and caused a very unpleasant scene, that was the last straw.

Evans is disappointed. He believes in the little league program and has continued to be involved back in his old neighborhood all these years because he sees the good it does.

He doesn't want the mean streets to win, and he doesn't want his son to give up on the neighborhood where Evans was raised. Evans knows that bad things happen sometimes in the "hood," but he also knows that good baseball programs help transform the lives of many inner city kids.

He believes that "If you give the kids a good program with a lot of structure, kids will enjoy it and remain committed to baseball."

Structure is vitally important. "As many kids come from structureless homes, they experience structure for the first time within the context of the little league. Small things like scheduling, logistics planning, and contact management help the kids learn new things that they can use throughout their lives."

In fact, Evans suggests that even more can be done with the kids to facilitate their skills acquisition and to promote learning. Specifically, he says, "let the kids help fill in some of the resource gaps." For instance, "fields need to be cleaned—let the kids help do," Evans says, "painting is needed, teach the kids how to do it. Phone calls have to be made, letters have to be mailed out, etc.—bring the kids into all operational aspects of the little leagues," Evans suggests. It would serve two purposes: It would impart additional skills, and it would make them stakeholders. If anyone attempts to scribble graffiti on something they newly painted, the kids will protect the property as stakeholders in it."

Little leagues require a lot of volunteer time, and not everyone has the time to devote; therefore, it's critical to develop a reward system for the kids to motivate them to chip in more to help fill the resource gap: It's a win-win situation.

Edward Nottingham: ***James Mosher Coach***

Coach Nottingham top left

Coach Edward Nottingham graduated from Hampton University with a degree in architecture. He works for a construction company as its Director of Architecture. He likes to build things and manage projects; it's in his blood. He has an insatiable thirst to play and thrive in the game of baseball. He considers baseball the perfect game and "America's Game."

Nottingham cut his teeth in baseball with James Mosher's league as a player in 1977. At that time, James Mosher was a dominant city league and fielded extremely successful teams that played locally and within the Baltimore/DC region. Year after year, James Mosher won championships throughout Baltimore. The kids got exposure, which helped them play competitively in high schools and at universities. A few even signed major league contracts. Flash forward 30 years, and nothing has changed: Mosher still has fantastic athletes who, given the opportunity, could be very competitive against local and regional talent. The problem is that the "premiere" summer league programs are far better organized internally, and far better connected with the powerhouse high school, college coaches, and pro scouts. None of the coaches from premiere teams such as Mount St. Joseph, Calvert Hall, and Arundel come to scout talent at James Mosher, for a number of reasons. One, they don't know about the program because it's poorly marketed, and secondly, James Mosher kids don't tend to participate in the "showcase" events.

The James Mosher league can and should be stronger, no doubt, given the talent of its players.

There are many coaches in the James Mosher league that are intensely passionate about the game, and Nottingham is one of them. He constantly studies the game to learn how to be a better coach, while continuing to hone his own skill as a player. As he continues to play the game himself, he competes all over the world. The local "30 and over" team for which he plays has won two National Championships. As a member of a Florida-based "All Star" team, Nottingham won a coveted "World Championship" at the 2005 World Masters Games in Edmonton Ontario.

As a coach and father of two boys, Nottingham is dedicated to helping his eldest son, Edward III, his "shinning diamond," develop into one of the best well-rounded baseball players in the city. His son will soon graduate from the James Mosher league and intends to become part of a "premiere" team. Following the advice of one of the baseball coaches from Nottingham's alma matter, Mount St. Joseph, "Little Ed" will now begin to "enhance his baseball resume."

Nottingham is equally committed to seeing all of the kids he coaches in the James Mosher program progress in baseball, and his efforts are bearing fruit. For the past four years, he has coached kids starting at age 7 and he's grooming them in accordance with "gold medal standards" that will help them excel, he says. His team has been undefeated for two years and has won two "Baltimore City Sunday Rec League Championships." He knows that his team is ready to play the Maryland Orioles, the Putty Hills, the Yankee Rebels, and other elite teams.

The problem is that the majority of the talented kids don't have financial resources to join the *Maryland Orioles*, which cost $1,500, or the *Putty Hill Panthers,* which costs $2,000 for the summer. Clearly, more resources should be allotted from the city to help fill the gap. In the meantime, Nottingham, like many of the other coaches in James Mosher, digs into his pockets to help. What is needed now, from the entire village of baseball stakeholders, is more "reach in," not just "outreach."

Jim O'Connor: *Baltimore Recreation & Parks, RBI Program*

If anyone thinks that to be in the village you have to be African American, they are dead wrong. Case in point, O'Connor is a White male. His job in the Baltimore Recreation and Parks Department is to facilitate the RBI program. That is his job however, his passion is seeing inner city kids have a chance to play baseball.

He is so passionate about the subject that he called me (the author) from his hospital bed, where he was scheduled to have open-heart surgery the next day, to offer his assistance and express his support for this book. That he could be thinking of a thing like that at a time like that is truly amazing.

He was born in 1937 in Salisbury, Maryland. His father was a professional umpire, and encouraged his son to be the same. He resisted for a while and obtained a degree from Mt. St. Mary's College in Emmitsburg, Maryland, and subsequently taught math at inner city schools for many years. When he could no longer resist the call to baseball, he quit his job and attended professional umpiring school in Florida. With his certification, he began umpiring in the minor leagues in 1971. He had to work his way up from Class A, to Class, AA, and finally to Class AAA, just like his father before him.

Unfortunately, the pay hadn't gotten much better since the time his father umpired. He only made $2,500 for seven months work, and that was before taxes, and he had to pay all of his own expenses, including staying in hotels and traveling to the games to umpire. Of course, he had to subsidize his lifestyle, which he did by raiding his pension fund and his savings, but alas, the money ran out, so in 1975, he had to return to teaching. All together, he taught for 40 years, and when he retired from the school system, he returned to his first love, baseball. His job is to schedule the umpires for the RBI games.

He knows that all of the fields aren't good throughout the city; and he knows that some of the RBI teams could be more robust, and that perhaps the program itself could be enhanced, but in his view, the most important thing is that baseball is happening in the City of Baltimore. More baseball and better baseball would be great, but the most important thing to do right now is to keep it alive. In fact, he says, "baseball is keeping me alive."

Joe Durham: ***Former Negro League and Baltimore Orioles Player***

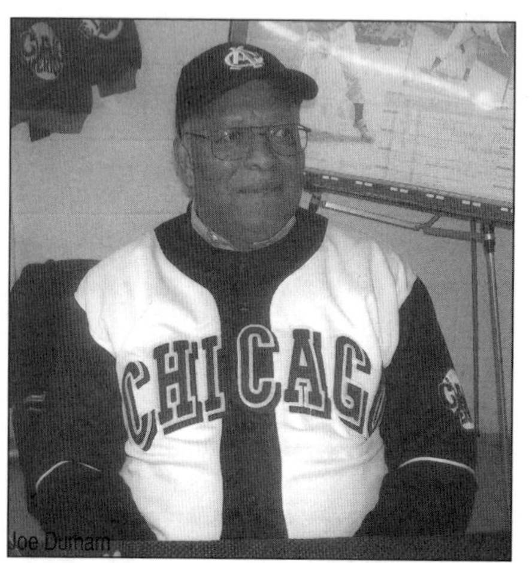

Joe Durham

Durham was one of the lucky ones: He made it to "The Show." Born in 1931 in Newport News, Virginia, he has dedicated his whole life to baseball. He started out with the Negro League team, the Chicago Giants, in 1952. The next year he switched to the St. Louis Browns, and was on the move until he landed with the Baltimore Orioles in 1954, where he remained, with a few interruptions like the Korean War, until the end of his career.

He has the distinction of being the **first African American to hit a home run with the Baltimore Orioles,** and he has been hitting them ever since, on and off the field. For over two decades he pitched batting practice for the Orioles, and he also coached in the Minor Leagues for the Orioles. During these times, he became intimately involved with the physics of motion, which is why he has been in a state of shock for about three decades as he has increasingly observed that African American inner city kids are afraid of the ball. He can't believe it. When he grew up, the kids in his neighborhood were practically glued to baseball. In fact, they glued bats together, strung some balls together, and made due in order to play their beloved baseball.

Durham laments that baseball has taken a back seat to other sports in inner cities. Nevertheless, he continues to sound the clarion call for baseball. He never stops coaching; he is coaching somewhere, passing on the game that he loves to somebody at all times. He mostly coaches in the county now, Randallstown, where he lives with his wife of five decades, but he believes in the power of baseball to transform inner city lives. Every chance he gets, he passes on that message and his knowledge to anyone who can catch it.

Al Bumbry: *Former Baltimore Orioles Player*

Bumbry, a former MLB player for 12 years, knows what it takes to "grow" African American baseball players. In his case, his mother made all the difference in the world. Her greatest influence was in ensuring that Bumbry kept up his grades and maintained a positive outlook on life. His father taught him baseball, but his mother and father both attended all of his baseball games. Raised in a small town in Virginia, his family of nine children was poor but rich in values and discipline. It paid off for Bumbry because he did attend university and received a scholarship. There was one time while at university he lost sight of his goals and was in danger of losing his scholarship, but his mother's voice in the back of his mind made him pull himself up and get it together. If he had lost that scholarship, it would have been the end of his future, he says.

Bumbry was lucky in another regard: He was one who made it out of the Orioles Minor Leagues into "The Show," and, what was even better, he didn't have to stay in the minors that long. After only a year and a half in the minors, he was recruited into the MLB for the Orioles, where he remained for 12 years as a center fielder.

Today, his son Stephen is following his footsteps, and not because his "Dad" put any pressure on him to do so. His son had choices and played soccer, football, basketball, and baseball. The funny thing is, his father was intrigued by the prospect of his son playing soccer, but his son chose baseball on his own accord. Bumbry speculates that it was all of the exposure that his son had to baseball—from traveling with his father, to watching MLB players in action to hanging out with baseball players— that made him choose baseball over the other sports he played. Also, he once got hurt playing football, and that left a bad taste in his mouth.

Stephen Bumbry plays on Virginia Tech's baseball team and is one of the few African Americans playing for the *Youse's Maryland Orioles*. He has a future in baseball.

For other African Americans to similarly have a future in baseball, Bumbry Sr., suggests that the most pressing and immediate need is to address the problem of single moms. The problem is not just that fathers are absent. It's deeper than that. It's about core values. Just like his mom helped instill values in him, all mothers can play a critical role in helping to instill the right values in their children. Importantly, the values instilled must de-emphasize material things and wealth. Bumbry remembers that oftentimes when he met young African American kids, all they wanted to know about was the kind of car they drove, and whether he lived in a mansion. "Kids need to be motivated to find the good in themselves not just the pot of gold laying out there somewhere outside of themselves."

"Surrogate fathers, with the right set of values, are needed to mentor kids living in single female-headed households," Bumbry suggests. What is also needed, he suggests, is for the MLB teams to put clauses in the contracts of their African American players to give back to kids in inner cities. The presence of role models matter. It's not just about providing equipment or financial resources: African American kids want to interact with successful African American baseball players. More matching grant programs would also be a good idea to encourage stakeholders in the community to put forward ideas that can help revive baseball in inner cities.

George Eccles: *Owner, Black Diamond*

George Eccles

Eccles is not a baseball player and doesn't have any children who played the game. He intersects with baseball in another way by selling Negro League memorabilia. This gives him a unique perspective of the demand side of the equation. His firm, Black Diamond, doesn't only sell Negro League memorabilia they also sell other African American-centric nostalgic goods. Since 1991, when Eccles formed Black Diamond, he has sold Buffalo Soldiers, Tuskegee Airmen, Rucker Park Basketball, New York Brown Bombers, and Negro Leagues memorabilia to African American and non-African American buyers. As he sells his goods through shows and exhibitions, he is in direct touch with his buyers. What sells most, he says, is Negro League memorabilia. He speculates that the reason why it sells the most is because he always has former Negro League players on hand

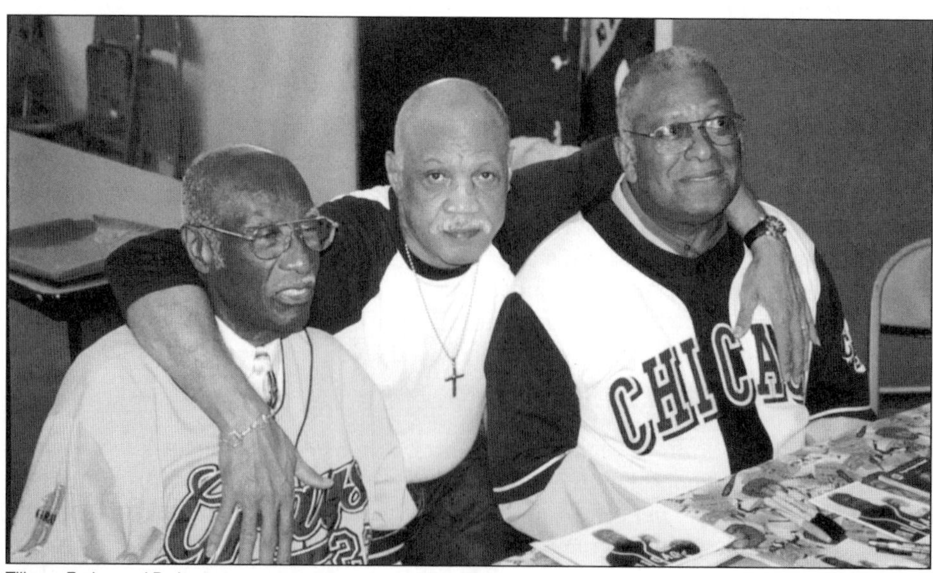
Tillman, Eccles, and Durham

who can explain the history of the Negro Leagues. Mamie "Peanut" Johnson often participates, as does James Tillman, Joe Durham, and other former players.

African Americans are not the main sellers or buyers of such nostalgic goods, according to Eccles, Whites are. Whites are better and more broadly educated than African Americans. They have read about the Negro Leagues and about the other seminal events in African American life. In fact, Eccles has observed that there is a "lost African American generation," which is the middle age group. However, younger or much older African Americans are in touch with their history, Eccles says. "They are the ones who purchase the nostalgic goods."

Eccles's experience underscores that when African Americans know more, they become interested, which is why having the Negro League players on hand is so important. It follows that by educating African Americans more about the opportunities in baseball, they, too, may become more interested in the game.

This chapter provides a small glimpse of what's involved in getting inner city kids from home to home plate, but there's much more involved than could possibly be captured in just one book. The main "take away" is that baseball is happening in inner cities.There are many people involved in it behind the scenes, and many people have a stake in it, but to see what's going on with baseball in inner cities, observers must "switch on" their attentiveness and gaze to see that which is often overlooked.

The next chapter, *"Diamonds Are A Girl's Best Friend,"* provides insight into the complex problem of reviving baseball in inner cities. It underscores that the revival can't happen without African American women helping to lead it.

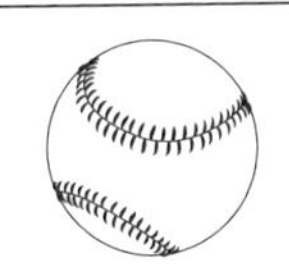

A James Mosher Little League Team

Diamonds Are a Girl's Best Friend

Diamonds Are a Girl's Best Friend

Just as diamonds are a girl's best friend the converse is also true. It's not a stretch to say that the survival of baseball in the African American community depends on women.

This isn't the first time in history that the importance of women has loomed so large in the survival of baseball. During the World War II period, Philip K. Wrigley, owner of the Chicago Cubs and a chewing gum factory, wondered what would happen when guns were needed more than gum and ball players were needed to fight the war? Once women began to build tanks, airplanes, trucks, and ships during the war, Wrigley realized they could also help by playing baseball. In his view, baseball's very survival depended on them, so in 1942, he formed his professional women's league to keep the game alive in the hearts and minds of society, while the men were at war.

Today, African American women are as important to the game of baseball as women were during the period of WWII, but for different reasons: Today, women are more urgently needed off the field, as supporters of their sons and daughters who play ball, and as baseball executives and businesswomen.

However, just as the future of baseball was in doubt during the war, its future is in doubt among the African American population. And, as women were called upon to step up to the plate to support baseball during the war period, African American women are being called upon today to step up and help resurrect baseball in inner cities.

The parallels don't end there. When the men were away during WWII, women stepped up to the plate and played ball. Now that Black men are away from their homes today—*for different reasons*—it's largely left to the women to keep baseball alive in Black communities.

African American women were always important to the game of baseball, but often behind the scenes. By contrast, as heads of household in many inner cities, the job falls on the single mothers to advocate for the public and private investments in baseball they need to keep their children in the game.

Women are pressed to make judgment calls on how to spend their limited disposal income, and on which games to support their children in playing. They must allocate their time to watch their children's game, take time to learn the game, and encourage their children to grow and develop in the game. To do this, they must have a clear vision about the opportunities in baseball.

Just as baseball players must learn the fundamental "tools" to play, African American women must have the "tools" to learn about baseball and the opportunity it presents. Resources are the key, since it takes resources to educate women about baseball, and it takes resources to keep "em" in the game.

Many African American mothers are young single heads of household. In their positions, a lot is coming at them very fast all at once, as fast as a baseball coming at them at over 100 mph. It's breathtaking.

Unlike trained "turkey spotters," who learn as a children how to "spot" situations and call them in an instant, many African American mothers lack vision and don't have a game plan for progressing in life. They also lack the information to be able to "spot" the difference between what is good about one sport versus another. What they presume is that basketball and football are ways out of the ghetto. According to Lapchick (1984), "the high visibility of African American athletes and the low visibility of successful African Americans in other professional industries, create this expectation and approach in our youngsters."

One thing African American mothers are clear on is that baseball is good for their young children. For many young African Americans mothers in inner cities, baseball is not only a community development tool, it's a life saver. It keeps their children out of trouble, and supplies positive male role models for them, but beyond this, little is known about baseball opportunities for their children going forward.

Simply put, African American women are suffering from "information poverty" in respect to their knowledge about baseball and the opportunities it presents.

How, is the question, can information gaps be addressed, and how can the interest and focus African American women have on baseball, while their children are still in little league, be built upon?

Taking the "pulse" of where African American women are in respect to the game is critical. There are two sides of the story: The first involves the past, and the second involves the current situation. Both are discussed below.

African American Women & Baseball: *The Early Years*

Just as baseball is part of African American history, it's part of the history of African American women. Thus, one can't talk about such a large part of history without including all sides of the story.

African American women have a story in baseball to tell and it covers the field. From these stories one thing is clear: Woven together, the contributions of Black women to baseball are threads in a tapestry of support, perseverance, and sweet victory.

The threads of support of Black women for their partners and family members who played ball are brightly colored in the tapestry; the threads of their perserverance hold the tapestry together, but dotted sparingly around the edges is *gold trim*—these are the threads that are distinguished from all others.

During the Negro League era, three women wove in the gold: **Toni Stone**, **Mamie "Peanut" Johnson**, and **Connie Morgan**. They were trailblazers as players of the game who experienced sweet victory on the ball field. Not content to stand behind the men, they played right along side of them on their own field of dreams in the Negro Leagues.

They loved baseball, and not just in the abstract; they loved to play ball, hardball, and they were good at it. In fact, they were professional ball players and skilled athletes, just like the men, and they acquired their love for the game the same way the men did: They played on sandlots on a daily basis from the time they were little girls. They received daily instruction from male family members in how to play the game, and they learned how to throw, catch, and pitch just the same way the boys did. When baseball was "*hot*" in the Black community, it was considered "*cool*" to play—by both women and men.

> Lyle (Toni) Stone became the first Black woman to play professional baseball when she joined the Indianapolis Clowns of the Negro American League in July 1953. Hailed as "an excellent fielder and accurate thrower," the St. Paul, Minn., native began playing with boys' teams in high school. At 22, she was spotted by Clowns talent scouts who signed the second baseman to a $12,000 single-season contract.

Stone played from 1949 until 1955, with the New Orleans Creoles and the Indianapolis Clowns. The Clowns captured the Negro American League championship in 1952 with both Toni Stone and Hank Aaron at bat. Connie Morgan was a right-handed second-"baseman" who joined the Clowns at 19 years of age in 1954. She started in an all women's league (where she had a .368 batting average) before joining the Clowns in 1954. She was signed as a replacement for Toni Stone (who was traded to the Kansas City Monarchs after 50 games). Mamie Johnson (nicknamed "Peanut") was the first woman to pitch in the Negro Leagues. She built an impressive record of 38 wins and only 8 losses in her career.

Among these pioneers, Mamie "Peanut" Johnson, who was born on September 27, 1935 in Ridgeway, South Carolina, is the sole survivor. Everyone wants to know her story.

A Conversation With Mamie "Peanut" Johnson: "A Strong Right Arm"

Everyone wants to hear Mamie's story about playing in the Negro Leagues, but few really want to hear the answer she gives. Her story, quite simply, is about loving to play baseball, nothing more and nothing less. She flat out refuses to tell stories about the two other women who played and the personal behind the scenes stories of the male players. The truth is, she didn't care about any of those things. All she cared about

Mamie "Peanut" Johnson

was playing baseball. No one can really imagine what it was like for her to play the game or how much it meant to her psychologically. The truth is, *she loved baseball from the inside out.*

Upon further reflection, is it really so difficult to understand why Mamie loved playing baseball so? Consider the times. Halfway through the 20th century, things were beginning to change in the African American community, and Black women helped to usher in many of those changes. In fact, when Mamie "Peanut" Johnson played ball, from 1953 to 1955, Black women played a central role in two of the most important events for African Americans. Their change agency set the stage for *Brown v. Board of Education* of Topeka, Kansas, when the Supreme Court ruled unanimously against school segregation, overturning its 1896 decision in *Plessy v. Ferguson*. Also, one woman, *Rosa Parks*, in refusing to give up her seat on a Montgomery, Alabama bus triggered a successful year-long African American boycott of the bus system.

Perhaps these triumphs sent a subliminal message to Mamie that signaled that the time was ripe for her to break into "a man's world" to play hardball.

Mamie also had another motivation to join the Negro League: It was her only alternative. She would have welcomed the opportunity to play with the All-American Girls Professional Baseball League (AAGPBL), but they didn't welcome her. It was already a hard sell for Wrigley to promote the concept of women players to the baseball franchise owners back in 1943, but going a step further to include Black women on teams would have been unthinkable. The issue of femininity took center stage:

> *...Wrigley contracted with Helena Rubenstein's Beauty Salon to meet with the players at spring training. After their daily practices, the women were required to attend Rubenstein's evening charm school classes. The proper etiquette for every situation was taught, and every aspect of personal hygiene, mannerisms and dress code was presented to all the players. In an effort to make each player as physically attractive as possible, each player received a beauty kit and instructions on how to use it.*

By contrast, White society still bought into the "Jim Crow" era depiction of Black women as "Mammy." From slavery through the Jim Crow era, the Mammy image served the political, social, and economic interests of mainstream White America. Mammy was completely de-sexualized and de-feminized, and was far removed from the majority's concept of beauty and femininity.

Make no mistake: Mamie was not a "Mammy"—not only appearance-wise—but also in terms of attitude and demeanor. The "Mammy" caricature was portrayed as an obese, coarse, maternal figure who had great love for her White "family," but who often treated her own family with disdain. Although she had children, sometimes many, she was completely de-sexualized. She "belonged" to the White family, though it was rarely stated. Unlike "Sambo," she was a faithful worker. She had no Black friends; the White family was her entire world.

It's the subservience part of the portrayal that really gets to Mamie. Anybody who knows Mamie will tell you that her defining personality characteristic is that she *"ain't taking nothing from nobody."* It started back in her childhood.

Mamie knocked on the doors of the White female teams of the time asking to be let in, but when they shunned her, it strengthened her resolve to be the best baseball player she could be, no matter what. She aimed to go one better than the White female players: She decided to play with the boys, and in the process set one of the highest watermarks for any woman in the history of baseball in America.

Indeed, Mamie knows how to play hardball, on and off the field. Now in frail health, her feisty spirit remains in tact. Upon visiting her in the hospital recently, she could be found "pitching" to the doctors from her bedside. Clearly, she is still very much in the game. She let the doctors and nurses know in no uncertain terms that they better not throw her any curve balls. She wanted it straight, and wanted to be dealt with straight up every step of the way.

If you want to get a smile from Mamie, however, just turn to the subject of baseball and her face lights up. Mamie "Peanut" Johnson may be down, but she is not out, and as long as she is still up at bat, her heart is filled with joy at the mention of the word baseball.

Her love of the game demonstrates what can happen when there is a perfect storm of factors that come together to support one's love of the game. All the elements were in alignment in Mamie's story: She had a male figure, her uncle, who was knowledgeable about the game and who taught her on a daily basis. She lived in a rural area where there were few sports alternatives to playing the game. She had access to wide open spaces; and everyone around her played ball. The only factor that didn't contribute to the formation of the perfect storm was her gender, but even that couldn't hold her back.

Long before Title IX, which defacto forced schools to include girls on their teams, Mamie empowered herself to play baseball. What she lacked in stature, she made up in nerve; she not only played ball, she had (nerve).

Title IX of the Education Amendments of 1972, is a 37-word law enacted on June 23, 1972 that states: "No person in the United States shall, on the basis of sex, be excluded from participation in, be denied the benefits of, or be subjected to discrimination under any education program or activity receiving Federal financial assistance." Although the most prominent "public face" of Title IX is its impact on high school and collegiate athletics, the original statute made no reference to athletics. The legislation covers all educational activities, and ... applies to non-sport activities such as school bands and cheerleaders, as well as non-social fraternities/sororities, clubs, and organizations.

Her uncle may have taught her to pitch a ball, but she was the one with the gumption to make a "pitch" to join the Negro Leagues. She had the nerve because she had the goods, which she had acquired as a result of practicing day after day in the hot sun in rural South Carolina. It was only natural that she became good at it, and though some at the time may have considered it unusual for a female to play hardball, it was a natural outcome of her mastery over the game. Day after day, she knew she was practicing for something. She was going somewhere in baseball, no matter what it took, and if the White women's team would not accept her, then there was another field for her dreams: The Negro Leagues.

"It was 'straight up' fun playing in the Negro Leagues; it was a special time," Mamie said. She loved traveling around to all those cities to play games, even though life on the road was hard for Negro League players. "Many hotels and restaurants would not serve Black people, and hotels were hard to find." When Mamie was on the road, instead of staying in hotels or barns with the men, the team arranged for her to stay in people's homes. Imagine how special it must have been for a poor Black girl from rural South Carolina to travel around America to play the most popular sport at the time?

In a 2001 article entitled: *Girls Playing with the Boys, and Boys Playing with the Girls*, Zoe Meyer discusses issues that often arise for women who play a man's game:

> … For a female to "break into" a male sport is probably one of the most difficult parts of being an athlete. The main argument [against it] is that the female body is not made to correctly function while participating. Also, the idea that the women will lose their femininity if they play with men is another reason to keep them off the field and out of the ring. For women to be taken seriously in a male dominated sport they have to not only be the best female in the ring, gym, or wherever, they also have to be the best overall athlete.
>
> Traditionally, women are thought of as more fragile, and less aggressive than men. The costs to a woman playing with a man in the ring or on the field are more numerous than simply getting laughed at and called names. …The men will usually play their hardest, if not harder in an attempt to push the women to their limits and eventually

> make them quit. Also, since the woman is in a male dominated sport, the chances that there are other females out there helping "the cause" are very small, which makes it even harder for her to be taken seriously.

The foregoing applied ten-fold to Mamie's situation when she played with the Negro Leagues.

It was a profound and extraordinary accomplishment for a woman of color to pitch major league baseball in such legendary stadiums such as Yankee Stadium, Comiskey Park, and Griffith Stadium; it was not only one of the most thrilling experiences any athlete could have, it was phenomenal.

When people ask Mamie to describe how it was playing with the guys, she isn't happy because that's not the important question for her. Ask her about her right arm, however, and she will be engaged in the conversation.

The 1940s were a turning point for African American in economic terms. Those in urban areas experienced relatively large wage gains relative to White women, sharp declines in agricultural and domestic service work, and significant increases in formal sector employment. Mamie wasn't from the inner city however; she was from the rural south where the economic prospects for woman like her weren't bright.

The wages Mamie earned in the Negro Leagues were in significant contrast to what she might have earned in a regular job back home. The opportunity baseball afforded her to see America, while doing something she loved, meant more than the money, however.

Not that the money didn't matter. Just as playing professional baseball was a big deal for the few selected White women who played in the AAGPBL who earned salaries ranging from $45 to $85 a week, in many cases making more than their parents, Mamie's earnings were also a big deal for her family. Mamie's mother, like many single African American mothers today, played the central role in supporting the dreams of her athletic daughter. It all worked out, proving that dreams really do come true.

Should African Americans strive to revive baseball in the inner cities? Should African American women play baseball? Absolutely, is Mamie's answer. "Yes, any thing a women is capable of doing they should be able to do it. They should have the opportunity to do it," says Mamie.

Mamie wants to see baseball revived in inner cities, and has contributed what she could to help make it happen. For years, she was a baseball coach in Maryland, but it wasn't easy. It wasn't like the old days when kids loved baseball. She tried to teach baseball to people who didn't want to learn it, and had to deal with interfering parents in the process. Never one to take an insult lightly, she finally had to give up coaching. Though she can't claim to know all of the ingredients that are required to revive baseball in inner cities today, she knows for sure that African Americans have the talent to "knock the ball out of the park."

Effa Manley: An Owner's Perspective:

Effa Manley, known as the Queen of the Negro Leagues, became the first—and only—woman elected to the Baseball Hall of Fame in 2006. Though she did not play the game on the field, she played the game off the field; her induction into the Hall of Fame underscores the importance of being an economic player in the game. The following information about Manley, written by Leslie Heaphy, was retrieved from the Baseball Hall of Fame website.

As a businesswoman in a primarily man's world Effa Manley wanted to be a winner. Though the only woman among an industry of male owners, Manley got her wish in 1946, when the Newark Eagles, owned by her and her husband Abe, won the Negro League World Series, defeating the famed Kansas City Monarchs. Manley ran the day-to-day operations of the club and helped build a winner for the city of Newark, both on and off the field. Her election to the National Baseball Hall of Fame as the institution's first woman electee is a reflection of her commitment to baseball and civil rights, serving as a tribute to her leadership, vision and her dedication to creating respect for Negro league baseball.

Born on March 27, 1897, Manley grew up in Philadelphia, but her commitment to the game and civil rights began when she moved to New York following high school. Often found at Yankee Stadium watching Babe Ruth, Manley dedicated her time to local social organizations and causes. For example, in 1935 she walked the picket line in a successful campaign to get local businesses to hire black employees, a "Don't Buy Where You Can't Work" campaign.

While attending one of the World Series games in 1932, Manley met her future husband, Abe, and the rest was history. Nearly 15 years her senior, Abe had already established his reputation in the local community as a baseball man. Together they forged a partnership that resulted in the rapid rise to fame of the Newark Eagles, a team they owned from 1935 until she sold the club to a group of investors in 1948.

Manley's involvement in baseball in the 1930s and 1940s came at a time when women's roles were still dominated as homemakers. Her position as co-owner of the Eagles included handling contracts and travel schedules for the Eagles, and she quickly gained recognition across the league for her ability to promote the team. Fellow owner Cum Posey, also among the 17 electees to the Hall of Fame this summer, remarked that the league could learn something from Manley's keen sense of promotion. Manley also displayed personal care for the team's players on and off the field, assisting players with jobs, serving as godparents to some, and purchasing a $15,000 bus for the team's travel, always working to get players the best available accommodations on the road.

Perhaps Manley's greatest contribution as an owner would come in her final years with the Eagles. Following Branch Rickey's signing of Jackie Robinson from the Negro leagues to play Major League Baseball, Manley fought for compensation for team owners. A few months following Robinson's entry into the major leagues in 1947, Manley and the Negro leagues received compensation for Larry Doby, the first African American to play in the American League, thereby establishing a precedent for player compensation. The move showed the legitimacy of the Negro leagues, giving the leagues a measure of respectability never before seen from the majors.

Throughout her ownership, Manley pushed the envelope to develop a better league, emerging as a leading voice among Negro leagues owners. "She is a good businesswoman, and most of the men club owners could take a few tips from her," wrote Chicago Defender reporter Fay Young in December 1943 on the meeting of the Negro American League.

Manley also used her position with the club to promote a variety of causes and benefits. The team invited soldiers during World War II to Eagles games for free. The club hosted benefits for causes such as the Harlem Fight for Freedom Committee, the Newark Community Hospital and world champion sprinter John Borican. One of the benefit games featured a "Stop Lynching" theme, with ticket takers collecting donations and wearing sashes to promote the cause.

The Eagles boasted a number of excellent players during Manley's tenure as owner, and their success culminated in a 1946 Negro League World Series triumph over the Kansas City Monarchs. The great Eagles rosters included future Hall of Famers Ray Dandridge, Leon Day, Larry Doby, Monte Irvin, Biz Mackey, Mule Suttles and Willie Wells. Other All-Stars on her teams included Fats Jenkins, Dick Lundy and Max Manning.

Following her ownership tenure, Manley co-authored a book on black baseball with Leon Hardwick, and she donated her scrapbook to the National Baseball Hall of Fame. She also wrote letters lobbying for Negro Leaguers to be admitted into Cooperstown. In 1980, at the Negro Leagues Reunion in Ashland, Kentucky, the players paid special tribute to Manley for all she did for black baseball, shortly before her death in 1981.

When she found a closed door, Manley kicked it open to improve her league and her team's playing conditions. Because of her contributions to the Newark Eagles and the Negro leagues growth, Manley will be remembered forever as a member of the National Baseball Hall of Fame.

Her epitaph reads, "She loved baseball."

Rachel Robinson: A Partner's Perspective

There will perhaps never be a complete account of the contributions made by the wives of Negro League players. Those who are still around to tell their stories, tell an interesting story indeed. Their stories make it clear that their own characters and determination had to be as strong as that of their spouses. Just as much was required of the players, much was also required from their wives, much more than meets the eye.

Among the many untold number of African American women who traveled the roads less traveled with their baseball player spouses, some remain who are able to paint a vivid portrait of the incredible times they experienced. Rachel Robinson, widow of Jackie Robinson, is one such woman. Her story provides a unique window into a special time in the nation's history.

She continues to be active today, and is leaving her own mark as an activist and leader through the Jackie Robinson Foundation.

> The Jackie Robinson Foundation (JRF) is a public, not-for-profit national organization founded by Rachel Robinson in 1973 as a vehicle to perpetuate the memory of Jackie Robinson and his achievements. Serving as an advocate for young people with the greatest need, the Foundation assists increasing numbers of minority youths through the granting of four-year scholarships for higher education. The Foundation provides much more than financial support. While each Jackie Robinson Scholar receives up to $7,500 a year in financial support, they also become an active member in the Foundation's unique Education and Leadership Development Program, which is an extensive mentoring program that includes attendance at workshops, assignment of a peer and a professional mentor and placement into summer internships and permanent employment.

Ten years ago, Rachel Robinson spoke with students for whom she painted a rich portrait of the events she experienced with her husband, baseball pioneer and civil rights activist Jackie Robinson.

Interview with Rachel Robinson:

Rachel Robinson, the wife of Major League Baseball pioneer Jackie Robinson, answered questions from students on February 11, 1998, during a live interview. Mrs. Robinson is also the founder of the Jackie Robinson Foundation, which provides educational and leadership opportunities for minority students nationwide.

Did you experience much in the way of racial discrimination growing up? Did Jackie? Had anything changed by the time he started to play ball?

I was born and raised in northern California. Racial discrimination was very subtle. For instance, if we went to the movies, as we entered the lobby, the usher would direct us upstairs to the balcony. We were being segregated almost without knowing it.

When I went south for the first time in 1947, I was shocked by the legal discrimination where I had to use a drinking fountain labeled "for Negroes only;" or where I had to use a Negro women's bathroom in the airport.

Jackie grew up in Pasadena, California, where discrimination was even more blatant and humiliating. For instance, he could not swim in the YMCA pool, except on a day for Negroes. So, Jack experienced discrimination in a much more powerful form.

How did you and Jackie Robinson first meet? What was your first impression of him?

I was a freshman at UCLA and he was a senior. He was Big Man on campus, because he was the first four-letter man at UCLA — that is, he starred in all four major sports. I was introduced to him by one of his teammates on the football team. I was extremely shy, but I was rather pleased to see that he was also shy in that encounter. However, my impression of him was that he had great self-confidence, and I was pleased to see that he was not arrogant. It's a trait I detest. He was extremely handsome, with a wonderful smile. And he was clearly comfortable and proud of being a black man.

In the 1940s I was very impressed by that fact. Not all of us could carry our racial identity with such pride.

Did Jackie Robinson experience discrimination in the army?

Oh, yes. In the 1940s the armed forces were segregated. The black soldiers did not have the same accommodations and facilities to use as the white soldiers.

Jack had applied for officers training school to become an officer, but the army initially refused to review his application. Joe Louis, the world championship boxer, happened to be in the same unit as Jack at Fort Riley, Kansas. Joe wrote Washington, D.C., protesting discrimination in the army, and succeeded in getting the army to allow Jack and others to go for officer training.

The sad part of this part of his life is that while we were at war overseas, Jack was at war at home on the army base.

Was there discrimination on the college teams he joined?

No, not at UCLA. However, they did play southern teams, and had to be conscious of the vicious tactics that teams would plan. Tactics like ganging up with unnecessary roughness on a black player. A tactic like that can be hidden in a football game, where there's always a form of "ganging up."

When Jackie started playing for the Brooklyn Dodgers, did you travel with him? How were you accepted by the other wives, players, and people you met?

When Jack began with the Dodgers in 1947 — by the way, I never called him Jackie. The name didn't have the intimacy that calling him by his given name had. Anyway, in those days wives were not permitted to travel with the team. The teams were saving money, and the men had roommates.

Typical of those days, in terms of women, we were given a "treat" by being allowed to travel with the team maybe once a year. Today, in contemporary times, wives get elaborate treatment. They not only travel; the have suites, limos, etc. Do I sound jealous? The whole situation was different then. It was more like a plantation system.

Initially one or two wives attempted to make me feel more comfortable as we sat in a special section of the ballpark for wives. But I think that the tensions were as evident in the stands as they were on the field. I became particularly close to Joan Hodges, the wife of Gil Hodges, Betty Erskine, the wife of Carl Erskine, and Pee Wee Reese's wife, Dotty, as well as the wives of the black players — Roy Campanella and Don Newcombe.

How difficult was it for Jackie to honor his agreement to be silent for two years and not respond to negative behavior?

Jack made a pact with Branch Rickey, the general manager of the Dodgers, and a pioneer in his own right. He would not respond to provocation regardless of what it was, or how much it hurt.

He was physically and verbally abused, particularly when he was on the road, in certain cities. The taunts angered him, sometimes frightened him, but he turned away from them.

I think the lesson for us is: if you have an overriding goal, a big goal that you're trying to achieve, there are times when you must transcend the obstacles that are being put in your way. Rise above them. Jack wanted to integrate athletics. He could not afford to create an incident on the field that would interfere with reaching this goal.

There had been predictions (at that time) that if you integrated sports, there would be riots in the stands and on the field, and races could not play together. He had to demonstrate that this was incorrect. Jack did so at considerable personal sacrifice. He was a personality who would usually fight back in an instant if he sensed that he was being mistreated. But he knew that he had to turn the other cheek for a short period of time — two years. That was a very clear part of the pact. So, he could bide his time knowing that it would come to an end, and he could soon be himself.

How did you both react when the Brooklyn Dodgers offered Jackie the chance to play in the major leagues? What did your families think?

This offer came as a total surprise to both of us. We were very excited, but we didn't know what it really meant in the larger sense. At the time, Jack needed a job. He'd just gotten out of the army and we wanted to get married. So initially, we were just pleased that we could carry out our plans. Our families were extremely happy for us, and somehow knew that if Jack were given an opportunity, he could make the most of it.

How did Jackie feel when other African Americans entered Major League Baseball?

Jack always said that being the first to break the color barrier was important. But it didn't prove anything in the long run if there was not a second. In other words, he wanted to see the door opened for minorities. So, he was thrilled when Roy Campanella became the second African American in the National League and Larry Doby became the first African American to play baseball in the American League. It meant to us that real social change was occurring in that system.

What was the worst or scariest experience you faced while Jackie played Major League Baseball? What was the worst experience for your husband?

From time to time we received hate mail. And because it was necessary for Jack to continue to perform, and because taking those messages seriously meant I would live in fear, we ignored the mail. Then, one day, we received a letter stating that Jack would be shot from the stands in a particular city. That was scary. We turned the letter in to the team, and asked that some measures be taken to protect Jack. It was hard then to believe that one could be killed because of one's race.

And yet, we knew of the lynchings in the South, and we knew that the potential for violence always existed in the North as well.

What was Jackie's experience playing in the Negro American League? How did it compare to playing in the National League?

Jack played for one year with the Kansas City Monarchs — the team that Satchel Paige made famous. He was impressed by the caliber of play, and the unique way that the Negro leaguers performed. He learned a great deal from them, and enjoyed the camaraderie.

What he hated about playing in the Negro Leagues was the way the players had to live — traveling through the South on buses, unable to stop at hotels, unable to enter restaurants, unable to use restrooms. He found it thoroughly humiliating.

The Negro Leagues were flourishing for a time, and it's ironic that Jack's being signed by the Dodgers signaled the demise of the Negro Leagues.

What was it, in your opinion, that gave Jackie so much courage?

I believe that he derived his sense of himself — his life mission, and the courage to carry it out — from his mother, Mallie Robinson. She was an extraordinary woman — courageous, determined, extremely religious, and self-reliant. She had been a sharecropper in Georgia. Her husband left her with five small children. So, she packed them up and took them to California, all alone.

Mallie managed to purchase a home for the family from her salary as a domestic worker. And she created an environment that was filled with positive values, as well as love. She was THE major influence in Jack's life.

A lot of people admired Jackie. Who was Jackie's hero?

In the early 1940s, Joe Louis, boxing's world heavyweight champion, was our hero. We felt that he didn't just fight in a ring, but he was battling the world on our behalf. He was fighting for respect, opportunity, and our place in America.

Later on Jack met Martin Luther King, Jr. in the 1950s and early 1960s, when the reverend began organizing for the civil rights movement in the South. What Jack admired most about Dr. King was his nonviolent protest, and his use of organization and strategies that drew on the human spirit, and his sense of being entitled to all that America promised.

Did you or your husband ever regret that he decided to play in what had been an all-white league? Did Jackie ever feel like quitting?

No, we never regretted the decision. There were times when he felt like quitting, but he never expressed to me any intention to quit. He fought back by performing with excellence, and — as many sports writers said — he would answer the critics with his bat.

How did your three children feel about being part of such a famous family? Was it hard for your children growing up?

Only one of my children, Jackie, Jr., the firstborn — and obviously the one named for his father — suffered greatly. From a very early age, like at 2, he was being compared to his father by other people, and virtually being told that he could never be as great as his father. He lived under his shadow, and was pained by having to compete with this great man. It affected his work in school, his relationships with the family, and eventually led to serious encounters outside our home.

He enlisted in the army, fought in Vietnam, became a drug addict, and eventually went for rehabilitation. But he came to a tragic end despite his efforts to change. He was killed in an automobile accident in 1971, the year before his father died.

Sharon and David, the younger children, had to learn to share their father with the world. And sometimes that was difficult. But they have overcome the feelings, and are flourishing as adults, both giving back to society in their own way.

What was Jackie Robinson really like? Did he have a good personality?

I'm glad you asked that question, because most people only know his public persona: The tough guy always battling, very consumed with the struggles in America. But the family knew a different person. We knew a man very capable of great love and commitment. I always felt especially fortunate to be loved by him and to experience his great tenderness.

Even his vulnerability was more evident at home. He tended to be quiet and had great routines. He cherished the opportunity to gather the family together for dinner. Jack never drank or smoked, and felt that one respected the household by not using profane language at home — though I understand from his teammates that he could manage the language very well in the locker room.

He had a very strong sense of responsibility. Even in the post-baseball period, he worked very hard to get into the civil rights movement, and to work on behalf of others. He had an interesting statement to make about what life meant to him, which the Jackie Robinson Foundation now uses. It was: that a life is not important, except in its impact on the lives of others.

Are you a baseball fan now? Who is your favorite team?

Yes, I am a baseball fan. Not a rabid one. And my team will always be the Dodgers, despite their defection from Brooklyn. For me, affiliations tend to be lifetime.

How were you and Jackie involved in the civil rights movement? Did you ever meet Martin Luther King, Jr.?

When Dr. King was marching in Birmingham in 1963 Jack went south to participate with him. Thereafter, he was always available when Dr. King called. One of the things we knew from this experience was that Dr. King needed money for the movement. Jack and I established an outdoor jazz concert on our property to raise funds to be used as bail money for those who had been jailed for their actions. That was my particular involvement, and that

concert is still being held on the last Sunday in June in Connecticut. I now raise funds for the scholarship program of the Jackie Robinson Foundation.

Jack served on the board of directors of the NAACP for eight years, and was one of the chief fundraisers. He joined the Rev. Jesse Jackson in Chicago when he established Breadbasket and the PUSH organization. Informally, Jack kept himself involved all over the country as new movements were started, and new leadership appeared. His activities proved to me, and I think to others, that an individual can make a difference.

What do you think was Jackie's proudest moment? What has been your proudest moment?

I think I would say there were many proud moments in his lifetime, beginning with the birth of his children. We had always wanted a family, had learned to cherish family life from our own childhood, and so each birth brought great joy.

In terms of his profession, being elected to the Baseball Hall of Fame in the first year of his eligibility was a high point for him. He had not expected to win this honor because he had challenged the baseball writers often, and had antagonized some. And they were the ones who had to vote for him for this honor. So, this was a great thrill.

I consider myself to be one of those very fortunate people who have lived to see wonderful things happen. When my daughter Sharon graduated from Howard University and received her masters degree from Columbia University, I was tremendously proud and excited. When my son David went to Tanzania, Africa, and single-handedly established a rural development project in his village, I was in awe of his achievement, and thrilled to know that he was carrying on family traditions in a totally new area.

**Read more about David Robinson's coffee farm in Tanzania at: www.vanityfair.com/politics/features/2005/05/robinson200505.

I've said what I feel about the importance of family, so I have to tell you that I have ten grandchildren, and one great-grandchild, and every time they have their small victories, my life is enriched.

I am the founder of the Jackie Robinson Foundation. We provide four-year scholarships, totaling $20,000, and I'm happy to tell you that we have serviced over 500 young people. And we have a 92 percent graduation rate — which is the highest in the country for comparable programs.

I have had my own joys about myself; I was always very independent and strong as a child, but very shy. I have worked hard to conquer the shyness and to prepare myself to live as an independent person, and not just a woman living in her husband's shadow.

I went back to school after many years as a homemaker, got my masters degree in psychiatric nursing at New York University, and went to work in mental institutions. My husband was not very happy with my going to work, but fortunately we struggled with this issue of my being a separate person. Jack died at an early age, and though I was devastated by the loss, I have been able to carry on my own work.

What advice do you have for children today to continue what Jackie started in civil rights?

Last year was the 50th anniversary of Jack's breaking the color barrier. Among the many exciting things that happened was the amount of correspondence I received from children of all ages, from all parts of the country. What delighted me about the letters was that these children were curious about their history, concerned about the impact of the history on their lives today, and were thinking about what they should be doing to make this a better world.

I think at any age, one can look around in your own setting and in your own family and find ways to contribute to social change. When you see attitudes that hurt others, or limit their opportunities, you can say to yourself: what is my part in this? Can I be a catalyst for change in my school, on my block, in my church, wherever I am? The question is: do I have a responsibility for others? I would say yes because I passionately believe that we are linked as human beings. Our destinies are intertwined. And what is happening to me ultimately is having an impact on you. So, if someone is homeless, uneducated, without medical care, without support, I have to feel some responsibility for them, and do whatever I can think to do. We all need to stand up and be counted...

Spouses Carrying The Torch

Across America many African American women survive as widows of baseball legends. Though their husbands may not have been as famous as Jackie Robinson, their baseball accomplishments touched the lives of many in their respective communities, and beyond. Their spouses, like Rachel Robinson, carry the torch and often play a role in helping to lend their famous husband's names, and their own support, to help get kids involved in baseball. These women are "Pied Pipers." Clearly, there is a need for more intense "*reach in*" efforts by the MLB to bring them out of the woodworks to play a role in leading inner city kids to baseball.

Mrs. Geraldine Day, wife of baseball legend and Hall of Fame electee Leon Day who passed away in 1995, is an example of a spouse who is playing the role of "Pied Piper" for baseball through the Leon Day Little League in Baltimore, Maryland. Though she is experiencing a few health problems at the moment, and wasn't available to be interviewed, her work on behalf of the Leon Day Little and the Leon Day Park, speaks volumes.

> The founding of Leon Day Park has worked magic for the children and families who were neighbors of National Baseball Hall of Famer Leon Day ('95). Leon's love and involvement with children made it clear that the love of athletics is a key to keeping them off the streets and away from drugs. Peter Angelos, majority owner of the Baltimore Orioles, funded the diamonds, basketball courts, playground, lighting system, dugouts, and viewing stands at Leon Day Park in the Rosemont Community of downtown Baltimore. The playground is a source of pride that attracts families from all around, bringing the neighborhood together with great purpose.

Box 16
Leon Day
(1916-1995)

The most consistently outstanding pitcher in the Negro National League during the late 1930's and 1940's, Leon Day was a heady pitcher whose money pitch was his fastball. The 5' 9" 170 lb. Newark Eagle ace righthander had a good curve and change-of-pace to complement his speed. Not only was Leon a great pitcher, he was also a good base runner and a good hitter, with averages of .320, .274 and .469 to show for the seasons of 1937, 1942, and 1946. His best season came in 1937 when, backed by the Eagles' "million dollar infield," he finished league play with a perfect 13-0 record. Appearing in a record seven East-West All-Star games from 1935-46 won his only All-Star decision and set an All-Star record by striking out a total of 14 batters. In the 1942 game, he struck out five of the seven batters that he faced without giving up a hit.

Leon missed two prime years when he was drafted into the Army during World War II. After two-and-a-half years in an amphibian unit that landed on Utah Beach during the Allied invasion of France, he was discharged in February 1946. Returning to the Eagles, he picked up where he had left off, pitching an opening day no-hitter against the Philadelphia Stars and not allowing a runner past first base. This surpasses an effort earlier in his career (1942) when he struck out 18 Elite Giants, allowing only a bloop single over the shortstop. After the opening day no-hitter, Leon continued his pitching heroics, topping the league in strikeouts, innings pitched, and complete games; and finishing with a 9-4 record as the Eagles captured the pennant. Even though his arm was hurt, the veteran moundsman started two games in the World Series as the Eagles defeated the Kansas City Monarchs for the championship.

The hardworking competitor played six winters in Puerto Rico and in 1948 he played his second winter season in Cuba, finishing with a composite 8-4 record. The 1949 season, spent with the pennant-winning Baltimore Elite Giants, was his last season in the Negro Leagues. In 1951, he entered organized baseball at the age of 35, pitching for Toronto in the AAA International League. On March 7, 1995, the Veteran's Committee elected Leon Day to the Hall of Fame. Six days after learning of the honor, Leon Day passed away.

African American Women & Baseball *Today*

Who moved the field of dreams? It's now a whole new ballgame, especially for African American women.

The position of African American women in society has changed, and so has their connection to baseball. Some of the changes have been good, and some haven't been.

On the positive side, African American women have made great strides in politics, especially in Baltimore. It was a clean sweep recently for African American women in Baltimore when they won every major elected position (Mayor, President of the City Council, Financial Controller, and Attorney General).

Baltimore's 48th Mayor, Sheila Dixon, is the city's first female Mayor, and its first African American Mayor. She is also a single mother and a sports fan, which are two considerations that may bode well for her support of inner city baseball.

Mayor Dixon is a longtime supporter of the James Mosher Little League program and has rolled up her sleeves and gotten out there on the field to throw the ceremonious first ball of the game on a number of occassions. Furthermore, as a former instructor in the Head Start program, the Mayor understands how important it is to get a "head start," and how involvement in baseball at a young age can help African Americans learn skills and sportmanship that gives them such a head start.

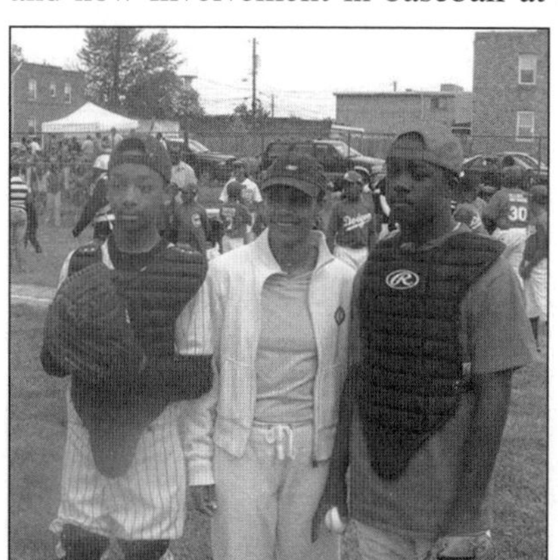

Baltimore Mayor Sheila Dixon with James Mosher Little Leaguers

Now, it's up to African Americans inner city stakeholders to make a compelling case to the Mayor and other city officials about the assistance they need to revive baseball.

There are a lot of ears listening these days in Baltimore, but it's up to the little leagues, African American parents, and other stakeholders to raise their voices more loudly to make their case for bigger investments in baseball in the inner city.

Sports Moms Wearing Many Hats

Numbering somewhere between 41 and 42 million, mothers are the behind the scenes players in every sport, and they are busy, very busy.

At no other time have parents needed to choreograph their lives to the split second as they do today. Mothers, in higher-income brackets try to keep track by all means possible: desk calendars, PDAs, BlackBerrys, 16 × 20 wall calendars, sticky notes, three-ring binders, and computers.

For African American mothers in lower-income brackets, it's exponentially more difficult to get a handle on all of activities involved in their lives, especially if they are single heads of household. For them, there are no desk calendars, PDAs, BlackBerrys, 16 × 20 wall calendars, sticky notes, three-ring binders, and computers. What they have is extended family living arrangements, where everybody chips in—grandmothers, cousins, brothers, and others to lend a helping hand. What the statistics do not convey is the extent to which subfamilies may live within the parental household, cohabit, or share their own household with other adult relatives.

Sheila A. Dixon (born December 27, 1953) is the 48th Mayor of Baltimore, Maryland. She was raised in the Ashburton neighborhood of West Baltimore. Her father, Phillip Dixon, Sr. was a car salesman, and her mother, Winona Dixon, was a community activist, active in her church, political causes, and member of local community groups. She attended Baltimore City public schools and is a graduate of Northewestern High School. She holds a bachelor's degree from Towson University and a master's degree from Johns Hopkins University. She is a former elementary school teacher and adult education instructor with the Head Start program. She worked for 17 years as an international trade specialist with the Maryland Department of Business and Economic Development and in 1987 won a seat on the Baltimore City Council representing the 4th Council District, where she served for 12 years. She became the city council president in 1999, the first African American woman ever elected to this position.

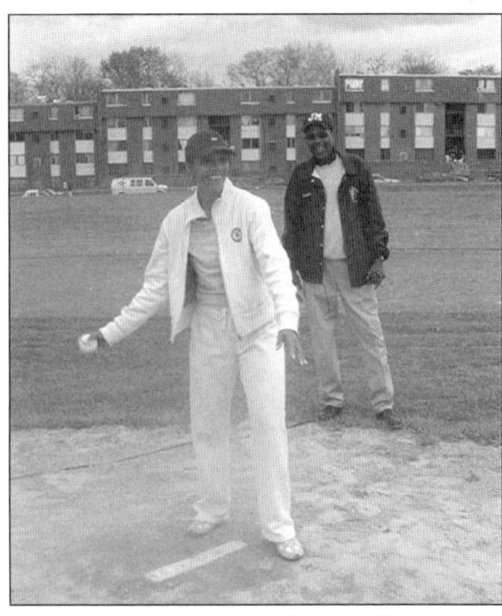

Mayor Sheila Dixon throwing out ball at James Mosher

According to the Census Department's decennial census, as reported in *The Black Population in the United States: March 2002*, as of 2001, 13 percent of all women were poor. The poverty rate for Black women (25 percent) was more than twice that for non-Hispanic White women (9 percent); for women 65 and older, the rates were 26 percent and 10 percent, respectively.

Courtesy of The Library of Congress

Despite shared living arrangements, mothers are the ones that have special obligations associated with raising athletic children. While typically not the ones who teach sons and daughters how to throw and catch balls, they're needed to teach them how to play the game of life.

Education commences at the mother's knee; every spoken word matters and every nuance is processed by the child who is searching for the meaning of things in a complex world. It follows that if mothers get behind baseball, their positive messages creep into the psyche of the child.

Recognizing the importance of education, Major League Baseball chose Jackie Robinson's daughter, Sharon Robinson, as an educational consultant. New York Times Sports Columnist William C. Rhoden sat down with her in 2001 to discuss the educational program she started with the MLB. The article is summarized in Box 17.

Box 17:
Sports of The Times; Jackie Robinson's Daughter Continues Job of Conquering Obstacles

By William C. Rhoden
Published: July 15, 2001

Sharon Robinson sat in an uptown coffee shop recently, enthusiastically describing the in-school education program she started along with Major League Baseball in 1997. The *Breaking Barriers in Sports, in Life* program, which is in 26 major league cities including New York, teaches adolescents the principles of confronting obstacles and ultimately clearing them. Robinson, 51, said that after rearing her son and serving as a midwife for more than two decades, her involvement with this program is the most invigorating undertaking of her life.

The curriculum consists of a video about her father, Jackie Robinson. The textbook is *''Jackie's Nine: Jackie Robinson's Values to Live By,*'' which describes the nine principles that guided his life. Those principles are courage, determination, commitment, persistence, integrity, justice, teamwork, citizenship and excellence.

During classroom discussion, students and major league players discuss what constitutes an obstacle, from the smallest to the largest, and effective ways to face it. The students then write essays about an obstacle in their life and how they negotiated it. Robinson and a panel of others read each essay and select the best three. The rewards range from a trip to a game for the entire class to team caps and other baseball items.

But "Breaking Barriers" is more than a token community outreach program in which teams hand out some bats and balls and trot out an athlete who tells the kids to keep their chins up and their noses clean. There are real-life issues and real-life solutions.

One girl wrote about refusing to live with her mother because her mother was in an abusive relationship. ''She opted to live with her grandmother and told her mother that until her mother got out of that relationship, she would not come back in the house,'' Robinson recalled.

A California boy wrote about the day he and his mother were going to school and his mother was shot. The gunman then shot himself. ''He wrote about how he was adopted by his grandparents and how he has been able to move beyond that moment by having therapy and the therapist making him relive it,'' Robinson said. ''He says he has found some level of happiness.''

Sharon Robinson represents a vast and deep tradition. She is the resounding human dimension of Jackie Robinson's legacy. One of her brothers died in a car accident after wrestling with drug addiction, the other works in Tanzania. Her mother, the indomitable Rachel Robinson, is as much a part of the legend and legacy as her father.

Sharon shared her father with the world. Her entire family paid the price for his pioneering act of integrating baseball in 1947. Her father's sense of mission compelled him to see himself as mighty Zeus, who seemed to carry an entire race on his shoulders until his death in 1972 at age 53.

''My father never complained about those early years in baseball,'' she said. ''It was a factual account, not a complaint: this is what happened, why I agreed to do that. What we got out of that, what we have to work toward, why we as family are going to be involved in civil rights. We bought into the concept that we were pioneers.''

Heroism can take a toll on the delicate psyche of children of the legend. Indeed, Robinson would have won her own contest.

''I got hit with life when I was 16 years old,'' she said. ''I had a boyfriend who was abusive, and I had never in my life been talked badly to, hit, not treated good. And it happened so quietly and insidiously, you don't quite understand what's happening until you're deep into it.''

Getting herself out of the relationship was Robinson's ''first test of my own ability to survive.'' she said.

''It was a wonderful preparation for life because from that point on, life got harder,'' she said. ''It doesn't get easier, whether it was my brother's drug addiction and worrying about him all those years and his eventual death. Then my father's death.''

Robinson had been divorced twice by the time she was 22. At age 24, she learned she had lupus.

But her greatest obstacle was overcoming a sense of dread that she was being raised in the shadow of a legend, a shadow that haunted her for many years. She described a museum-like room in her family's Connecticut home that held her father's trophies, plaques and awards.

''As I moved into adolescence, the anxiety of passing through that room began to build,'' she said. ''Nothing I was doing compared to anything that was in that room. I had Girl Scout badges and that kind of thing, but I never thought of them as accomplishments. That was the hardest part of having a father so revered out in the world, held up to such high standards. You hold yourself up to that same high standard and it's hard to feel like you're meeting it. I keep raising the bar.''

She cleared a personal obstacle in 1997, the 50th anniversary of her father's breakthrough in baseball. Robinson was invited to Seattle to throw out the first pitch on opening day. ''I was by myself for the first time,'' she said. ''Ken Griffey Jr. greeted me so warmly and the crowd was so loud and electric. It was very emotional.''

Robinson realized that moment that she was no longer under her father's shadow. She had a vision of how she could perpetuate his legacy in a way that would touch young people and teach them to confront difficulties in their lives. The next week, she contacted Major League Baseball about instituting a program that became "Breaking Barriers."

''The thing about my parents is that I watched them get up after major things," she said. ''My father was diagnosed with diabetes and I watched him continue to travel, take his own medicine in the mornings, fix himself breakfast, force himself to remain independent, despite the fact he had this chronic disease. We were committed as a family to social change… it became a lifelong mission."

Education matters in the development of children and so do sports, especially for boys, and perhaps most of all for African American boys in inner cities.

- Sports provide boys a healthy way to channel their intense physicality and aggression and feel strong;
- Sports help boys develop self-control and self-confidence;
- Sports provide a place in which boys can form friendships with other boys and are central to boys' social relationships;
- Sports help keep boys active and physically fit;
- Sports provide boys with increased social status. Research shows that male athletes across all sports are significantly more popular than non-athletic male peers, with the most popular group being those boys who play both contact and non-contact sports;
- Participation in sports makes it less likely that a boy will smoke cigarettes, use drugs, or think about or commit suicide (the suicide rate has almost tripled over the past forty years and is now the third leading cause of death among adolescents fifteen to twenty-four, with the rate for boys higher than for girls);
- Boys who play sports in high school get better grades and do better on standardized tests. In addition, it has been suggested that psychologically, Black male athletes think that they would have a good chance of playing professional sports if they attend college for at least two years. Therefore, they do whatever is necessary, academically, in high school to gain entry into college.

Sports are equally important for girls. In addition to the benefits girls get from playing sports, society itself benefits from the spirit of cooperation women and girls bring to sports. Baseball can provide an important outlet for little girls in inner cities in much the same way as it does for little boys.

Girls playing baseball with James Mosher

Take **Eshon Everett**, for example. She played in the James Mosher little league program when she was growing up. Today, she is a Mechanical Engineer for Boeing, where she tests the performance of wind tunnels, but early in her life she tested herself when she played baseball with the boys. She said:

> *"I learned so much from playing baseball. It taught me teamwork, how to listen, and it built my confidence. It also taught be about responsibility and accountability, and helped to shape my character. It also showed me that I could hold my own against the guys, which is a foundation experience that prepared me to be able to work alongside mostly men in the my profession today. I look on my boss as my coach, I listen to him, and I work well in teams; my experience playing ball at James Mosher helped me to play ball in life."*

Everett was one of the lucky ones growing up. Her father was a "Dad." He was a coach in the James Mosher program and coached her and her little brother too. It was a family affair, and "so much fun," Everett recalls. For Everett, it wasn't just the social aspects of baseball that she liked; she actually liked the playing game, and continues to play it today, and basketball too.

There are many benefits associated with girls playing sports, as Meyer (2001) observed:

> The benefits for a woman in a man's sport however are probably some of the greatest out there. She will not only most likely be the star and the sweetheart of the team, but she will also most likely get the most attention both in and out of the game. Also, the endorsements for a woman playing with men are unimaginable, especially with all the

feminists behind her and supporting her, she will most likely never have to worry about money again. The one problem with all of this though, is that she will probably have to be defending her sexuality constantly from those that think all female athletes are gay. However, if any woman can get through the taunting, and succeed in a male dominated sport, then she truly will have "made it" in the world of athletics.

According to the Census Department's decennial census, as reported in *The Black Population in the United States: March 2002*, as of 2001, among the 26.2 million Blacks and the 158.3 million non-Hispanic Whites 15 and older, 10 percent of each were divorced and about 6 percent of each were widowed, but 43 percent of Blacks had never married, compared with 25 percent of non-Hispanic Whites. Blacks were less likely than their non-Hispanic White counterparts to be currently married (35 percent and 57 percent, respectively).

Today, many women are "making it" in the world of athletics, and many more are having success subsequently in their professional careers. Their early successes on the field help them to strive for successes off the field.

The varied ways in which African American women are involved in baseball are well-kept secrets. Perhaps, they are best known for their involvement as mothers. However, African American mothers of young baseball players tend to fall into two camps: Those that fundamentally like the game, and those that have no affinity for it.

Allene McClary & sons

Take **Allene McClary**, for example. She is an example of a mother who actually likes the game of baseball. Her "Dad" was a baseball fan, and helped her to be one. McClary is a single mother with three sons who play in the James Mosher little program. She is a Dental Assistant, so her financial resources are fairly limited, but she lives in an extended family situation and has her parents and brothers who *step up to the plate* to help her to raise her three sons.

This is the way McClary sees it: On the one hand, she loves baseball and knows that it is good for her sons to be involved in it. On the other hand, she has some concerns about the extent to which her kids should focus on sports as a way out of the ghetto. She favors the academic route over the "sports-out-of-the-ghetto" model. She is committed to having all of her sons play baseball all the way through little league, but beyond that, she isn't sure what opportunities exist for them in baseball after little league. She also isn't sure whether they should be focusing on sports beyond the little league years at all. Insights shared by her and her three sons are summarized below.

Son # 1: Is a shy, academically focused youth. He is 14 years old. Though still shy, he entered baseball as a very shy kid. Over his years in baseball, which total 8 so far, he has become less shy and more aggressive on the field. In fact, when he started playing in the catcher's position, he really got involved, in almost every play, and was in a commanding position on the team. He likes baseball and has learned a lot from it, he says, but he doesn't prefer it to wrestling. He's not in a wrestling program at present, because his Mom will not allow him to partake, but from a distance, he believes that wrestling is more "*cool*" than baseball because "it's more of a contact sport," he says. He likes contacts sports, and what they stand for, but mostly, he likes the Internet, which he says is "*coolest*" thing of all.

Son # 2: Isn't shy at all; in fact, he has ADHD. It's been an uphill struggle for him to keep his eye on the ball. It is particularly hard for him to stay focused when he is not playing in a critical position on the team. During such times when he has to wait his turn, a minute seems like an hour. He has been in the James Mosher program for 6 years now, and is 10 years old. He is beginning to "get with the program," but for him, baseball is a duty that he is performing for his Mom. When asked what he thinks about baseball, he says, "It's good, you learn how to listen and pay attention." Does he love baseball though? No. He prefers football. Why does he prefer football? Because the guys are bigger, it's more of a contact sport, and it's "*cooler,*" he says. Is he playing football now? No, his mother won't let him.

Son # 3: He is just a little lad, 6 years old, and has played in the James Mosher program since he was 4 years old. Does he love baseball? Yes. He loves everything and everybody.

Mom: When Mom goes to watch her kids play, and she goes to most of their games, having made sure that her employer understands that no matter what, she must attend their games even if this means taking off from work, she actually pays attention to the game. She understands the game from her father, with whom she frequently attended baseball games, and is able to evaluate the quality of play. This puts her in a minority among the other Moms, she notes, "who are just sitting there talking on their cell phones, and not paying any attention to the games." She has no basis of camaraderie with those other Moms because it's a bifurcated situation; those moms who care about baseball and like the game, versus those who are only there

> out of necessity. In her camp of Moms who care about the game, she stands alone. She says that she doesn't know one single other mother who knows or cares about the game.

What McClary knows for sure is that African American women need to be educated about baseball. "They must be targets of well-crafted marketing campaigns that pique their interest in the game," she explains. As it stands now, African American Moms are more focused on football and basketball for their children. From a personal point of view, she can understand the appeal of the other sports, particularly that of football. She remembers when she was in high school, she only attended football games; she never attended baseball games. One of the reasons is that she liked how football players looked. "They are bigger, look more 'buff,' and they look like they could protect you," she says. By contrast, baseball players don't look like physical specimens. They don't look like they could protect you against the hard cruel world. Living in the heart of gang territory in inner city Baltimore, McClary is always focused on the need for protection.

African American Women As Baseball Professionals

There are numerous ways in which African American women are involved as professionals in baseball. Some work in the outreach departments of MLB teams, some, like Sharon Robinson serve as consultants, some work for the MLB directly, and some hold senior positions with MLB teams, among other positions. There is scope, however, for deeper involvement.

Information about the many ways in which African American women may be involved as professionals in baseball is not widely known. More importantly, it is not clear how their unique knowledge of the African American community is tapped to help formulate strategies to revive baseball in inner cities. It is one thing to help implement a policy, it's another to help craft the policy on the front end and to lend their authentic voices, knowledge, and experience to the thinking that goes into the policies before they are set in stone.

In addition to having African American women in the "outreach departments" of MLB teams, they are needed to play a bigger role in "*reaching in*." They have the potential to be powerful role models and "Pied Pipers" to help other African American women envision the possibilities in baseball, both for their children and for themselves as professionals.

Educating African American women about baseball is one thing, and educating them about opportunities for them as professionals within the MLB is another.

African American Female Sportswriters & Broadcasters

One new frontier for African American women in—and around the game of baseball— is as sportswriters. Admittedly, there aren't many African American female sportswriters, but to the extent there are any, they too could potentially be "in the village" as "Pied Pipers" helping to get other African American women interested in the game.

Claire Smith is one of the few African American female sportswriters and a positive role model.

Smith is not only a positive role model who demonstrates the diverse ways in which African American women can be involved with sports, she also knows a lot about the game of baseball. She wrote an article in January 2000 that provides deep insights into what it takes for women like her to do what she does; it's a story that African American women in inner cities would be interested to hear. The article is sumarized in Box 18, says it all.

Box 18:
"No longer focused on locker room access, women find that covering sports conflicts with having a family life"

By Author: Claire Smith
Published: January 1, 2000

The sports world, which likes its entertainment untainted by real-world issues, seldom accepts progress without a prod. Its participants, frighteningly disconnected from the world around them, too often don't even realize the currents, issues and changing times roiling society.

This is why I had to smile at the way in which a handful of black baseball players wrestled around baseball's record of intolerance after Al Campanis exposed the game's dirty little mindset on race in 1987. Campanis, then the general manager of the Dodgers, shocked the sports world by opining on national television that blacks lacked "the necessities" to hold certain management positions much the way they lacked buoyancy, ergo no black Johnnie Weismullers.

The '87 season that was to serve as a placid, but benign celebration of Jackie Robinson's breaking of baseball's color barrier, was awash with controversy from day one. This much I knew as I stood in a major-league baseball stadium waiting to begin my sixth year covering the New York Yankees for The Courant in Hartford, Conn.

Dave Winfield, the Yankee's all-star right fielder and future Hall of Famer, called me prior to the season opener. Whispering conspiratorially, Winfield — an African-American — informed me that he and other black players had been discussing the Campanis incident when they reached what was apparently a startling conclusion. The players realized that not only was I a woman, but an African-American as well! The newly discovered distinction would assuredly earn for me a greater degree of cooperation from "the brothers," not to mention a scoop or two, Winfield declared with great solemnity and solidarity.

I had to smile. For the first time ever, being African-American had finally overshadowed my other lonely outpost: standing sentry as one of the few women reporters to work in the major league press boxes. In 1987, there were precious few women covering major league baseball; you could count them on one hand. When I left the national baseball beat in 1998, my departure brought the number of women holding that job to zero. However, women in increasing numbers do cover Olympic sports, collegiate athletics, tennis and men's and women's basketball.

I have never claimed to be in that first wave of either African-Americans or women to cover professional sports in America. Wendell Smith, Sam Lacy and other members of traditionally African-American news organizations started the long, tortuously slow journey from the colored sections of the bleachers to the press boxes the moment Robinson took the lead on the field for the Brooklyn Dodgers.

As for women, the walls came tumbling down in the 1970s when the courts agreed with the contention that professional sports teams had to right to deny women journalists equal access. Pioneer reporters such as Mary Garber had covered sports for decades while handicapped by arcane rules limiting their contact with male athletes. Syndicated columnist Elinor Kaine and Melissa Ludtke of *Sports Illustrated* were the first to successfully argue for their right to walk through locker room doors in order to fully do their jobs. Tracy Dodds, Diane K. Shah, Jane Gross, Melanie Hauser and Mary Schmitt followed, trailblazers who, like Robinson, changed perceptions in the workplace and in life in extraoradinary fashion just by insisting they be treated in an ordinary but fair fashion.

Today, [2000] there are by some counts well over 500 women working in the once-male-dominated worlds of sports media as well as for pro teams, leagues and sports-related industries, though still relatively few of these women are beat reporters covering major league teams. Each year, hundreds attend the national convention of the Association of Women in Sports Media, which was founded in 1987.

The fact that women have come of age in these traditionally male industries isn't so much seen in the fact that an organization such as AWSM exists, but rather that locker room access (and the attitudes and behaviors of the athletes) is no longer the dominant subject at AWSM gathering. The receding hot-button topic of the 1980s has been replaced by issues such as juggling work and family responsibilities, managing finances, and attempting to secure quality of life in the midst of what this line of work demands…

Smith is a sports columnist for *The Philadelphia Inquirer*. This article originally appeared in *Nieman Reports*. Source: *http://www.asne.org/index.cfm?ID=74*

The number of African American women sportswriters is low, but the number of African American women who are radio and TV Broadcasters in the MLB system is so low it's not even reported. Overall, the percentage of women broadcasters decreased from two to one percent from 2005 to 2006, according to *The 2006 Racial and Gender Report Card: Major League Baseball* (Lapchick, Ekiyor & Ruiz, 2006).

During the 2006 MLB season, Whites held the same 79 percent of the broadcasting positions as in the 2005 Report. African-Americans held three percent, down one percent, while the percentage of Latinos stayed at 17 percent. There are only two Asian broadcasters in MLB (Lapchick, Ekiyor & Ruiz, 2006).

The point is, for however few African American women there may be in sportswriting and in the media, they nevertheless have powerful voices that could be raised even louder to help educate African Americans in inner cities about opportunities in baseball.

AFRICAN AMERICAN WOMEN BASEBALL TEAM OWNERS

This is where the field gets really small. In fact, there aren't any African American baseball team majority owners, according to Lapchick's *2006 Racial and Gender Report Card.*

As of 2006, there also weren't any African American team CEO/Presidents.

Majority Owners

	%	#
2006		
White	96.6%	27
African-American	0%	0
Latino	3.4%	1
Asian	0%	0
Other	0%	0
Women	0%	0
2005		
White	96.9%	31
African-American	0%	0
Latino	3%	1
Asian	0%	0
Other	0%	0
Women	0%	0

CEO/President

	%	#
2006		
White	100%	32
African-American	0%	0
Latino	0%	0
Asian	0%	0
Women	7.1%	2

An extraordinary thing happened in 2006 that the Report Card does not capture, which is that one African American woman became a minority owner of an MLB team. Effa Manley would have been proud.

Faye Fields

Faye Fields is the lucky one. She didn't knock on baseball's door; it was the other way around. Fields was invited to the table. Now that she is at the table she takes her job seriously. Always a baseball fan, thanks to her brother who "designed" her into a fan when she was growing up, she knows the game and attends most games during the season. Whereas her brother taught her the game being played on the field, she is now in a position to teach him, and other African Americans, how the game is played off the field.

The front page story of a May 4, 2006 *Washington Post* article read:

> *"After 17 Months, Baseball Introduces Nats' Owners Lerner Group Pledges to Work Closely on Stadium."*

The "Nats" are the Washington Nationals MLB baseball team. The article explains, "A group of area businessmen led by developer Theodore N. Lerner was awarded ownership of the Washington Nationals yesterday and pledged to build a first-class baseball organization by investing heavily in player development and working closely with the city on construction of the team's new stadium on the Anacostia waterfront."

The article further explains:

> Lerner, who has made a fortune in real estate across the Washington region over the last five decades, was informed of the decision by Major League Baseball in a telephone call from Bud Selig, the league's commissioner. It brought to a close a 17-month ownership search for the franchise that was moved to Washington from Montreal before the 2005 season.
>
> Lerner, 80, was selected over seven other bidders who each had agreed to pay the $450 million sale price set by Major League Baseball, whose 29 other owners bought the struggling Montreal Expos for $120 million in February 2002.

Seated in the photo below, taken from the May 4, 2006 Post article, Faye Fields indeed got a seat at the head table.

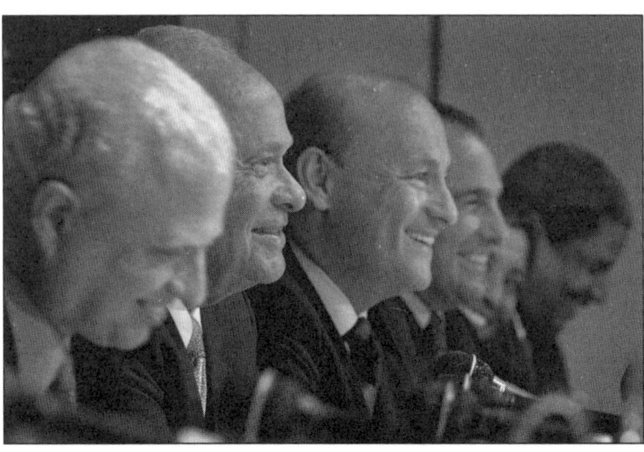

The Nationals' ownership group, which includes, from left, Mark D. Lerner, Theodore N. Lerner, Stan Kasten, Robert K. Tanenbaum, Faye Fields, and Rodney E. Slater (others not shown).

It wasn't easy to get to the table. Fields played all of her cards right throughout her life, never imagining becoming a baseball owner, but simply always doing the right thing and making the right moves.

Fields has been a small business owner for a very long time; today, as one of the minority owners of the Washington Nationals, however, she owns a piece of a large enterprise. She brings a lot to the table. Perhaps her most important contribution is to lend her perspective as an African American woman about how to revive baseball in inner cities. She also brings valuable lessons she has learned as a small business owner and President and CEO of *Integrated Resource Technologies* (*www.irti.com*).

There is an interesting parallel between what she has accomplished in her life's work in her own firm and what she is doing with the Nationals. In both cases, she is "*breaking barriers*." She is not just talking about it; she is doing it, quietly but most assuredly. In her day-to-day business, her ability to "break into" federal government contracting was aided and abetted by the **U.S. Small Business Act of 1953**, which stipulates:

> Only through full and free competition can free markets, free entry into business, and opportunities for the expression and growth of personal initiative and individual judgment be assured. The preservation and expansion of such competition is basic not only to the economic well-being but to the security of this Nation. Such security and well-being cannot be realized unless the actual and potential capacity of small business is encouraged and developed...

The take away point is this: Breaking into anything is hard, but it can be done, and when it is done, it is done through the facilitation and advocacy of stakeholders.

Just as local elected officials in Washington, DC demanded minority participation in the baseball ownership consortium, and as small business owners rose up in the 1950s to demand consideration in government contracting, African Americans throughout inner city America have the power today to put pressure on their elected officials, the MLB, and on themselves to revive baseball in inner cities.

Baseball has been a closed shop for a long time, but the doors are beginning to open. For those who haven't been at the table, it will take time to learn how the game is played and to discover how to take advantage of all of the economic opportunity that is associated with baseball. One thing is sure: "The journey of a thousand miles begins with a single step."

It time for African American women to "step up to the plate."

There is "gold" in the diamond, which is the subject of the next chapter. There is a lot at stake and a lot of opportunity. Instead of limiting options to a few sports, the message, particularly for African American women, is clear: There are opportunities in every sport. The decision to opt out of baseball is irrational in economic terms.

GOLD IN THE DIAMOND

GOLD IN THE DIAMOND

There are a lot of ways to make money in baseball and a lot of people making money in baseball in different ways.

Andrew Zimbalist, a Professor of Economics at Smith College, is one of the foremost authorities on the subject of how money is made in baseball. His 1994 book, *Baseball and Billions: A Probing Look Inside the Big Business of Our National Pastime* tells the story, starting from the early baseball barons, to examining franchise finances and player's salaries, to examining how money is made in the minors. Delving into all of these issues is an ambitious undertaking that is outside of the scope of this book. The more modest aim of this chapter is to focus attention on those aspects of the "money picture" that have a bearing on what has transpired to diminish the participation of African Americans in baseball, and on key considerations for the revival.

This is a story told in two parts. The first part focuses on overseas player development, and the second part directs attention to the story of how current President George W. Bush leveraged his ownership of a baseball team all the way up to the Oval Office. These two examples are given for a reason: Collectively, they demonstrate that it "takes a village," and a real grass roots effort to break down barriers in baseball. Ultimately, the challenge of reviving baseball in inner cities in America is all about the power and money in the game. Power players are not only on the field. The "real" power players and heavy hitters are always off the field.

Factors That Have Contributed To Diminishing The Participation Of African Americans in Baseball

As has been demonstrated throughout this book, there are numerous internal and external factors that have contributed to diminishing the participation of African Americans in baseball. In economic terms, however, there is perhaps one factor that contributes most significantly to the situation, which is overseas player development, some say, at the expense of player development in the United States. A proponent of this view, sportswriter Diane Grassi, wrote an insightful article in 2006 on the subject, presented below.

WHY THE MLB FAVORS OFFSHORE PROSPECTS:
WHO GAINS AND WHO LOSES?

By Diane M. Grassi

On May 28, 2006 Barry Bonds succeeded in hitting his 715th home run to pass Babe Ruth's homerun record and now second to Hank Aaron's Major League Baseball (MLB) all-time home run record of 755, it is representative in a number of ways of the present state of MLB. Specifically, the state of the game's future in the African-American community comes to mind. And it might be an appropriate time to reexamine the decline of participation of the black athlete in baseball, which is a far more multi-faceted problem than commonly expressed.

While there is a dearth of interest among young boys and teenagers in the black community participating in organized baseball, the reasons most often provided are shortsighted and often too easy to come by. Without an honest discourse between the leaders of the black communities throughout the United States, as well as some candor coming from the offices of MLB, what seems an insurmountable problem to attract blacks to baseball, will forever remain.

And although it is simply too easy to blame any one entity for all of the fall-off of black players in baseball, the primary beneficiary, of ignoring players from the U.S. including white players, remains MLB. And it must be held accountable, regardless of myriad cultural reasons attributed to children's lack of interest in baseball, predominantly in the inner city neighborhoods, for its lack of investment in them.

On February 28, 2006, MLB opened its first Urban Youth Academy in the U.S. At a cost of $3 million that took three years to complete, with the idea shopped around for six, MLB Commissioner Bud Selig clucked, "This is the first of what I hope is a series of academies all over America." The facility is located at the campus of Compton Community College on 10 acres of land in Compton, CA, south of Los Angeles. It includes two regulation size baseball diamonds, a youth field and one for girl's softball and a 12,000 square foot clubhouse with locker room, weight room and other training facilities. It is expected to be a prototype for other U.S. facilities, through the Urban Youth Initiative, which will serve not only as a catalyst for reviving baseball but a place for inner-city youth to enjoy each summer and after school.

Starting in June 2006, 125 children each day are expected to participate and to be given instruction by professional level coaches on playing the game. The monetary investment, however, was not solely supplied by MLB. $70,000.00 was collectively donated by Enos Cabell, Jr. and Tim Purpura, GM of the Houston Astros for batting cages and $500,000.00 was donated by L.A.'s Anaheim Angels. Access to classrooms and computers are being made available by Compton Community College. Compton was picked primarily as so many African-Americans from MLB's past arose from Compton, but also because the college donated a number of its facilities. It takes on average three years to build a Major League stadium. It is stunning how long it took to put in four ball fields and a clubhouse with so little financial investment from MLB and whose idea largely came to the Commissioner's Office as a grass roots effort.

In 1989, former Major League player, John Young, developed a program called RBI or Reviving Baseball in Inner Cities in South Central Los Angeles for children ages 12-18. In 1991, MLB got involved and assumed its administration. MLB then teamed with the Sporting Goods Manufacturing Association from 1993-1996 in providing grants to various cities demonstrating financial need. After five years, Young went national and by 1997, RBI collaborated with various chapters of the Boys & Girls Clubs of America. However, MLB and its individual teams have only provided $15 million for RBI since 1991.

The RBI program now includes both boys and girls and its objective is to also include nurturing children's interest in school along with baseball as the main component. It claims that it has helped more than 150,000 children in more than 200 cities worldwide play baseball. And its *Quick SMART*! Program addresses the issues of alcohol, tobacco and other harmful drugs with city youth. Says Roberto Clemente, Jr., who founded the RBI program in Pittsburgh, "RBI keeps kids out of trouble and off the streets, while at the same time teaching them to stay in school. The educational components help them realize their potential and to receive college scholarships based not only on athletics, but academics." But one can question the program's expansion worldwide before the job is done in the U.S.

"Campos Las Palmas has set the standard for what a baseball academy should be and we're extremely proud of the work done here, not only on the field, but in the community as well." No, this is not another baseball academy planned for the U.S. but a quote from Frank McCourt, owner of the Los Angeles Dodgers, upon his visit to the Dodger's Dominican Republic baseball complex, in celebrating its 20th year anniversary, earlier in 2006. And while no one can find fault with the individual efforts of the RBI program nor with the idea of Urban Youth Academies in the U.S., it is necessary to contrast those programs with over the $60 million dollars each year which MLB and its individual teams pour into Latin American countries for player development.

Most MLB teams have more than one such facility in Latin America with the most located in the Dominican Republic, followed by Venezuela. When Camp Las Palmas opened in the 1987 season, it was the first facility of its kind and became the universal prototype for all MLB teams in Latin America. It sits on 75 acres of land, equipped with two full and two half baseball fields, a dining room, kitchen, recreation room and two two-story dormitories accommodating 100 players. In addition, it provides lessons in adapting to American culture, classes in English, and nutritional counseling.

Players stay up to 30 days at a time and can be signed at age 16 unlike players in the U.S. where players must at least complete high school or be 18 years of age. If they are enrolled in college, U.S. players must wait until the age of 21 to be signed. But then they go into the draft, which clubs claim deters them from investing in any development of U.S. players, as another club could end up as the beneficiary of such efforts. Also, Latin America does not face competition from the sports of basketball and football as baseball does in the U.S., therefore giving MLB many more prospects to choose from.

It is crucial to understand that offshoring of Latin American baseball players is arguably directly proportional to the loss of African Americans being developed in MLB. Black players were at their peak of their composition in MLB in the late '70's and early '80's or roughly 27% of all players. Today that total hovers around 10%. However, it is the combination of other factors which make the Latin American factor even more decimating to the black athlete's chances of ever making it to the Major Leagues.

Ideologies include the increased incarceration of young black males, the lack of positive role models and the lack of two parent families as contributing factors. They, however, cannot necessarily be declared the primary determinants of the lack of blacks' participation in baseball. It is argued that expense is a factor, as it supposedly takes $100,000.00 to build a baseball field and that even if there are baseball fields available, maintenance costs are necessary too. But urban and rural African-Americans played baseball on sandlots and played street stickball for generations, long before pristine $100,000.00 fields were considered a prerequisite to playing baseball.

Others argue that the National Basketball Association (NBA) has done a far better job at marketing to black youth, who rarely ever go to MLB games. And making the National Football League (NFL) is far more attractive than an arduous and lengthy learning process on the way to earning a MLB contract. Both the NBA and the NFL although now require at least a year of college play, are a fast track on the way to fast bucks for those lucky enough to make it. Still, the family fabric not only in the inner city, but more pronounced there, has destroyed the learning curve necessary to build a baseball following. Baseball requires a father or father figure such as a youth leader or mentor to have an impact upon, what used to be considered the National Pastime, the inner-city child. And if they are not hooked by age 13 or 14, it's hard to get them interested later.

Requisite hand-eye coordination skills do not come to children naturally and must be learned, unlike the immediate impact of shooting a basketball or running with a football. It takes patience and fortitude for those skills that must be nurtured. Historically, such nurturers were fathers. But also absent today is the presence of present MLB players who do not involve themselves with the community like Hall of Famers, Hank Aaron, Willie Mays, Frank Robinson and Reggie Jackson did. The black MLB player today must step up even more so, especially because of the lack of male role models in the black community.

The dissolution of the once three-sport player has also added to the demise of baseball in the inner city. Many public schools only field a football team or basketball team and have dropped baseball altogether. Intramural programs, the victim of budget cuts, only heightens the chances that black youth will be absorbed into gangs, due to lack of organized programs for them.

And for college baseball players, scouting is limited and even more so for the black baseball athlete who rarely competes in baseball in college due to the small scholarships awarded for baseball. Even Howard University has dropped its baseball program, which one would think is a no-brainer for the development of African American baseball players, given its vast appreciation of black history. The National Collegiate Athletic Association only allows for 11.7 baseball scholarships at any given time for a team of 30 players on a roster. Full scholarships are rare. Football, however, is allowed up to 85 scholarships and basketball gets 13 for a roster half the size of baseball's. Both programs are provided far more full scholarships.

Frank Robinson, now 70, and presently the Manager of the Washington Nationals after holding several positions within MLB, became part of the first generation of great black players who followed Jackie Robinson's breaking the color barrier in 1947. And Frank Robinson holds today's players accountable. "People don't see minorities attached to the community or going home and giving something back. Now the stars and the top players, they hide. They don't go into the community. They don't go back into the inner city or where their roots were. Baseball is now third, maybe fourth in the [inner-city] household."

Yet, the baseball draft instilled in 1965, with stricter age limits, combined with MLB's vastly increased development in Latin America over the past 20 years, remain the biggest impediments, along with the lack of MLB's moral will, in increasing the African-American presence in MLB. Much like the ill-fated acceptance of the offshoring of U.S. manufacturing jobs by U.S. multi-national corporations, MLB has enjoyed the same misguided regime, regardless if it ultimately hurts the American athlete.

Commissioner Selig stated after the 2005 season that gate receipts, merchandising revenue, team revenue- sharing and acquired broadcast rights revenue were at all-time highs in MLB. He likes the public to know that, given his abysmal management in other areas such allowing steroids in baseball over the years, the 1994 strike, the handling of the sale of the Montreal Expos, including his lack of involvement with the black community. However, while baseball enjoys such "good times," like its multi-national counterparts, MLB does not reinvest in the U.S.

Much like cheap labor overseas appears to be a required component of U.S. industry, similarly the benefits of signing and investing in baseball players has been relegated to Latin American players and more recently in Asia, where the rules of the U.S. do not apply. So instead, MLB has found new ways to circumvent its problems by merely

skipping over U.S. players. And while the African-American community has seen the starkest decline in participation, the white community is also losing ground to foreign players. More than 40% of major and minor league players are born outside of the U.S., with nearly 30% comprising the major leagues. It is predicted that by 2007 over 50% of all major and minor league players will be Latin Americans.

Prior to 1965, teams could contract with any high school graduate that scouts identified. Since it was believed that this advantaged only the wealthier teams, MLB imposed the draft. U.S. citizens could no longer be signed immediately, starting the cycle of lack of development investment by particular clubs. Along with supposedly eliminating the exploitation of underage players, the age restrictions followed. However, a player can be signed to a MLB contract at age 16 in Latin America with the clubs spending several years developing those players far earlier. By the time a U.S. player reaches 18 or 21 if they are in college, they are years behind Latin American players. Secondly, the contracts offered the Latin American undeveloped players are far less than those offered drafted U.S. prospects. And prior to 1984 there was no age limit on signing Latin American players who were signed as young as 12 or 14.

Since developing players is a big expense, MLB simply went after the "cheap and unregulated labor." Sound familiar? And for foreign and U.S. players of similar talent levels the expected recompense for U.S. players is much lower given the lack of property rights in developing him and what is expected to be a shorter career. If it is a choice between two players of equal talent in the U.S. or Latin America, the MLB club invariably chooses the foreign or Latin American player.

While white players who are affluent or have a family willing to invest resources to have their sons join available teams outside the inner city, the road still remains a gamble due to the outright scouting delays of Americans, given the preference of the cheaper talent. Unless a draft choice is truly bankable, the chances of that prospect succeeding are contingent upon his former training either from college or paid for opportunities from family. And U.S. baseball players do not have the benefit of competing at academies like those in Latin America, often run like baseball boarding schools with seemingly unlimited budgets.

In conclusion, much like the U.S. watches its industries and institutions being sold bit by bit to foreign entities, it will take the will of the community, not just the black community or the white community, but the American community, to fight for our young people and to show them that America is worth fighting for. We can no longer afford to isolate ourselves from each other regardless of our color or ethnicity. For this fight is far more than the one between basketball and baseball. It is symbolic of the erosion of that which once identified America and was a staple of the family and by extension our neighborhoods. And contrary to popular belief, the hijacking of America's National Pastime is not unimportant, but is indicative of a dangerous trend in the U.S. And we owe it to ourselves as Americans to not only save our children in the process but in turn to save our country.

Bio: Diane M. Grassi

Diane M. Grassi is an electronic and print media columnist, of independent thought, who provides in-depth reports and articles on multiple issues on U.S. public policy and government affairs, concerning key federal and state legislation, including court decisions, all relative to the interests of average Americans.

Intellectually honest and original reporting without an agenda, Ms. Grassi likens herself as a facilitator to her readers, looking beyond the headlines in providing in-depth analysis from research.

Ms. Grassi's writing also covers topical issues for her readership, which includes in-depth analysis about sports in relationship to society and culture. Her goal through her writing is to present factual content to the reader on the important issues of the day, including the sports world.

Originally from the New York City area, Ms. Grassi resided, attended college, did post-graduate work and was a professional in NYC for most of her life. She earned a Bachelor's Degree from the Manhattan School of Music, one of the most highly recognized music conservatories in the nation. Ms. Grassi then spent over 15 years working in a legal capacity in the music recording and publishing industry, with respect to intellectual property rights and legal protections.

Ms. Grassi's credentials include a paralegal degree and certification from the New York University School of Law, graduate study in Public Administration with a concentration in government at the Pace University Graduate School of Public Administration, also in New York, and she attended the California Western School of Law in San Diego, CA where she did graduate work in law.

Ms. Grassi is a features columnist for numerous online sports media publications including the Black Athlete Sports Network (Blackathlete.com), The Biz of Baseball, Sports-Central.org, Sports Fan Magazine, E-Sports Media Group, the Diamond Angle Magazine, amongst many others.

You can find her highly regarded articles on U.S. public policy online at: the New Media Journal.us; Renew America.us; Hawaii Reporter.com; Veterans Today.com; Amherst Times.com; Elite TV.com; American Chronicle.com, the Common Voice.com, Associated Content.com, Army.com, amongst many others.

And on radio, Ms. Grassi has been a regular guest on the Bruce Elliott Show on WBAL-AM in the Baltimore/D.C. area; a regular commentator on the Niel Young Show of WEZS-AM New Hampshire; and appears regularly on KTTK-AM Salt Lake City, and KPHX Phoenix on both the Jeff Farias Show and Cynthia Black Show. She has also been a featured writer for the following print publications in Nevada: Liberty Watch Magazine, What's On Magazine; the Las Vegas Penny Press. And in the NYC area she is a government features writer for the Westchester Times Tribune.

A resident of the southwest for over a dozen years, and now in the Las Vegas, NV area, Ms. Grassi's writing and media experience is a composite of her past educational, professional and advocacy backgrounds. As she demands much of herself when taking on new projects and challenges, she demands no less of her readers. Contact: dgrassi@cox.net

The Money To Be Made In Baseball

Any African American who thinks that there's no money to be made in baseball is not seeing the picture. When the Negro Leagues were first formed, it founders had their eyes on the money in the game. Somewhere along the line, African Americans lost sight of the ball. It's time to refocus on it, however. An article, which explains how current U.S. President George W. Bush leveraged his ownership of a baseball team to make millions, says it all, and underscores that money is power.

Box 19:
THE 2000 CAMPAIGN: BREAKING INTO BASEBALL; Road to Politics Ran Through a Texas Ballpark

By NICHOLAS D. KRISTOF
Published: September 24, 2000

For those who mock George W. Bush as a daddy's boy who slouched through life reaping the dividends of his name, the lovely Texas Rangers baseball stadium here is a useful rebuttal.

Walking around the Ballpark in Arlington as it was under construction in 1993, Mr. Bush explained proudly to a Texas reporter, ''When all those people in Austin say, 'He ain't never done anything,' well, this is it.''

This stadium is the house that Bush built -- and the one that allowed him, in a sense, to become a presidential candidate. As the owner of a baseball team in Arlington, a Dallas suburb, Mr. Bush laid the groundwork for his race for the governor's mansion, and that in turn may prove his steppingstone to the White House.

As an owner, Mr. Bush proved himself an outstanding manager, still remembered fondly by the players who pitched and batted for him, by the fans he wooed, even by the executives he fired. Mr. Bush helped turn the Rangers into a greatly improved team, and he presided over the complex arrangements for the new ballpark, one of the finest in major league baseball.

Mr. Bush became a multimillionaire in the process, setting himself up financially for his run for the presidency. In one blow, he acquired not only wealth but also the resume he would need to triumph in politics.
Yet a close look suggests that Mr. Bush got the opportunity to be a baseball owner mostly because of his connections. Moreover, his investment was immensely profitable in part because he and his co-owners were shrewd bargainers who charmed and bullied the city of Arlington into giving them a great deal, with the local taxpayers paying more than $135 million to help build the Rangers a stadium.

''The largest welfare recipient in the state of Texas is George W. Bush,'' said Mark S. Rosentraub, a sports economist who formerly taught in Arlington and is now at Indiana

University. ''The numbers speak for themselves. You cannot accept $135 million from the taxpayers of Arlington and then be against welfare.''

Mr. Bush and his fellow owners even got the local government to seize the property of other landowners and, in effect, hand it over to the Texas Rangers so that they could make a profit on it. All this was shrewd business and a tribute to Mr. Bush's savvy and vision, but critics complain that it is hard to reconcile with his speeches about limited government and private property rights.

''If a conservative is one who believes in limited government, this whole transaction shows how hypocritical it is for Bush to claim to be a conservative,'' said Jim Runzheimer, a lawyer in Arlington who opposed the public subsidy to build the stadium. ''He got the government to pay his expenses, and that flies in the face of capitalism.''

Yet Mr. Bush was simply doing, exceptionally successfully, what sports franchises everywhere have frequently tried: getting taxpayers to swallow some of their business costs. And to the extent that Mr. Bush's job at that time was to make money for the team's owners, he was eminently successful.

A longtime friend of Mr. Bush's and a fellow Rangers' owner, Roland W. Betts, noted that the criticisms in effect confirm Mr. Bush's success in doing his job.

''Didn't he profit off Arlington?'' Mr. Betts asked. ''Is it politically right to pit one community against another? Well, you have to say that at that point, George wasn't the governor of Texas. He was a general partner, he was a fiduciary, and a fiduciary's obligations are to perform well for investors. And that's what he did.''

'I Just Grabbed On to It'

George W. Bush has frequently claimed to have cobbled together the deal to buy the Rangers in 1989. ''I was like a pit bull on the pant leg of opportunity,'' Mr. Bush said in a long interview about his past. ''And I just grabbed on to it. I was going to put the deal together. And I did.''

But that is a bit like Vice President Al Gore claiming to have taken the initiative in creating the Internet: there is something to it, but it is also an exaggeration.

The initiative, Mr. Bush acknowledges, came from Bill DeWitt, a businessman and friend of the family. Mr. DeWitt had heard that the Rangers were on the market and wanted to recruit Mr. Bush as a partner to buy the team.

The attractiveness of Mr. Bush as a partner had little to do with his business ability; at that time, his business record was a bleak one involving faltering oil companies. Rather, Mr. Bush was useful because his father was then the president, and because he and his parents were longtime friends of the seller, Eddie Chiles. If anybody could get a good deal buying the team from Mr. Chiles, it would be Mr. Bush.

Sure enough, Mr. Chiles said he would be delighted to sell the team to Mr. Bush. So Mr. Bush, always a brilliant fund-raiser, persuaded a group of relatives and acquaintances to invest in the team. But most were not from Texas, and the baseball commissioner, Peter Ueberroth, wanted the teams to have local owners. Mr. Bush was flummoxed.

At this point, Mr. Ueberroth and other baseball executives persuaded a Texas financier, Richard Rainwater, to help buy the team. By all accounts, the attraction of Mr. Bush in the deal was his name and connections.

''It certainly helped,'' Dr. Robert W. Brown, then the president of the American League, said of Mr. Bush's status as First Son. Dr. Brown, a former Yankee third baseman better known as Bobby, added: ''He came from a very prominent group. I was very friendly with his father. So it wasn't just a strange happenstance.''

Mr. Bush's path to becoming a baseball owner was remarkable because at first he did not put up a cent of his own money. Instead, he borrowed $500,000 from United Bank of Midland, a Texas bank of which he had previously been a director, and used it to buy a stake in the team.

Wayne Merritt, who was then the president of the bank (it has since been merged out of existence), said he could not discuss the loan because it was ''Mr. Bush's private business.'' But Robert A. McCleskey, Mr. Bush's longtime accountant, said that as collateral for the loan, Mr. Bush had pledged oil company stock then worth more than $900,000.

In any case, a year later Mr. Bush sold the stock and paid off the loan. He also raised his investment in two stages to a total of $606,000, or 1.8 percent of the team.

Mr. Bush himself seemed to acknowledge the advantage that came with his name.

''Being the president's son puts you in the limelight,'' he told a reporter for Time magazine after buying the team. *''While in the limelight, you might as well sell tickets.''*

Throughout his life, baseball has been one of Mr. Bush's truest loves. As a child, he collected baseball cards and was a catcher on the all-star Little League team in Midland, Texas. As governor, he decorated his office with his collection of baseballs autographed by the likes of Ted Williams and Joe DiMaggio. And even these days on the campaign plane, he perks up when baseball teams are mentioned and seems more intimate with the fine print of the sports pages than of the foreign news pages.

Mr. Bush's passion for baseball and his deep understanding of it helped him as he settled into his new role as an owner. While he initially grated on some Texans who saw him as a spoiled rich kid playing on his connections, he worked hard and impressed people in the baseball world.

Instead of watching games from an enclosed suite, as many owners do, Mr. Bush sat and ate peanuts in Section 109, Row 1, behind the Rangers' dugout. He got to know all the hot dog vendors and ticket-takers by first name, tirelessly introduced himself to fans and aggressively cultivated reporters.

Jim Reeves, a sports columnist for The Fort Worth Star-Telegram, recalled that he had initially been skeptical of Mr. Bush, thinking that he had gotten the opportunity to be an owner simply because of his name. But Mr. Bush then wooed him, golfing with him twice and stopping frequently to chat, and Mr. Reeves changed his views.

''I saw him as a down-to-earth guy,'' Mr. Reeves recalled. ''He would come to spring training and do his running and hang around the weight room or the clubhouse and stop and chat about the team.''

''He was,'' Mr. Reeves added, ''excellent with the media.''

Mr. Bush also worked to charm the players, dropping by the clubhouse and socializing easily with them. He came across as the direct opposite of the stereotype of an imperious, pretentious owner.

''From the get-go, I liked him,'' said Kenny Rogers, who pitched for the Rangers then and rejoined the team this season. In particular, Mr. Bush became friendly with Nolan Ryan, the legendary pitcher who had just agreed to sign with the Rangers when Mr. Bush's group bought the team.

Mr. Ryan had been expected to play just one year with the Rangers before retiring. But he ended up playing five years, and when he was inducted into the Hall of Fame last year, he wore his Rangers cap, even though he had played more seasons with other clubs.

The Rangers had ranked sixth in the American League's Western Division the two years before Mr. Bush came on board; they clawed their way up to second place by his last year of full-time involvement. Since then, they have won the division three times, although it's not clear how much credit if any Mr. Bush should get for that.

Mr. Bush had a particular knack for getting media attention, beginning when he got his mother, then the first lady, to throw out the first ball in a game. He also managed to get his father photographed wearing a Texas Rangers cap, and he took advantage of his family's prominence by giving speeches throughout the region proclaiming the virtues of baseball and urging people to go to games.

All this promotion paid off. The Rangers had never drawn as many as 1.8 million fans in a season in previous years, but attendance exceeded 2 million each year of Mr. Bush's stewardship.

It was less obvious to the fans, but Mr. Bush also proved an astute businessman and a first-class manager. In his presidential campaign, he sometimes describes leadership using the model of a chief executive in business, and that is what his colleagues remember him as: a leader who set an agenda, inspired those around him, acted predictably and was comfortable delegating authority.

Owners in baseball are notorious for being haughty and difficult, but Mr. Bush cultivated the opposite image. Instead of micromanaging -- suggesting a pitching change during a game, for example -- Mr. Bush proved then (as now) relatively uninterested in details and happy to delegate to those beneath him. It is hard to find anybody who worked in the ballpark who did not like him and did not periodically chat with him.

''He always picked my mind about what Latinos went through in baseball and, indirectly, what Latinos went through in the U.S.A.,'' said Luis Mayoral, who was then the Latin American liaison for the Rangers. ''We'd kid a lot in Spanish. He'd see me in the distance and raise his arms and say 'a la victoria.' ''

It helped that Mr. Bush came across not as a rich boy but as a notorious cheapskate. He regularly wore shoes with holes in the soles, until a fellow owner, Edward W. Rose III, bought him a $150 pair of fancy Italian shoes at Neiman Marcus.

''And then he took them back,'' Mr. Rose laughed. ''The way he remembers it, with his convenient memory, is he traded them in for two shirts. But that's not the way it really was. Actually, he traded them in for cash.''

Sometimes Mr. Bush made management mistakes -- the Rangers traded away Sammy Sosa on his watch, although Mr. Bush simply approved a decision that had been made well below him -- but his management style also won him fierce loyalty. Tom Grieve, then the Rangers' general manager, says that owners typically try to tell tales of their old college baseball days to show off, but Mr. Bush won his heart by doing the opposite.

''George came in here and said, 'Tommy boy, let me tell you about my days with the Yale freshman team,' '' Mr. Grieve recalled with a chuckle. ''You know it's going to be funny, because that's like a high school junior varsity team down here. And he was the relief pitcher! And he says how one day the pitcher really screwed up, and the coach decides to pull him, and George is really excited and thinks he's got his big chance.

And then the coach calls in a second baseman even though he'd never thrown a pitch. And Bush says, "That's when I figured my aspirations of becoming a major league player might not be achieved."

Although he charmed people, Mr. Bush was not a patsy. In the end he fired three key people: Mr. Grieve as general manager, Bobby Valentine as manager, and Mike Stone as president. Mr. Stone declined to talk about it, but Mr. Valentine and Mr. Grieve rave about the man who fired them.

...While in baseball, Mr. Bush demonstrated a grasp not just of tactics but also of strategy. His central strategic goal was to get a new stadium for the Rangers without making the owners pay for all of it.

A Huge Public Investment

The old Arlington Stadium was a mess.

Built in the early 1960's as a minor league ballpark and later remodeled with extra seating, it lacked the scale -- and the lucrative extras like sky boxes -- that these days help generate revenue for a professional baseball team. The previous owners had spoken with the city of Arlington about renovating the stadium, but studies had suggested that would be prohibitively expensive.

On the other hand, a new stadium would cost close to $200 million, and the owners were already saddled with debts and did not want to inject more capital into the franchise.

So what could they do? Get the people of Arlington to build them a new ballpark.

The efforts to get public financing have raised eyebrows because they seem to conflict with much of what Mr. Bush has stood for as a politician. While running for office, he has always called for limited government and low taxes, and the 2000 Republican Party platform in Texas (which he does not publicly embrace) explicitly states, ''Public money or public powers should not be used to fund or implement any private projects such as high-speed rail or sports stadiums.''

Yet the Rangers negotiated a huge public investment of taxpayer money, largely by hinting that without it they might leave. To a place like Arlington, already overshadowed by neighboring Dallas and Fort Worth, the Rangers were an emblem of local pride, and the possibility that it might lose the franchise was shattering.

...In the end, the two sides in Arlington agreed on a deal in which the city would put $135 million into building a stadium; the Rangers would get $17 million in cash to pay off a debt, while giving the city land worth considerably less than that; the Rangers would get virtually full control over the project but be exempted from obligations of ownership like paying school taxes; and the Rangers would have the right to get the entire stadium complex for nothing after 12 years of paying a modest rent. (It would have been foolish for the Rangers to take the stadium, even for nothing, because then they would have had to pay taxes, and the later owners of the team gave up that option to buy the stadium.)

The Rangers also contributed a sum to the ballpark that was originally put at $90 million. But this was arguably illusory, and the owners were not asked to invest a penny of fresh capital. Instead, the team raised its share by dedicating future revenues from seats, luxury suites and concessions -- in the stadium that the city was building for them.

''The taxpayers took it in the shorts,'' said William M. Eastland, an accountant in Arlington who studied the agreement and came to oppose it. Mr. Eastland, a lifelong Republican, emphasizes that he supports Mr. Bush in the election -- indeed, he was a Bush delegate at the Republican National Convention -- but he still objects to public financing of the stadium.

''You can call it anything you want, but it's corporate welfare,'' Mr. Eastland said. ''And I don't like corporate welfare.''

Still, whatever one thinks of such deals for sports complexes, they have become frequent.

''It's one thing to say, 'Why are we building this for owners and for right fielders who get $14 million a year?' '' said Jeff Smulyan, who owned the Seattle Mariners when Mr. Bush ran the Rangers. ''But the reality is that if you want a ball team in a place like Arlington, there has to be a public-private partnership.''

...Professor Rosentraub calculates in his book about stadium economics, ''Major League Losers,'' that governments in two places, Seattle and Cleveland, provided more than $500 million in subsidies for sports, and four others provided subsidies of more than $300 million. St. Louis was so desperate to get a football team that in the mid-1990's it built a $280 million stadium to attract any football team that might be feeling restless. It worked: the Rams moved in from Anaheim, Calif.

On the other hand, after voters rejected a series of four proposals for public financing of a new stadium for the San Francisco Giants between 1987 and 1992, the team went ahead with a new $320 million ballpark that was privately financed, and that has been widely praised.

In Arlington, there was plenty of controversy about the subsidies for the Rangers, but the verdict that really mattered came from the voters in January 1991. The city's contribution was to be paid by an increase in the sales tax, and that had to be approved in a referendum. With a huge turnout, voters endorsed the agreement and the sales tax increase by almost a two-thirds majority.

''Who is the final judge of whether you made money on the backs of the city of Arlington?'' asked Mr. Rose, Mr. Bush's fellow owner. ''Is it some journalist who wants to sell papers, or the people who think or know that they made a good deal?''

While the stadium is clearly popular, there is disagreement about the economic outcome. Supporters note that the local economy is booming and credit the ballpark.

''There's no question that the ballpark made a huge difference for this franchise,'' said J. Thomas Schieffer, who succeeded Mr. Bush as general partner of the Rangers. ''But we think the citizens of Arlington benefited as much as the owners did.''

Professor Rosentraub, in contrast, attributes the boom to the vibrant metropolitan area and new malls. The stadium itself, he asserts, was a losing economic investment, although he adds that he has nothing against voters who want to lose money as a way of boosting civic pride.

''I'm not saying I don't like it,'' Professor Rosentraub said of the stadium. ''I like it. I'm a baseball fan. It's just that it's a regressive tax taking money from the poor and middle-income people and shifting it to a very wealthy group of people. It's a redistribution of wealth upward.''

Aside from the public subsidy, another aspect of the ballpark project angers some people.

While the Rangers' owners arguably had enough land for the new ballpark and parking lots, they foresaw that one way to make money would be to own and develop property around the new stadium. Over time, a popular stadium could make the surrounding land more desirable so that it could be profitably transformed into strips of hotels, restaurants, gas stations, office buildings or even houses.

The owners always tried to keep their partnership agreement secret, but a copy of the 110-page document, obtained recently, lists among the purposes of the partnership not just profiting on baseball but also ''owning, managing, operating, exploiting, selling or disposing of real estate.''

As Mr. Bush told a local reporter after buying the team, ''The idea of making a land play, absolutely, to plunk the field down in the middle of a big piece of land, that's kind of always been the strategy.''

The problem was that some of the land belonged to other people.

As a politician, Mr. Bush has repeatedly sided with the property rights movement, which aims to protect property owners from government attempts to take land or limit its use. Often this issue comes up in environmental cases, and the national Republican platform this year -- which Mr. Bush's aides helped mold -- has an entire section titled ''Protecting Property Rights.''

''In Texas, in my first term, we enacted one of the strongest property rights laws in the nation,'' Mr. Bush declared in a speech on the environment late last year. ''As president, I would follow the same policies.''

But when Mr. Bush was running the Rangers, the team got Arlington to use its power of eminent domain to seize private land for the new stadium complex. At one level, this was simply one more way for Arlington to give the Rangers an incentive to stay. But the practice raised questions about fairness.

Confidential memos among the Rangers owners became part of the public record in subsequent litigation, and they paint a picture of the owners casting a proprietary eye over the area and then telling the city what land to seize. In one internal memo, for example, an owner referred to a privately owned parcel and told the other owners that it ''sounds like another condemnation candidate -- if you want to work the site into your master plan.''

Judging from the memos, Mr. Bush was not directly involved in the mechanics of the condemnation. But he supervised those who were, and the process reflected his own philosophy of how to make money in baseball: move beyond tickets and hot dogs to seek new sources of revenue.

The Mathes family was one of those that tangled with the Rangers when they were under Mr. Bush. The family, the heirs of a television tycoon named Curtis Mathes, owned a piece of land near the stadium, and agreed to sell if the price was fair.

What would be fair? The city had previously paid $10 a square foot for a sliver of that same property to expand a road, Horace B. Kelton, a family member and spokesman, said. But in the end, court documents show, the city warned off another potential buyer and seized the property for less than $1.50 a square foot.

The Matheses went to court, and a final settlement gave the family more than $11 per square foot.

''It took us seven years and we spent millions of dollars on legal costs,'' Mr. Kelton said. ''It was grossly unfair, until it was rectified by the courts.''

The Rangers see it differently. Mr. Schieffer notes that property values had fallen in Texas and insists that it was the Matheses' lawyers who hijacked the process and got more than the land had been worth.

After the settlements, the Rangers, tough bargainers to the end, refused to pay, noting that the legal obligation to pay lay with the city of Arlington. It was only last year, after Mr. Bush and his group had sold the Rangers, that the new owners agreed to repay the city for the losses.

''They made a heck of a deal,'' Glenn Sodd, the lawyer who represented the landowners against the Rangers, said of Mr. Bush and his fellow owners. ''If he was the architect of it, it indicates some brains on his part.''

But Mr. Sodd, who said he had voted Republican in every presidential election since 1968, added that he would not vote for Mr. Bush this time around because of what he said was his repugnance for the ''dirty pool'' played by the Rangers owners.

''My concern is whether billionaires and powerful people are going to run the government the way they ran that deal,'' Mr. Sodd said. ''Otherwise I'd be voting for the guy. If it weren't for this nightmare we went through, I'd be voting for him.''

One of the skills Mr. Bush demonstrated with the Rangers was an ability to disagree with people without coming across as disagreeable.

It was that talent that almost led his career in a different direction, one that would have

kept him in baseball and out of politics. There had been a bitter dispute among major league owners about Fay Vincent, the baseball commissioner and an old friend of the Bush family. Mr. Bush had been Mr. Vincent's most vocal supporter, but in the end the other owners -- led by Bud Selig, the owner of the Milwaukee Brewers -- forced Mr. Vincent to resign.

Even though Mr. Bush was on the losing side, he was widely respected among the owners for his conciliatory style and commitment to baseball, and some suggested that he be appointed to replace Mr. Vincent as a way of healing the rift among the owners. Several friends say that in early 1993 Mr. Bush was very interested in the job.

''George wanted to be commissioner, and Selig said he'd support him but didn't,'' Mr. Vincent said. ''And if George had become commissioner, he wouldn't be running for president. So if he's elected, he'll owe the job in some way to Selig.''

Mr. Selig, who was then acting commissioner and eventually was given the job permanently, has a different memory. He said he recalled no specific discussions with Mr. Bush about him getting the job, adding that in any case a decision on a new commissioner was put off until long after Mr. Bush had decided to run for governor.

When he began campaigning for governor, Mr. Bush's full-time involvement in baseball came to an end. But he retained his financial interest until 1998, when he and his fellow owners sold the Rangers -- very shrewdly, at the top of the market -- for $250 million.

It was a good deal for all the owners. The limited partners, who had leveraged their capital with loans, made a 450 percent profit on their investment. And Mr. Bush did far better.

As general partner of the Rangers, Mr. Bush was paid $200,000 a year. But, more important, he was rewarded with a provision that after the investors got their money back plus 2 percent interest per year, he would get a gift of a 10 percent share of the remaining profits.

The result was that **his investment of $606,000 turned into $14.9 million**. In addition, he is likely to receive a final distribution of another $1 million or $2 million over the next year. That will amount to at least **a 2,500 percent profit**.

Any student of history, politics, economics, management, operations research, or indeed, anyone who wants to know "the real deal," need look no further that the foregoing examples; it's all there. From the need to form strategic alliances, to the need to form public-private partnerships, to the need to leverage social capital, to the need to lower costs and maximize profits, information presented above provides real world examples of how economic theories play out in the "field."

For African Americans who want to stay in the game, the message is clear: They need to really get in "the game," and the game is not only about being a ball player; it's about playing ball.

Getting A Piece of the Action

There's big money in baseball and small money; it's advisable to keep's one eye focused on both. In terms of the big money, as can be seen from the foregoing, it either takes a lot of connections, a lot of money, or a lot of social capital to break in. So far, no African American has broken in as a majority owner. The time is coming, however, as slowly but surely African Americans, like the minority partners of the Washington Nationals team, are beginning to put a foot in the door.

"Small" money opportunities abound in baseball, which doesn't necessarily require a lot of capital or contacts; it simply takes focusing one's gaze on the opportunity, doing one's homework, and getting in the game. Millions are being made in baseball card trading, in betting, in memorabilia goods trading, and investing, for instance.

There are also opportunities for small businesses through the MLB's *Diverse Business Partners* program.

> The mission of the **Diverse Business Partners** program is to promote efficiency and profitability for Major League Baseball and its Clubs while extending Baseball's ability to contribute to the economic growth, strength and well-being of diverse communities. In 1998, Commissioner Allan H. (Bud) Selig, authorized the creation of the DBP program, an economically driven business initiative established to cultivate new and existing partnerships with minority- and women-owned businesses, by increasing opportunities for minorities and women to participate in the procurement activities of MLB.
>
> In October 2001, MLB announced an aggressive new public phase of the program, expanding its outreach efforts in order to raise additional awareness for the program and show interested vendors how they can participate. Since the formation and initial implementation stages of the DBP program in 1998, MLB has incurred expenditures in the hundreds of millions with minority-and women-owned businesses, making DBP an industry-leading program. In addition, the DBP program has complemented supplier diversity initiatives implemented by sports authorities for the construction of professional ballparks.

An African American woman, Wendy Lewis, Vice President, Strategic Planning, Recruitment and Diversity, is responsible for overseeing the program for MLB.

See Appendix 5 for information on the financial status of MLB teams.

African Americans need to check out the economic opportunities in baseball. To do that, they mustn't check out of baseball; they must stay in the game and start getting into the "real game," which is about capturing some of the *gold in the diamond.*

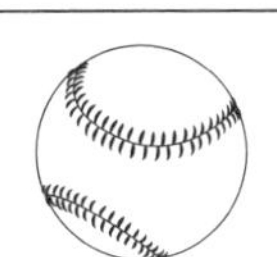

"WANTED" PIED PIPERS TO LEAD AFRICAN AMERICANS TO BASEBALL

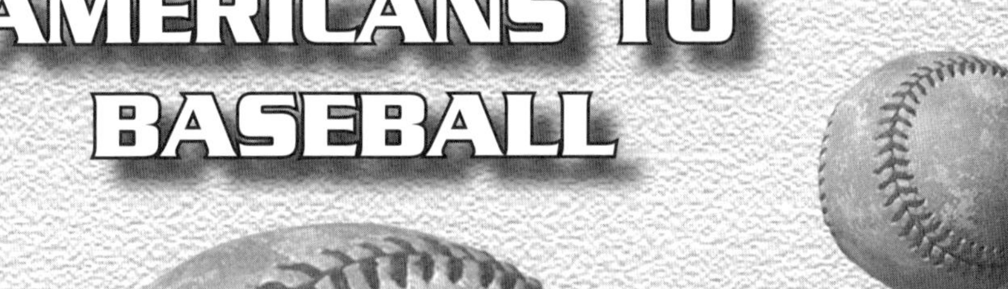

"WANTED" PIED PIPERS TO LEAD AFRICAN AMERICANS TO BASEBALL

In presenting my research on the low percentage of African American boys in youth select baseball, I am often asked at regional and national conferences about the reason for concern over why there are so few black youths playing the game at the highest competitive levels. If African American youth choose not to play the game, that's their decision. Why should there be any concern about a boy's decision to play one sport and not another? I have a three-part response, as follows.

First, there is a rich heritage and historic relationship between African Americans and baseball. The Negro leagues go as far back as the major leagues, and the brand of black professional baseball that developed outside the major leagues was like no other brand and became integral to African American culture. Jackie Robinson, Monte Irvin, Larry Doby, Ernie Banks, Willie Mays and other African Americans, who were among the first wave of Negro leaguers to enter the major leagues, sacrificed pride and sometimes spirit to show that they belonged in the majors. At a 1997 ceremony at the Hall of Fame in Cooperstown, Hall of Fame second baseman Joe Morgan paid a tearful tribute to Robinson and thanked him for blazing the trail for him and other African Americans. Do those sacrifices lose historical significance when only 8 percent of Major Leaguers are African American? Does the heritage of 100 years of Negro League baseball and its historical imprint on African American culture fade when only 3 percent of youth select ball players nationally are African American?

Second, any organization that doesn't develop or use the resources afforded it to improve its product and to represent the communities it serves becomes a lesser organization. In this case, the organization is Major League Baseball and the resources are the potential talents of African American youth.

Third, the low percentage of African American youth in select baseball is at best an indication of the unequal distribution of baseball facilities and playing opportunities in various communities and, at worst, an example of communities' failures to ensure that youth have access to the sports of their choice, regardless of the neighborhood. My research indicates that the best baseball youth facilities and playing opportunities are often found in the suburbs, not in the urban core.

Research on African Americans and Baseball

For the past eight years, my research has explored not only the number of African Americans playing youth select baseball, but also the reasons behind what seems to be an indifference to the game among African Americans. That indifference is exemplified by the low number of African Americans who attend major league games (some research shows that between 3 and 6 percent of major league crowds are African Americans) and the low number of African Americans playing college ball and in the major leagues (African Americans comprise 8 percent of the players on the 2006 major league rosters and 6 percent on the 2006 rosters of NCAA Division I schools.)

For many U.S.-born baseball players, the road to the professional ranks begins early with youth baseball and, more specifically, with "select" baseball. Select, or traveling team, baseball is characterized by teams that procure players via tryouts or invitation, compared to "recreational" youth baseball, in which all youths who sign up are given opportunities to play. Select baseball is most often sponsored by private organizations, individuals or local businesses. Recreational baseball, as characterized by some youth sports officials, consists of city park leagues, YMCA-sponsored leagues and other forms of baseball sponsored by umbrella organizations, such as Major League Baseball's Reviving Baseball in the Inner Cities (RBI) program. There are other differences between select and recreational, or "rec," baseball. Generally, recreational baseball leagues offer a limited playing schedule, compared to schedules played by select teams. Youths in recreational ball may play between 12 and 25 games for the season. Select teams will play an average of 65 games each season, according to a sample of 350 teams across the U.S. Some teams in that sample played as many as 160 games a season.

The difference in exposure to the game between select and "rec" players becomes apparent when watching both brands of baseball. On several June mornings in 2007 I watched a number of select baseball teams at the Super Series and Triple A baseball tournaments, which were held in Omaha, Nebraska during the College World Series. Those tournaments draw hundreds of teams throughout the country. Later in the day I traveled to local YMCA fields to observe teams playing in a league sponsored by that organization. The differences in the level of playing skills between the select ball players and those in the YMCA were obvious and in some respects stark. For example, pitchers on select teams exhibited better control, threw at greater velocity and could mix change-ups and fastballs. Some could even throw curveballs and sliders for strikes. Pitchers on the YMCA teams were more likely to have trouble throwing strikes and rarely changed speeds or threw different pitches. YMCA pitchers were more concerned with getting the ball to the plate, much less with throwing different pitches. It stands to reason that select players, more so than YMCA players, are able to hit a variety of pitches with authority, and extended observation shows the offensive superiority of select players when compared with YMCA players.

Select players also seemed to understand the fundamentals of defense better than YMCA players did. Select infielders, for example, were more likely to assume an appropriate fielding stance and position when the pitch was thrown. Double plays in select games were not unusual. The same cannot be said for the defense at YMCA games. YMCA players often had difficulty throwing across the diamond to get a groundout. On a few occasions those players had to be instructed on the correct position of the glove when catching the ball.

I do not draw attention to these differences to disparage recreational baseball. My observations show that "rec" players have as much competitive drive and desire to win as their select baseball counterparts. But such differences do serve to illustrate the amount of time and training select players devote to improving their baseball playing skills. To my knowledge there is no research on the differences in training and preparation between select and "rec" players. However, I have interviewed dozens of select team coaches about their players. It is common for select players to have their own private hitting, pitching and/or fielding instructors during the off-season. That instruction can carry into the season and be in addition to the coaching the players receive from their teams. An increasing number of youth baseball "academies" have opened during the past few years and not only sponsor and support select teams, but also offer year-round instruction.

Coaches say many select players see such instruction and playing time as an investment to their futures as high school and college ball players. A study of college baseball players nationally seems to support that. A survey of almost 350 college players showed that 9 of 10 played an average of 6 years of select baseball and the average age at which they started playing select ball was 11. More than 98% of the respondents also played all four years of high school baseball and reported that an average of six of their high school teammates also played select baseball. The majority of those who, as select players, pitched, played first base, shortstop, outfield or catcher played those same positions in high school. For some college players select baseball served as the roots of learning to play a position at which they remained for their high school and at least part of their college careers. This was the case most often for catchers and pitchers. Second basemen and shortstops, while not sticking with their positions after they began playing in college, played other infield positions post-high school.

The impact of select baseball becomes clearer when considering how professional baseball has become increasingly dependent on colleges and universities as a source of players. Of the 3,000 players in MLB's first-year player draft in 2005 and 2006, 64% were recruited from college. In applying the results from my study of college players, 864 of the approximately 1,500 in each of the first-year player drafts the past two years played select baseball as youths. This serves as an indication of the ultimate influence of select baseball on the professional ranks. If select baseball is the well from which more than 57% of players in the first-year draft spring, then profiling select baseball may serve as one indicator of what the U.S.–born contingency to Major League Baseball will look like; and as of 2007, it would appear that there are few African Americans in that contingency.

The crux of my research has involved profiling select teams. During the past eight years I have surveyed approximately 450 youth select teams from 27 states. Of the almost 5,000 players on those teams, slightly more than 3 percent are African American. Year to year the percentage has varied between 2 and 4 percent. The percentage of Hispanic youth on the teams I have surveyed has increased during the past five years, and last year accounted for about 6 percent of the players I surveyed. If select baseball is the beginning of the pipeline to the professional ranks, as my research indicates, then you can expect to see even lower numbers of African-Americans in major league baseball in the years to come.

The diminishing number of African Americans at the major league level contrasts starkly with those numbers more than three decades ago, when almost one third of major leaguers were African American. The decrease in numbers becomes more intriguing when compared with African Americans' involvement with the game during the 1930's and 1940's. During those decades, Negro Leagues baseball was a major economic enterprise for African Americans (although white owners and booking agents, like Nat Strong, remained entrenched financially in the leagues). Negro Leagues baseball assumed a cultural stature for African Americans that few institutions rivaled. Almost 50,000 (mostly African Americans) attended the Annual East-West Game (the Negro Leagues' equivalence of the All-Star Game) during the 1940's and, as Buc O'Neil related, African American churches would schedule their services to accommodate attendance at Negro League games.

Possible Reasons for the Demise of Baseball in African American Culture

What has happened during the course of 60 years to create such a rift between African Americans and baseball? There is no direct answer. Some baseball scholars, such as Gerald Early, contend that African Americans' interest in baseball waned with the dissolution of the last Negro League team around 1960 and the retirement of former Negro League players who made it to the major leagues. It may be more than coincidental that the African American players who were on the major league rosters in the 1970's, when the number of African Americans in the American and National Leagues reached its zenith, would have been the last generation of youth to have followed Willie Mays, Monte Irvin, Ernie Banks and other Negro League stars who entered the majors. But the dynamics of that rift are more complicated and are driven by social and psychological forces. Exploring all or most of those dynamics is not possible within the scope of this essay. But most fall under three categories: intrapersonal, interpersonal, and cultural.

Intrapersonal: Studies on the formation of self-identity and self-awareness can be found in various disciplines. Those studies reveal that social, cultural and physical environments are major forces in the molding of self-identity and awareness of self.

Sociologists, such as Anthony Giddens, noted that people gain a sense of security or well-being from the everyday practices that they've adopted over the years. These practices become absorbed into and part of the fabric of one's sense of self. As Giddens noted, such practices are constrained by available resources and shaped by various social and cultural elements. When Giddens' concepts are applied today, those elements could include significant others, exposure to mass communication, social institutions (from schools and churches to neighborhood groups and clubs) and the physical environment. Familiarity with a situation or location breeds comfort, or at least a feeling of ease, with that situation or location.

For most African American male youth, particularly those living in the urban core, playing baseball is not a common practice or routine to which they are exposed often and early in life. The often matriarchal family structure, a lack of discretionary time and income, the lack of baseball-related facilities and the lack of neighborhood baseball role models may contribute in varying degrees to a young black's sense that baseball is not part of his personal landscape nor of the culture to which he commits his self-identity.

Feeling comfortable playing second base or being a point guard in basketball or a quarterback in football all require familiarity with the game and playing field and some degree of encouragement or confirmation from a role model or significant other. In many cities baseball facilities and neighborhood role models are scarce in the urban core and resident youths have few opportunities to learn the game. Basketball hoops are more plentiful and small basketball courts are better suited to cramped urban areas, and that can make it easier for youth to gain more experience in the fundamentals of basketball than in the fundamentals of baseball. As stated earlier, familiarity breeds comfort and comfort can lead to enjoyment and continued interest.

Interpersonal: Peer group membership is one of many extensions of self-identity. A male adolescent or teen often selects peer groups and friends based on how well they fit his self-identity. Many select baseball teams that I have surveyed started with a small peer group whose common interests included baseball. Those peer groups often played together as a select team for years and even into high school. As one parent of a select team player explained, "Jim loves to play baseball, but he wouldn't love it as much if his friends didn't play it."

Studies have shown that peer groups often use sports interests as a common bond. For African Americans, according to one study, that bond is basketball and wearing basketball apparel is one way youths expressed their membership in a peer group. There are numerous studies to indicate that youth are more likely to become interested or involved in a sport when they see members of their peer groups playing or following that sport. An African American player at the NCAA College World Series in Omaha, for instance, lamented that it was somewhat discouraging not to see more black players on college baseball diamonds and at the College World Series.

Significant others and authority figures may also contribute to interpersonal factors that inhibit or facilitate youth interest in sport. Many coaches whom I've interviewed cite parents as major influences in their sons' interest in playing baseball. Writings in educational psychology and cognitive development explore the role of parents and other authority figures in the formation of childhood interests. Sociologist S.F. Philipp has shown that African American parents are more likely to identify basketball as the sport they would like to see their children play and African American youth are more likely than other minority groups to be encouraged by school coaches and officials to play basketball.

Overall interpersonal communication and exchanges help an individual to form relationships and to ingest the interests those relationships and that communication

include. But those relationships not only mold a person's identity and presentation of self, they also reflect the greater culture in which those relationships are forged.

Culture: Baseball has lost much of its cultural capital among African Americans; and what baseball has lost, basketball has gained.

Baseball offers fewer opportunities for extemporaneous expression that other sports may offer. For example, "stuffing" the basketball lends itself to physical expressions of grace and acrobatics and the speed in which the game is played provides instant dramatics and powerful dynamics in compressed time. Such styles of athletic expression could fall in the category of what Richard Majors has called "cool pose." Cool pose is culturally sanctioned expressions, symbols, movements, and occurrences. Such expressions, according to Majors, can be an important part of self-identity for African American males. That such expressions and occurrences are commonly accepted throughout the African American culture (while others are not) shows the impact culture can have on self-identity. Some scholars have called this fusion between culture and self identity as "collective identity." That is, youth take cultural cues from peers and mass media on what is desired behavior and what is not. Youths incorporate those cultural cues into expressions of identity and use those to solidify their position within their peer group and among significant others and also use them to identify themselves with their culture. Indeed, mass media helps to underscore for youth what is sanctioned culturally and what is not. Some athletic shoe manufacturers, for example, have used pick-up games on an inner-city basketball court as the backdrop in TV ads touting their products; and spokesmen for the shoe manufacturers historically have been National Basketball Association stars who are African American and who set the tone for cool pose in their sport. Youths are much less likely to see a Major League Baseball player who is African American touting athletic wear or any product for that matter.

The Way Forward: It Takes a "Pied Piper"

Deciding which sport, if any, to follow as a fan or to play is a process driven by intra- and interpersonal forces and the cultural environment. Such forces can facilitate or restrain a person from developing an interest in a particular sport. This essay is by no means intended to give an exhaustive catalog of factors and forces that impinge on the development of sports interests. Instead, it is intended to provide a basis for understanding the process that drives certain youth to certain sports.

This essay is also intended to serve as a reminder that an unequal distribution of sports facilities and sports mentoring programs means that some children do not have the option to play certain sports, not because of their lack of interest but because of where they were born and raised. This understanding and realization are necessary if baseball is to regain some cultural status among African Americans and if actions are to be taken to help baseball to regain that status.

Some communities have implemented programs aimed to increase interest and participation in baseball among inner city minorities. Major League Baseball launched its Reviving Baseball in the Inner Cities (RBI) program to do just that, although that program has met with limited success, based on the small number of African Americans who have entered the major leagues since the RBI program was created in the late 1980's. But there are several examples of community-based programs that have been successful, at the very least, in exposing young African American males to baseball. In Omaha, Nebraska, a mid-town youth baseball league with mostly white players extended an invitation to students at a predominantly black grade school to join the league for the summer. Almost 30 African American children played in that league, while league coaches and officials provided one-on-one instruction and equipment and waived the league fees for those children.

Others have also stepped up to the plate. For instance, in Washington, D.C. at Garrison Elementary School, former Baltimore Orioles pitching prospect John McCarthy directed a program, called Elementary Baseball. McCarthy, who after college was signed by the Orioles and played for its rookie league team, began Elementary Baseball in 1994 not merely as a baseball instruction program, but as part of a literacy program. McCarthy used baseball as a "reward" for grade school students who agreed to participate in a one-on-one reading program and showed progress week to week. McCarthy worked with third graders, most of whom were African American, but eventually expanded the program to all students at the elementary school. He said he used baseball as a vehicle for teaching children that perseverance pays off and improving one's skills in both reading and baseball demands a commitment of time and energy.

Other youth baseball officials have praised McCarthy's program, and for good reasons. Framing baseball as an incentive and reward for learning other skills in life puts the sport in a more attractive context and provides an overall perspective for sports in general. Baseball skills, like others, must be learned and the more adept a person becomes at those skills, the greater the enjoyment the person experiences in performing those skills. Such a philosophy, however, must be introduced to youngsters very early in life and applied consistently through the years, and that requires someone who is dedicated to teaching that philosophy and using baseball to do so. A "resident" baseball mentor is not something most inner city neighborhoods have. North Omaha, which is predominantly African American, was fortunate to have had, what one youth baseball coach called, a "pied piper." The late Hubert Moss coached Little League baseball, as well as girls' fast pitch softball, for decades. His Little League teams won several local championship tournaments in the 1990s and he helped sustain Omaha's Martin Luther King Youth Baseball League.

Moss faced numerous challenges keeping baseball alive in the urban core. T-ball for grade school children didn't exist in North Omaha and he said most of youths living in Omaha's north side didn't "start playing until they're 10 years old." With most of his young players coming from one-parent families and lacking transportation to practice and games, Moss found it difficult some years to maintain a team. "Kids don't want to walk," he said. "They won't walk. I've lost some good ball players, because I had to travel all over town to get kids."

Lack of playing facilities and disinterest in the community contributed to the Martin Luther King League's woes. "I had 7 coaches quit in one year," he lamented. "They just fade away. They don't have time, or there's something else they've got to do." Even for North Omaha's "pied piper" of baseball, the lack of interest and participation in the game became discouraging. A few years before he died, Moss told me, "When it comes to baseball, they [African American youth] aren't interested like some people are. But I think if someone would come out here and talk to these kids about baseball, it might soak in. It might. It used to be in '89 we had a lot of kids who wanted to play ball. We had a strong league. But now they stay away."

Moss confronted and understood the obstacles baseball organizations face today in re-establishing for African Americans the cultural validity of the game. Moss also recognized the importance of the role he played and that a community baseball mentor, who will work with youth consistently and regularly, is an essential ingredient for increasing the number of African Americans involved in the game. Unfortunately, too much emphasis has been put on building new baseball facilities and not enough on personnel who will use those facilities to teach baseball. New facilities may generate initial interest, but it takes "a pied piper" to sustain that interest and to make sure it's carried over from summer to summer. Without such instructional consistency and long-term dedication to teaching baseball to inner city youth, the game will remain outside the cultural purview of African Americans.

Biography
Dave Ogden, Ph.D.

Dave Ogden is associate professor in the School of Communication at the University of Nebraska at Omaha (UNO). Ogden received his Ph.D. in 1999 from the University of Nebraska-Lincoln.

Before joining the staff of the University of Nebraska in 2001, Dr. Ogden was an associate professor at Wayne State College. He served as director of public affairs at the University of Nebraska Medical Center from 1984 to 1988, and has worked as a reporter/news writer for KFAB and Metro Networks.

Ogden's research focuses on baseball and culture, with specific emphasis on the relationship between African American communities and baseball. Since 1995, he has presented his research at the National Baseball Hall of Fame Conference on Baseball and Culture in Cooperstown, N.Y.; Indiana State University's Conference on Baseball in Literature and Culture; the *Nine* Spring Training Conference in Tucson; and at other national research meetings. His work can be found in *Nine: The Journal of Baseball History and Culture*, the *Journal of Leisure Research*, the *Journal of Black Studies*, and *Great Plains Research Journal*. He is currently co-editing a book, *Reconstructing Fame: Race, Sport, and the Redemption of Once-Tainted Reputations*, which will be released in Fall 2008 by the University of Mississippi Press.

Some of Dr. Ogden's recent publications include:

"The history of black baseball at Forbes Field." A chapter for the book, *Forbes Field: Revisiting a Classic Ballpark*, Angelo Louisa and David Cicotello (eds.), Jefferson, N.C.: McFarland & Company, 2007, 55-66.

"Major League Baseball and myth-making: Roland Barthes' semiotics and the maintenance of image," *Nine: A Journal of Baseball History and Culture,* Spring 2007, *15*(2) 66-78

"Are anti-spit tobacco campaigns striking out? A survey of Iowa and Nebraska college baseball players," *Great Plains Research Journal*, *16*(2), Fall 2006, 195-201, (co-authored with Dr. Mike Hilt, Dr. Teresa Lamsam, and Professor Hugh Reilly).

"Josh vs. Satchel: Legends, their leveling effect and their cultural longevity," *Baseball/ Literature/ Culture, Essays2004/2005*, Peter Carino (ed.), Jefferson N.C.: McFarland & Company, 2006, 117-127.

"Using Giddens' structuration theory to examine the waning participation of African Americans in baseball" (co-authored with Dr. Randall Rose), *Journal of Black Studies, 35*(4), March 2005, 225-245.

Revival Strategy

Revival Strategy

In one of his last interviews, famous Negro League Player and Founder of the Negro League Museum Buck O'Neil was asked: "Weren't you mad that you got snubbed by not being inducted into the Baseball Hall of Fame?" He replied, "If I was going to get mad, I would have gotten mad when they didn't let me into the University of Florida, because when they didn't let me in, I didn't get a chance. By contrast, I got a chance to be voted on for the Hall of Fame, I just wasn't voted in, and I am not mad 'cause I had a chance. All I asked for in life was a chance."

It seems from all uncovered in this book that African Americans have a chance to revive baseball in inner cities, but a chance doesn't mean a plan. A game plan is needed.

What I have seen from my experience in working in over 100 countries in the developing world is that when things fall apart, it takes a village to put them back together. Everyone must work together, hand in glove. Collective action, social activism—it takes a grass roots movement to pull it all back together again.

As shown throughout this book, things have fallen apart for African Americans and baseball in inner cities, for many reasons. Now that it has happened, what should be done about it, and whose interest is it in to do anything about it?

Answering the second part of the question first, it's clear that it's in the interest of African Americans to keep baseball alive in inner cities because baseball represents an additional option for them. No one in their right mind wants to knowingly throw away hard earned options. Keeping the option open doesn't mean that every African American has to prefer baseball to other sports; it simply means that an option remains open for those who might prefer and excel at baseball.

It's also clear that it's in the interest of Major League Baseball to keep the sport alive in inner cities, for a number of reasons. Take the case of Baltimore, for instance. The Orioles have been losing for some time. What are the chances that suburban fans will travel into the city to watch a losing team? Importantly, over time, without being able to demonstrate the relevancy of the sport to inner city residents, proposals for new stadia and for economic development concessions that have helped baseball be so profitable might not be so convincing in the future.

So far, the MLB has been lucky. Few, having seen all of the faces of Black players on the baseball field, know that the participation of African Americans in baseball has diminished to the extent it has. Few elected officials who support baseball understand how irrelevant baseball is becoming to African Americans. At the same time, the visual picture of the absence of Black fans in the stands hasn't sunk in either. It's just a matter of time before the whole support infrastructure for baseball in inner cities comes tumbling down. It's already happening. There are stories of athletic departments at schools and universities that are beginning to sabotage their own baseball programs because they would prefer to spend limited funds on more popular sports like basketball and football.

Baseball is hanging out there on its own, without a "bench." While no one is watching, slowly but surely, and city by city, the resources for baseball are being diverted and re-directed to those sports that are more effectively marketed to the African American inner city community.

Tackling the subject of how to revive baseball in inner cities is, like much else in this book, a story told in two parts.

The first part concerns MLB's role in the revival, and the second part concerns the role of the main stakeholders, the African American community. These roles must be played out in tandem.

The MLB's Role In The Revival

Vision, leadership, and financial commitment are the three essential ingredients required of the MLB to turn the situation around. Vision is needed to provide direction; leadership is needed to move toward the goal; and a greater financial commitment is needed to more effectively "*reach in*" to inner cities to lend a hand up.

Just as the McDonalds Corporation provides a successful enabling environment for its franchises to flourish, the MLB Commission needs to do a better job in helping its franchises meet the demands of a changing society.

The "*McBaseball*" analogy is appropriate in many regards. For instance, one of the key contributions of the corporation is marketing to uphold the brand. McDonalds marketing always takes changing demographics into consideration to ensure that the message is considered "cool" to the target audience. The overarching message of all McDonalds commercials is that it is "cool" to eat at McDonalds. As has been shown in Chapter Two of this book, it's all about being seen as "cool" to be able to attract and maintain today's audiences. Baseball could learn a lot from the McDonalds' example.

Another page out of the McDonalds leadership book can also be taken in respect to training.

One of the hallmarks of McDonalds is its intimate knowledge of its audience. The corporation has a *Price Purchasing Parity (PPP) Index* that is the envy of economists the world over; it holds the key to information about the ability of each household to purchase hamburgers in every zip code, in every state, and in every location in the world. The point is this: Because McDonalds knows its customers, it knows how to train its owner/operators to deal with the situation they find themselves in from zip code to zip code, in each location, in every place it operates.

The relevance of the analogy for the MLB is that each of its baseball franchises operates similarly in a specific location. Likewise, the population in those locations must be understood and accommodations to them must be made. The fact of the matter is that baseball stadia are located in inner cities where there is often a large African American population. To ignore that fact, and to operate as if an oasis in a desert of blight, is neither a visionary nor a sustainable strategy.

Switching the analogy to basketball, there is no question that it has figured out how to capture the hearts, minds, and "soles" of African Americans in inner cities. The question is which page of its playbook can be borrowed to learn how to more effectively market to the target population. Two issues come up over and again in conversations with African American fathers about the draw of basketball for their adolescent sons. Secondly, basketball scouts reach further down to follow younger kids than baseball and, basketball camps are more affordable, more rewarding, and more fun because scouts and professionals attend and interact with the kids.

By contrast, where are the opportunities for inner city kids to mingle with baseball heroes, and where are the scouts who are looking at them early in their careers and encouraging them to play up?

Tracking and developing talent at an early age among inner city youth appears to be an opportunity that is lost to basketball. Basketball scouts hear the ping of every basketball dunked in the inner city. By contrast, no one is following the African American child from Tee-Ball up through the little league and beyond in inner cities. By the time the child shows up in the RBI program, it's too late to have intervened to capture his heart, mind, and "soles." In the absence of a fight, "Pied Pipers" for basketball and football easily lead children to their sports.

Leadership is needed. A lot is at stake.

An important leadership role for the MLB is to encourage its African American ball players to reach back to African American communities. As has been demonstrated throughout this book, heroes matter and having a connection to the community matters. The NBA gets it, which is why they are increasingly putting clauses in player's contracts to ensure that they are connected with African American communities and to worthy causes.

It's not necessarily a hard sell. Players like Torii Hunter are already giving back (*The Torii Hunter Project*), and he's not the only one. An article posted on MLB's own website in August 2007 shows that reviving baseball in African American communities is important to African American players, both past and present.

> COMPTON, Calif. -- Chuck Smith may have recently hung up his spikes, but he hasn't moved too far from the game.
>
> When the former Florida Marlins pitcher (2000-2002) moved back to his hometown of Cleveland after retiring from baseball, he wanted to find a way to give back to the younger generation of up-and-coming players.
>
> Smith, 37, was involved in the Cleveland Baseball Federation, a youth program run by the City of Cleveland, from ages 7 to 13. The baseball league there has since joined Major League Baseball's Reviving Baseball in Inner Cities (RBI) youth program. Smith said he enjoyed participating in the league when he was a kid, and due to MLB's involvement, it has only improved since he played there.
>
> "The amount of money that's been put into the program, they can have more camps, entice kids to get more involved with baseball, and buy equipment for kids that can't afford it," Smith said. "It's a great program."
>
> When Smith returned to Cleveland in 2006 after last playing baseball in Korea and Taiwan, he got in touch with Tim Wells, his former Cleveland Baseball Federation youth coach, who is now the sports manager for the City of Cleveland's division of recreation. He expressed interest in helping out, and Wells got him connected with the RBI program.
>
> "He called me up and asked me and my younger brother if we were interested, since we're products of the program, in coming back and helping out," said Smith. "And I said, 'Sure we were. ... I'd love to come to coach and give something back.'"
>
> Smith said he feels there's a lot of potential among youth in Cleveland, and as a former Major Leaguer, he wants to encourage African-American kids to play and help improve their baseball skills.
>
> "I just thought that it's part of my job to help create more athletically-sound players to get back out on the field and compete for positions in the Major Leagues," he said.

Smith is now helping Cleveland RBI manager Pete Guerra as the pitching coach for the RBI program. This week, he is with the Cleveland RBI seniors team at the RBI World Series, the championship round of the RBI program, in Compton, Calif.

"These kids have been playing above and beyond what we thought they'd be playing at," he said. "When we first started coaching, these kids were really raw. They had ability, but having ability and actually putting it to work are two different things."

Smith said in July at the RBI Regionals tournament in Pittsburgh, the kids performed at the level the coaches had known all along they were cabable of, which was encouraging.

"They played at a high level and they were consistent," said Smith. "Seeing that, it just makes you smile.

"That's what keeps me motivated and keeps me going, seeing these kids being consistent," he said.

Smith works specifically with the pitchers in the 16- to 19-year-old age group.

"I'm really impressed with the progress that these kids have had over these last couple months, and the courage they've shown to compete against these other teams that are from warm-weather states," he said.

Chaz Leftridge, 19, is one of the pitchers on the Cleveland RBI seniors team. This is his first year participating in the RBI program, and he said he has enjoyed working with Smith.

"This is my first Major Leaguer I've been in contact with so much," said Leftridge. "Where it feels like not just being a fan, but someone more of like a parent figure or a coach that you can actually relate to -- he's coming from a community that I'm accustomed to, because we live very close to each other where we grew up."

Leftridge said Smith has helped him with his pitching mechanics.

"He's adjusted my arm slot, to make it less stressful on my shoulder," Leftridge said.

Cory Douglass, 19, is also a pitcher on the Cleveland RBI seniors team. He said working with Smith has been an "awesome experience."

> "He works with your mechanics, pitching style," Douglass said. "He's talking to some schools for me, to get me into better schools." Douglass said he's learned a lot from working with Smith. "He's not like your average Major Leaguer, he's like a normal down-to-earth person, willing to teach anyone," Douglass said.
>
> Smith said he really likes the mission of the RBI program, in that it focuses on kids in the inner cities. "Major League Baseball has really recognized that there are some kids in our cities that can play baseball," Smith said. "They can give money back to the inner cities just like they're giving to these camps that are in Venezuela, the Dominican, Mexico.
>
> "All these baseball academies they have over there, they start bringing them here and giving these kids an opportunity to do something else other than walk the streets, it's an amazing thing," he said.

Encouraging more of this kind of "*reach in*" and "*give back*" from other African American former players is an important leadership role the MLB can play. Everyone needs inspiration; former players need to be inspired to be a part of the loop, and helping out in inner cities must appear to them to be within the loop. After all, ball players are team players, and they want to feel like they are still on the team. The MLB has the power to make them feel that they are still on the team.

The bottom line: The same economic development arguments that were used to get local political "buy in" and financing support for new baseball stadia in inner cities are the ones that the MLB is being encouraged to bring to fruition today, before it's too late. If baseball is not revived, everybody loses.

Major League Baseball has developed a number of initiatives over the years to try to keep African Americans in the game. While these initiatives are appreciated, are they enough and are they the right ones, and can they be leveraged further and/or coupled with new initiatives that rally the African American community around baseball?

These are important and pressing questions because every day that goes by that something isn't done is a day that football, basketball, and other competitor sports gain a stronger stranglehold. Future sponsors, volunteer coaches, supportive parents, public schools, local elected officials, fans, and other "would be" stakeholders for baseball are within the stranglehold.

Though baseball has had record attendance lately, it would be a mistake to be over confident; momentum is important, and the pendulum is swinging the other way. Social observers need look no further than the current 2008 U.S. Presidential race to understand momentum. Once the wind got behind Barack Obama's back, it became a "whole new ball game." The wind beneath his sails is from the people, from the bottom up.

Similarly, to revive baseball the wind must come from the bottom up, from the people.

The problem is today's primary stakeholders, young African American mothers who are often single heads of households, are not savvy politicians who know how to lead a revival. They don't even know that they need one. What they know is that baseball is helpful to their male children, but they take the little leagues for granted. They are also ill informed about what it means to have a future in baseball as compared with other sports. For this reason, leadership is needed from the Major League Baseball to "*reach in*" and lend a hand up.

The complexity of reviving baseball in inner city America has a parallel in developing country contexts, where there are so many dimensions to the problem that any attempts to address them feel like putting a finger in the dike to hold back gushing water that springs up in another directions.

What the World Bank learned after over 40 years in the development business is that it is incapable of spurring development solely from the "top down." Instead a "bottom up" approach is also necessary. Upon coming to this realization, the World Bank put forward an innovative approach called, "*Market Place of Ideas,*" which can be used as part of a strategy to revive baseball in inner cities.

Based on the belief that the people know what they need, the idea of the "*Market Place*" is to provide a framework and incentive structure to enable good ideas to spring up from the bottom.

A similar approach is needed to revive baseball in inner cities. Stakeholders must realize what's at stake for them, and so must the MLB. The strategy has to reflect of all these realities and aim to attack multiple facets of the problem, all the way *from home to home plate*.

The innovation of the World Bank's "*Market Place of Ideas*" competition is that it doesn't dictate what the answers should be in advance. Rather, the competition "unearths" knowledge that is lying dormant in communities, and unleashes and unharnesses a spirit and desire for transformation and change.

Similarly, a "*Market Place of Ideas*" competition could be an important linchpin in a strategy to revive baseball in inner cities among African Americans, and supporting and championing such an initiative is where MLB's leadership and financing come into play.

The African American Community's Role In The Revival

Just as the MLB has to step up to the plate, so does the African American community. It is clear that the African American community has to revive itself and to look at itself differently. Advocating for a baseball revival is only one part of a bigger equation that places emphasis on self-improvement and community development as a whole.

If a strategy to revive baseball provokes African American communities to take a harder look at their internal problems and to make a commitment to aim higher, then it will not only have played a positive role in terms of reviving a sport, it will have played an important role as a catalyst for broader social and economic development.

Tough issues have to be faced in the process. Chapter Three, *From Home to Home Plate*, shows that there are many problems in the home that need to be addressed. Chief among these problems is the absence of fathers in the home. It is a reality that has to be faced and a solution to bridging the gap has to be a linchpin of any strategy to revive baseball in inner cities, and indeed, to revive the inner city itself.

Many soul-searching conversations have to be held within the African American community as a part of developing a strategy to revive baseball. Some of these conversations have to be held in-house and some have to bring the community together hand-in-hand out in the open to confer together on how to put forward their best ideas for reviving baseball.

Clearly, a series of town hall meetings are needed throughout inner city America to focus the attention of African Americans on what's at stake for them if baseball disappears. African American mothers must be at the center of these conversations because more often than not, they are the ones raising the future baseball players virtually single-handedly. The research in this book indicates that they have very little knowledge of how baseball works. They know about little leagues but after that there is a black hole.

Step one, therefore, is to embark upon a conversation throughout inner city America with African American women about baseball.

Step two is to engage the hundreds of volunteer African American little league coaches throughout inner city America in the conversation to encourage them to believe again. They have been on an island for so long they have lost all hope of being rescued.

Step three, once the local "captains of baseball" are on board with the concept of a revival, entails all stakeholders joining hands, putting aside petty differences in order to start figuring out what is needed and what could be done, if given the chance.

To take advantage of the chance, African Americans have to strive toward bettering their own situations and to "*reaching up*" to achieve higher goals. This means less television, less eating, more school homework, more exercise, more baseball practice, more parent involvement, and more disciplined. There is no external initiative that can make this happen—it must come from the inside out.

It's hard to navigate a ship out of a storm; all hands are required on deck. In this case, the perfect storm has engulfed the African American community and has swept up baseball in the vortex. Both need to come out of it alive.

A "*Market Place of Ideas*" is what Buck O'Neil would have appreciated; it is a chance. It's not everything; it can't solve all the problems, but it can succeed in making important first steps toward finding grass roots solutions to the problem.

Twenty Reasons Why A "*Market Place of Ideas*" Is Needed As Part of a Revival Strategy

Assuming that there is a will in the African American community to revive baseball, and we believe there is based on what we have seen in Baltimore as an example, and assuming that the MLB also has the will to seriously tackle and support the challenge of reviving baseball in inner cities, there is a strong case to be made for why a "*Market Place of Ideas*" approach is the right way to get started. Arguments in support of the concept include that:

1. It will focus positive attention on the subject of baseball in inner cities;

2. It will focus attention of African American mothers on the game and include them as part of the solution;

3. It will enliven and invigorate the participation of African American males volunteers;

4. It will forge new reinvigorated strategic alliances between baseball institutions in the inner city;

5. It will involve politicians and increase their stake in and commitment to baseball;

6. It will teach an important civics lesson about the meaning of being a citizen and the importance of believing in one's self;

7. It will demonstrate how existing barriers limit the participation of African Americans and put forth possible solutions;

8. It will get a "buzz" going and garner a great deal of press across America about the importance of baseball in the African American community;

9. It will help African Americans realize the importance of the game to their families and communities;

10. It will force knowledge acquisition and learning about the game;

11. It will create a greater stakeholding in the game;

12. It will compliment and/or leverage existing initiatives;

13. It will promote learning about baseball and a greater appreciation about the game;

14. It will unearth good and actionable ideas that will strengthen the game in inner cities and put fans back in the stands;

15. It will put forward models of action that can be replicated, or sliced and diced for other applicability in other locations;

16. It will bring in new sponsors to help support the competition and the recommendations winners put forward;

17. It will be a positive demonstration of the interest of the African American community in the game;

18. It will be a positive demonstration of MLB's commitment to increasing the presence of African Americans in the game;

19. It has the potential to put forward ideas that improve the game, the learning experience, the audience viewing experience, and bringing forward valuable information about how to more effectively market the game in target communities;

20. It will provide an excellent opportunity for leadership at all levels throughout inner cities and for proactive leadership of the MLB on the subject.

Structuring the Competition

Little leagues are the first in the line as "Pied Pipers" and are, therefore, a logical choice as the first group with which to pilot the "*Market Place of Ideas*" competition. The importance of little leagues can't be overemphasized, especially in inner cities where many households are female headed; everything that they do and fail to do can make a difference. They also have a finger on the pulse of the community, know where all the problems are, and in many cases, they also know how to solve the problem, if given a chance.

The World Bank's initiative is a grant program. Similarly, there is a compelling case to be made for a grant program that MLB franchises financially support. At the same time, bidders should raise matching funds from local businesses to demonstrate that there is a broad coalition of stakeholders committed to the revival.

While supporters of the initiative would be the ones to design the competition, its design would stress bringing forth good and actionable ideas from grass roots stakeholders.

Food For Thought: Key Issues For The Competition To Address

It is clear that reviving baseball in inner cities is a challenge of "major league" proportions. It is no less complex than promoting development overseas. For this reason, it's impossible to imagine the solutions from on high, far removed from the epicenter of the storm. What the "*Market Place of Ideas*" competition can do is to give African Americans a chance to think about the problem and see what they can come up with to solve it. It's not about just about the MLB throwing more money at the problem: it's about African Americans throwing themselves into the problem to do what is necessary to solve it.

Recognizing that various MLB-sponsored initiatives already exist, the question is what can the competition bring forth to compliment existing initiatives, while going beyond them. The answers lie at every point, all the way *from home to home plate*.

Starting at home, in order for the competition to bring new value-added solutions it must tackle aspects of the problem that impose barriers at the household level, which are currently being overlooked. The key issues in this regard include: focusing on the mothers—educating them and helping them to understand what's at stake; the children themselves—inspiring them and helping them have a vision in which they see themselves in baseball, and ensuring that the vision stresses the importance of education; the "Dads"—encouraging them to either get involved, or if they are involved already, encouraging them to stay in the game.

The question that the competition needs to address, therefore, is what can be done that others may not have thought of, or that could be done better. No external consultant or outsider can answer these questions; the answers are *inside* the people and *inside* their knowledge base of what works and what doesn't work with members of their community.

The issue of knowledge sharing, or the lack thereof, looms large as part of the problem. As America's national pastime, over the years, many solutions have been found to various parts of the problem. Many of these solutions are playing out in the suburbs, but not in inner cities. For instance, best-case practices of how to be good "baseball moms;" of how to form strategic alliances for resource sharing; of how to manage little leagues organizations; of how to raise funds; of how to spark grass roots movements to get local officials to get behind the game; and of how to use technology and the Internet to share information, maintain databases, and to promote programs and players—are already happening in the suburbs. The trick is to infuse these lessons learned into the inner city.

As baseball continues to thrive in the suburbs while dying in inner cities, what new approaches can be unearthed through the competition to suggest ways of cross fertilizing from the suburbs to the city?

Within the cities themselves, it is clear that links in the chain of the baseball feeder system have been broken. Every link is operating independently, if Baltimore's example holds for other cities. The competition provides an excellent opportunity for stakeholders throughout the system to come together to put forward new ways of working together.

At the same time, the initiative can help fill in information gaps. It can also address the "inspiration gap" by being responsive to proposals that bring African American MLB players into the loop of support for proposed initiatives, and by encouraging the franchises to more vigorously support new ideas and new ways of connecting with the communities in which they are located.

Inspiration, which is probably the biggest missing piece of the puzzle, comes in all forms. From encouraging franchise scouts to "scout down" to the little league level, to marketing African American baseball heroes and encouraging them to connect with African Americans in the cities in which they play, to encouraging retired players to stay in the loop by helping out in inner cities, to supporting talented players and ensuring that they have opportunities to play on travel teams, to rewarding volunteer coaches, all initiatives help and are meaningful.

Little things like having award ceremonies and giving out trophies to retired players who do the most to help keep baseball alive in inner cities, to giving rewards and prizes to the best volunteer coaches, etc., give the signal that everybody is in the loop and playing on the same field. People want to be insiders, not outsiders. The MLB can make everyone feel that they are an insider and are on the team.

The competition could also make important contributions by unearthing new "*cool*" marketing ideas. To be sure, television commercials that feature old guard baseball heroes like Tommy LaSorda coming out literally from under the sink would have been totally "dodged" if the African American community had a say in the matter. As possibly one of the most "*uncoo*l" television commercials ever aired, clearly the MLB is in need of new ideas. Give a new target audience a say, and listen to the stakeholders. They know what appeals to them. Reward their opinions and strategies. Everybody can only win from it.

Listen to stakeholders about what's working and what's not working with the RBI program; they have valuable insights and potentially important suggestions for improving it and ensuring that it plays a greater role in helping African Americans climb up the ladder in their efforts to make it into "The Show."

Importantly, hear from stakeholders on the subject of new small business ventures that could play a role in connecting more African American youth to baseball. For instance, new informational websites, new instructional videos that aim to educate African American women about baseball and teach African American coaches in the latest coaching techniques are two ideas that readily come to mind. The stakeholders have many more ideas. They know what's needed. therefore, let their voices be heard and give them a chance to make a contribution.

At a time when baseball heroes like Roger Clemens are in the spotlight for alleged steroids usage, now is a good time to change the light from the ugly harsh glare of the spotlight to the soft rays of a positive limelight. The MLB's vigorous and quantitative support of a "*Market Place of Ideas*" initiative to get African Americans back in the game will shine a positive light.

The foregoing list is not exhaustive; it provides some ideas for starters. However, in the end, it is up to the African American community and Major League Baseball to come together to keep baseball alive in the inner cities. It's in both of their interests. Take a chance on a home run.

References

Barrow, H. (2006). The Decline of African-American Participation in Major League Baseball. A paper presented at the Florida State University D-Scholarship Repository (2006).

Conner, M.K. (1995). What Is Cool? Understanding Black Manhood in America. New York: Crown Publishers.

Earls, M. (2003). Advertising to the Herds. Paper presented at the Market Research Society, Annual Conference, 2003.

Farley, R. & Allen, W.R. (1988). The Color Line and the Quality of Life in America. The American Journal of Sociology, Vol. 94, (3), pp. 695-696.

Fort, R. Maxcy, J. (2001). The Demise of African American Baseball Leagues: A Rival Explanation Journal of Sports Economics, Vol. 2, No. 1, February 2001, pp. 35-49.

Gopnick, A. (1999). The Scientist in the Crib: Minds, Brains, And How Children Learn. New York: William Morrow.

Gray, H. (1995). Watching Race: Television and the Struggle for Blackness. Minneapolis: University of Minnesota Press.

Heaphy, L. (2006). More than a Man's Game: Pennsylvania's Women Play Ball. Paper presented to the Historical Society of Pennsylvania.

Humphreys, J.M. (2005). The Multicultural Economy 2005: America's Minority Buying Power. The University of Georgia Quarterly, Vol. 65, (3), Third Quarter.

Institute of Medicine. (2004). Childhood Obesity in the United States: Facts and Figures. Fact Sheet, September 2004.

Issacs, J. (2007). Economic mobility of black and white families. Washington, DC: Brookings Institution Press.

Kaiser Family Foundation (2005). Generation M: Media in the Lives of 8-18 Year-olds.

Kelley, R. (1994). Race Rebels: Culture, Politics, and the Black Working Class. New York: The Free Press.

Lamont, M. & Molnar, V. (2001). How Blacks Use Consumption to Shape their Collective Identity: Evidence from marketing specialists. Journal of Consumer Culture, Vol. 1, No. 1, 31-45 (2001).

Lapchick, R., Ekiyor, B., & Ruiz, H. (2006). The 2006 Racial and Gender Report Card: Major League Baseball. University of Central Florida.

Levine, D. N. (1972). Wax and Gold: Tradition and Innovation in Ethiopian Culture. Chicago, Il: The University of Chicago Press.

Long, M. (2007). First Class Citizenship: The Civil Rights Letters of Jackie Robinson. New York: Times Books.

Majors, R., & Billson, J. M. (1992). Coolpose: The dilemmas of black manhood in America. New York: Lexington.

Majors, R., Tyler, R., Peden, B., & Hall, R. E. (1994). Cool Pose: A symbolic mechanism for masculine role enactment and coping by black males. In R. G. Majors & J. U. Gordon (Eds.) The American black male: His present status and his future. New York: Nelson-Hall.

National Research Council. (2001). America Becoming: Racial Trends and Their Consequences. Washington, D.C.: National Academy Press.

Nickelodeon. (2005). U.S. Multicultural Kids Study.

Nightingale, C. (1993). On the Edge: A History of Poor Black Children and Their American Dreams. New York: Basic Books.

Ogden, D. (2005). The Demise of African American Participation in Baseball: A Cultural Backlash from the Negro Leagues. Paper presented at the People of Color in Predominantly White Institutions 10th Annual National Conference (2005). Omaha, Nebraska.

Ogden, D. (2004). The Welcome Theory: An Approach to Studying African American Youth Interest and Involvement in Baseball. A Journal of Baseball History and Culture ,Vol.12, (2), Spring 2004, pp. 114-122.

Ogden, D., & Hilt, M.L. (2003). Collective identity and basketball: an explanation for the decreasing number of African-Americans on America's baseball diamonds. Journal of Leisure Research, Vol. (35).

Overmeyer, J. (1998). Queen of the Negro Leagues: Effa Manley and the Newark Eagles. Lanham, MD: Scarecrow Press.

Pollack, W. (1999). Real Boys: Rescuing Our Sons from the Myths of Boyhood. New York: Macmillan.

Rhoden, W.C. (2006). Forty Million Dollar Slaves: The Rise, Fall, and Redemption of the Black Athlete. New York: Random House, Inc.

Robinson, R. (1998). Jackie Robinson: An Intimate Portrait. New York: Random House, Inc.

Rosentraub, M.S. (1999). Major League Losers: The Real Cost of Sports and Who's Paying for It. New York: Basic Books.

Noll, R.G., & Zimbalist, A., eds. (1997). Sports, Jobs, and Taxes: The Economic Impact of Sports Teams and Stadiums. Washington, DC: Brookings Institution Press.

Sampson, R.J., McAdam, D., MacIndoe, H., & Weffer-Elizondo, S. (2005). Civil Society Reconsidered: The Durable Nature of Community Structure of Collective Civil Action. Chicago, Il: University of Chicago Press.

Stadler, M. (2007). The Psychology of Baseball: Inside the Mental Game of the Major League Player. New York: Penguin Group (USA)

Sterkenburg, J.V. & Knoppers, A. (2004). Dominant Discourses about Race/ Ethnicity and Gender in Sport Practice and Performance. International Review for the Sociology of Sport: 39(3): (2004).

Thomas, J.M., Metzger, J., Ritzdorf, M., Ross, C., & Stiftel (1997). Race, racism, and Race Relations: Linkage with Urban and Regional Planning Literature. A Paper presented for White House Request for Race Literature.

U.S. Bureau of Labor Statistics. (2005). Women in the Labor Force: A Databook. Washington, DC: Author.

U.S. Census Bureau. (2007). Statistical Abstract of the United States: 2007. Washington, DC: Author.

U.S. Census. (2005). We The People: Blacks in the United States. Washington, DC: Author.

Watkins, S. C. (1998). Representing: Hip Hop Culture and the Production of Black Cinema. Chicago: The University of Chicago Press.

Watkins, S. C. (2000). Black Youth and Mass Media: Current Research and Emerging Questions. A Paper presented to the University of Michigan.

Wilson, D., Williams, J., Evans, A., Mixon,G., & Rheaume, C. (2003). Brief Report: A Qualitative Study of Gender Preferences and Motivational Factors for Physical Activity in Underserved Adolescents. Journal of Pediatric Psychology. 30 (3). pp. 293–297.

Winfield, D. (2007). Dropping the Ball: Baseball's Troubles and How We Can and Must Solve Them. New York: Scribner.

Zimbalist, A. (1994). Baseball and Billions: A Probing Look Inside the Big Business Of Our National Pastime. New York: Basic Books.

Additional References

Robert Harrison, "Negro Baseball"
http://www.fcps.edu/westspringfieldhs/projects/im98/im981/spo.htm

"New 'Buying Power' report shows blacks still outspend other ethnic segments"
http://www.targetmarketnews.com/Buying%20Power%20report%2003.htm

"The History of Negro Leagues Baseball."
http://www.nlbpa.com/history.html

Riley, James A. "History of Black Baseball and the Negro Baseball Leagues."
http://www.blackbaseball.com/introd.htm.

Links

Major League Baseball
http://mlb.mlb.com/index.jsp

Baseball Hall of Fame
http://web.baseballhalloffame.org/index.jsp

Negro League Baseball Museum
http://www.nlbm.com/

Black Baseball
http://www.blackbaseball.com/

Library of Congress
http://www.loc.gov/rr/perform/baseballlinks.html
http://memory.loc.gov/ammem/collections/robinson/

Appendices

Appendix 1

Torii Hunter's story says it all. It conveys that hardships come be overcome, no matter how painful they are. It also demonstrates that baseball can provide a path out of poverty, and most importantly, it shows that once delivered out of poverty, nothing is more important that giving back, and reaching back to pull others up. Though Torii recently signed a $90 million contract with the Los Angeles Angels as a Free Agent, he is never too busy to give back. He is indeed, an "Angel."

This book aims to inspire other "Angles" like Torii Hunter to emerge from inner cities throughout America.

Torii Hunter's Story

A message from Torii:

"Last year [2005] I shared a portion of my private life with *USA Today*. I felt a need to let people know that we all have issues and that regardless of the circumstances we all have an opportunity to make something of our lives. I did not grow up with a "silver spoon" in my mouth. I had to fight, scratch and claw for everything I have achieved. This is why the *Little League's Urban Initiative Program* was of interest to me. Perhaps there are some kids that need to know this story, but most importantly, they need to know that regardless of the circumstances, they can make something of their lives if they keep trying."

Father's drug addiction is driving Torii Hunter away
By Bob Nightengale, USA TODAY Sports Weekly

MINNEAPOLIS — It is nearly 3 in the morning. Torii Hunter is frantically pacing the house. He's making calls on his cell phone. He's waiting for someone to call back. No one is answering. No one is calling. Only torturous silence. He finally climbs into bed. Turns up the ringer on his cell phone. And makes sure the phone is an arm's length away.

And then cries himself to sleep.

"My dad — I love my dad," Hunter says softly the next morning. "After everything he's done, I would do anything for him. He knows that. He knows how much I love him.

"But I don't know what to do. I can't take this anymore. I can't keep living like this. Worrying every day. Every night. Wondering if he's all right. I've had enough."

Hunter shuts his eyes. He looks away. Blinks. His eyes are glassy and reddened.

"My dad used to be my inspiration," he says. "He was the reason I made it to the big leagues. I put so much pressure on myself just to make it. I thought, 'If I make it, I'm going to have the money I need to get him help.'

"I came to realize that money can't solve everything. Money can give you the means to be on the right track, but money can't change a person. Money is neutral. It can't make us a family again."

It sickens Hunter to admit this dark family secret. But on the eve of another empty Father's Day, it is time.

Theotis Hunter, Torii's father, is a crack addict.

"My dad is a good guy, and cool as you know what," Hunter says. "Everybody loves him. But I can't lie. I've never been close to my dad. Never. This thing was always there, and he was never around.

"As they say in the 'hood, his brain is kind of cloudy. I could tell all kinds of stories that would break your heart. There were so many times, hundreds of times, I'd see him messed up. I even went to jail for my dad."

"I just wish that my dad would understand that one person can mess up a whole family. It trickles down like a domino effect, and it knocks everybody over."

Hunter, 29, the Minnesota Twins' four-time Gold Glove winner and 2002 All-Star center fielder, says he will make his traditional call on Father's Day [Now with the Los Angeles Angels, 2008].

It won't be easy. It never is.

He will continue to pay his father's expenses.

Otherwise, he's done. No more chasing and worrying about his dad.

"I can't do it no more," Hunter says.

You couldn't understand, not unless you've had a loved one with a drug addiction.

Try searching the streets for your father, worrying whether he's dead or alive, only to find him stoned out of his mind at a crack house in Pine Bluff, Ark. Try being stopped by strangers and discover that you suddenly have half-brothers that you never knew existed. Try being awakened by calls late at night, learning that the electric company has shut off the power to your family's home and the mortgage company is threatening foreclosure.

"It's been so tough to take, especially early on in my career," Hunter says. "I put so much pressure on myself to get to the big leagues. I needed to make it just for my family. You talk about motivation.

"Even now, I may have a smile on my face all of the time, and people think that 'Spiderman' doesn't have a care in the world. They may think I'm a hero on the field. But they don't know what I'm going through. This is worse than anything you can imagine.

"It's just killing me inside."

THE PHONE RINGS, jarring Katrina Hunter, Torii's wife, out of her sleep in the wee hours last month at their home in Colony, Texas. There can never be good news late at night, and this time is no different.

Theotis, whom Torii had moved out of Pine Bluff to be near him earlier this year, is missing again.

Katrina hates to tell Torii. She knows the effect it will have. Torii says he can block it out once he steps on the field, but Katrina, his high school sweetheart, knows better.

She is well-versed on how Torii and his oldest brother, 32-year-old Taru, would stay up until 4 in the morning waiting for their father to come home, only to see him stoned or not show up at all. There were the times when they'd hide in the back of their house, pretending no one was home, when bill collectors came to the door. To this day Torii gets a sickfeeling just thinking about the times he and his brothers lived on nothing more than a loaf of white bread, spreading ketchup or syrup between two slices to make the hunger go away. Or the times he slept on a towel when the old mattress in his bedroom became too disgusting.

"You don't forget those things," says Taru, a personal trainer who rarely talks with his father. "Your daddy doesn't come up with money, and there's no food or power, what are you supposed to do? You're going to do that to your own kids?

"No child should ever have to go through what our daddy put us through."

Still, he is their father. How do you turn your back on him?

Torii, his mother Shirley, three brothers and one sister have tried to find a cure. They've sent Theotis to four, maybe five, rehabilitation drug centers. He spent six months one time locked up at a Houston rehab center.

"When he got out," Torii says, "I thought he was going to be fine. I even had him moved to Dallas to be close to me, and I thought he'd be clean forever. But before you knew it, nothing changed.

"People don't realize how powerful that stuff is. It just takes control of your life. And it ruins the life of everyone around you. I tell my dad that you need to stop. I tell him that he's doing nothing but hurting everybody in the family. He says, 'I'm going to stop.' But it never happened. He can't control it."

This time, in late May, no one knows what has happened to Theotis. No one has seen him in Pine Bluff. His brothers haven't heard a word in Dallas. And no one answers his cell phone.

Torii, who opened an account at Bank of America for his father, decides to investigate. He calls the bank and asks for recent transactions. There's $200 withdrawn at 9 on this Monday morning. Another $300 withdrawn at noon. Another $200 at 3 in the afternoon. And $500 withdrawn two days later.

"He doesn't think it's possible for me to know what he's doing, but come on, I know," Torii says. "What do you need that kind of money for, dawg? You don't need that coming from the 'hood. I don't even spend that. What else could he be doing but drugs?"

Theotis finally makes contact after the bank account is closed. He tells Torii that he was carjacked. The truck Torii bought him was stolen. He is fine, but the truck was gone.

"He was trying to tell me he was stranded and this and that," Torii says. "Come on, man, how can you be stranded in a city where you've got three sons and a daughter-in-law living? There's no way that's possible.

"That's why I shut him off. I can't give him money anymore. I'm done. I just can't. I'll pay for his bills, but if I give him cash, and something happens to him, it's my fault. I'm not going to be responsible for that.

"I know what he's doing from what I hear from the friends I used to have. They tell me what's going on. They tell the stuff he's buying.

"They know, because they're probably the ones who give it to him."

IT'S ONLY A FIVE-HOUR DRIVE from Dallas to his hometown of Pine Bluff, but Torii rarely goes back. He can't. Too depressing. Too many former friends who want him to hang out on the streets. Too many bad memories.

1995 Hunter family photo
The Hunter family, from left: Tramar, Theotis, Shirley, Torii and Tishque. Not pictured: Torii's brother Taru and sister Farolyn Denise

"Ever since that one night," Torii says, "I knew I had to get out of there. It was the worst night of my life. I knew if I stayed, my career would be over.

"That night almost cost me everything."

Taru says: "That was the night none of us will ever forget. That's when I wanted my dad out of my life."

It was Oct. 11, 1994. Torii had just finished his first full season in professional baseball, hitting .293 with 10 homers and 50 RBI at

Class A Fort Wayne, Ind. He was living up to the billing as the Twins' $450,000 first-round pick in the June 1993 draft.

Torii, still living at home, left the keys on the counter to his new Ford Explorer. He woke up the next morning, and the truck was gone.

So was his dad.

He spent four days desperately searching the streets for his father. Finally, one night, he found his truck. Parked in the back of a crack house. He walked toward the apartment with his friends, kicked in the door, and there was his father passed out on the floor.

Torii didn't know whether his dad was dead or alive. He was hysterical. He threw punches at everyone he could. Baseball no longer mattered. He wanted to lash out at everyone responsible for stringing out his dad.

"I was so hurt, I was beating everybody in there," Torii says. "I'm 17 years old, and I'm mad as hell. I'm crying. My friends are crying. I didn't expect to see my dad like that. I thought he was dead. I was so mad I grabbed the keys, took my friend and drove to Conway, Ark."

Torii and Basil Shabazz, the 1991 high school athlete of the year in Arkansas who was drafted two years earlier by the St. Louis Cardinals, drove to visit one of his cousins at the University of Central Arkansas in Conway. Torii went upstairs to the dorm room to play dominoes. Shabazz, exhausted, took a nap in the truck.

Campus police drove by, saw Shabazz sleeping and knocked on the window. Shabazz, thinking someone was trying to rob him, pulled his registered gun. Shabazz was handcuffed, and Torii was whisked away from the dorm room.

"I'm telling them who I am," Torii says, "but the cops are hollering, 'Do you mind if we search your truck?' I said: 'Sure, search all you want. I got nothing. I didn't do anything. I didn't have no alcohol or anything.'

"They searched and searched and searched, digging in the back seat, and what do you think they found there? They found an old marijuana joint and a pipe, sprinkled with crack. I tell them it's not mine, but I didn't want to say it was my dad's either. So we go to jail."

Torii was released the next morning on $2,500 bail. The charges were eventually dropped. The Twins were furious but stood by Torii. Shabazz, ranked by *Baseball America* as the Cardinals' No. 4 prospect, was released.

"My dad might have cost Basil his career," Torii says, "and nearly cost me mine. What was I going to do, tell everyone my dad was on crack? I couldn't do that. I still wanted to protect him."

Taru, who was not only the big brother, but the father Torii never had, couldn't stand it. His father hurt him enough growing up. He wasn't about to let him destroy Torii.

"I waited for my dad to get home that day," Taru says, "and I was so mad I hit him. I actually had fisticuffs with my own father. He started crying. He started saying how sorry he was. But if you're really sorry, then why keep doing this? He knows what he's doing. He's hurting everybody just to make himself happy."

With another Father's Day approaching, Torii would love to remember the good times with his dad. But he knows something is wrong when he can recall only one. It was the time his dad came home when Torii was 9, took the boys out on a boat and spent the day fishing on the Mississippi River.

"It was the best time we ever had," Torii says. "He was teaching us how to hook worms. He jumped in the water. Everything. I remember looking over at my dad, and thinking, 'Man, why can't we do this all of the time?'

"Really, except for that, I don't remember anything else that was good. Just the bad."

Torii shuts his eyes, reflects on his past, and winces. Another memory, from the ninth grade, still haunts him.

"I remember my favorite jacket, my Chicago Bulls jacket, was missing for a week and a half," Torii says. "One day, I see it laying in the house and my dad sleeping on the couch. I knew he must have taken it. So I grabbed it and wore it to school.

"My teacher asked who knew the answer to this question, and I raised my hand. Something fell out of my jacket. It was a crack pipe. It was burnt on both ends. That's the first time I knew he was using crack. I knew he drank and smoked marijuana, but I didn't know that.

"I was sweating, dawg, because if you're caught, you're out of school. Forever. You're done for the rest of the year and got to repeat ninth grade. So I raise my hand and ask to use the bathroom because my stomach hurt. I ran to the bathroom, opened up the back of the toilet, wiped my fingerprints off and dropped it in the back of the tank.

"I was crying and everything I was so scared. I wiped my eyes, went back to the classroom and didn't say anything for a long time.

"I never did tell my dad until (May). And once I told him, that's when he went missing. I don't know if he got depressed or what. Or if that's the reason he left. But he took off. It's the last I talked to him."

Theotis Hunter, 55, was last seen in Pine Bluff. He had moved in January to Dallas, joining his four sons. He has been back in Arkansas for nearly two weeks. He doesn't call. No one knows where he's staying. Messages left at the homes of his mother and uncle have been unanswered.

"We know he's OK, but that's all we know," says Shirley, a second-grade teacher who divorced Theotis in 1999, vowing to keep the family together until their youngest son, Tramar, graduated from high school. "We're still very close friends. He's a good man. He really is. I tried to stay (in the marriage) as long as I could, but I wanted him to get better. It just seems like it's getting worse."

Theotis worked the graveyard shift for 23 years as an electrician for the Cotton Belt Railroad, but he was laid off in 1998 and filed for Chapter 13 bankruptcy in March 2001.

"You pray and try to get wisdom from God," Shirley says. "He's the one who gave me strength all of these years. It's in God's hands now."

Torii, who has four sons (Cameron, 13; Torii Jr., 10; Darius, 10; and Monshadrik, 9), plans to place a Father's Day call this Sunday. He'll leave a message. He doesn't know if it will be returned. Really, it will be no different than when he was growing up.

"I don't ever remember him being around on Father's Day," Torii says. "I remember we'd make a card, or our mom would buy a card, and we'd leave it out for him. I figured he got them, but we never heard anything. But no matter what's going on, and I know it doesn't look good, he's still my dad. He's put me through so much, and it's been so tough on all of us. He put my mom through so much. She's the strongest person I know. But I love my dad. I'll always love him. It's just that if he wasn't sick, I wonder what kind of person he'd be."

Torii, who entered the week batting .277 with 10 homers and 39 RBI, says he needs to stay dispassionate about his dad for his sanity. He decided three weeks ago to stop worrying about his dad, believing he was only hurting himself. Since then, he is hitting .359 with five homers and 16 RBI in the past 19 games compared to .234 with five homers and 23 RBI in the first 39 games.

"I'm at a point now where I can't worry about it anymore," Torii says. "I've got a family of my own now. I've got to worry about my own kids. My mind is finally clear."

Torii sounds convincing. But those close to him say it's simply not his nature. This is a proud man who bought homes for his three brothers in Dallas, is paying for his two younger brothers' college education at North Texas State, and is having a home built for his mom and grandparents in Pine Bluff. He also donates time and money to underprivileged youth in the Twin Cities.

Can he really stop worrying about his own father?

"I'm happy now, I've got that peace of mind," Taru says. "I've learned that you've got to move on. If my dad prefers that sickness even though he's hurting everyone around him, you can't let him ruin everything for you.

"I'm not sure Torii can let it go. I mean, he (Torii) has done so much for this family. He's taken care of all of us, our mom, and all of the poverty. But even after doing all of that, there's one thing left.

"Our father is still sick. And until that goes away, it's like you really haven't accomplished what you wanted in life. It's like your life ain't complete. Try living with that."

For information about Torii Hunter's baseball career, see:
http://mlb.mlb.com/team/player.jsp?player_id=116338

Appendix 2
Negro League Teams Index

From the 1880s to 1950 literally hundreds of all-Black professional and semi-professional baseball teams played throughout the United States. While at times black baseball at its top levels enjoyed the benefits of organized league structures, most teams played in loosely organized circuits or as independents. In the common parlance all are referred to as "Negro League" teams. The list below is by no means a complete list of all the teams that competed in the 70-year history of Negro League baseball; the compilation of the list is an ongoing project.

- Atlanta Black Crackers
- Baltimore Black Sox
- Birmingham Black Barons
- Chicago American Giants
- Cleveland Buckeyes
- Cuban Stars - East
- Detroit Stars
- Indianapolis ABCs
- Kansas City Monarchs
- New York Black Yankees
- Newark Eagles
- Pittsburgh Crawfords
- Austin Black Senators
- Baltimore Elite Giants
- Brooklyn Royal Giants
- Cincinnati Tigers
- Cleveland Cubs
- Dayton Marcos
- Homestead Grays
- Indianapolis Clowns
- Memphis Red Sox
- New York Cubans
- Philadelphia Stars
- St. Louis Stars

Appendix 3
Getting into the Game: How Baseball Works and How Players Are Assigned

Major League Baseball (MLB) is the highest level of play in North American professional baseball. More specifically, Major League Baseball refers to the organization that operates North American professional baseball's two major leagues, the National League and the American League, by means of a joint organizational structure which has existed between them since 1903. Major League Baseball teams play a 162 game season. The American League operates under the Designated Hitter Rule, but the National League does not (inter-league, all-star and World Series game rules are determined by the home team's league rules). In 2000, the American and National Leagues were officially disbanded as separate legal entities with all rights and functions consolidated in the commissioner's office. MLB effectively operates as a single league and as such it constitutes one of the major professional sports leagues of North America.

Major League Baseball is controlled by an agreement that has undergone several incarnations since 1876, then called the NL Constitution, with the most recent revisions being made in 2005. Major League Baseball, under the direction of its Commissioner, Bud Selig, hires and maintains the sport's umpiring crews, and negotiates marketing, labor, and television contracts. As is the case for most North American sports leagues, the 'closed shop' aspect of MLB effectively prevents the yearly promotion and relegation of teams into and out of the Major League by virtue of their performance. Major League Baseball is mostly funded by private enterprises, but also partially funded directly by public taxes. MLB maintains a unique, controlling relationship over the sport, including most aspects of minor league baseball. This is due in large part to a 1922 U.S. Supreme Court ruling in Federal Baseball Club v. National League which held that baseball is not interstate commerce and therefore not subject to federal antitrust law despite baseball's own references to itself as an "industry" rather than a "sport." This ruling has been weakened only slightly in subsequent years.[1] [2]

The production/multimedia wing of MLB is New York-based MLB Advanced Media which oversees MLB.com and all 30 of the individual teams' websites. Its charter states that MLB Advanced Media holds editorial independence from the League itself, but it is indeed under the same ownership group and revenue-sharing plan. MLB Productions is a similarly-structured wing of the league, focusing on video and traditional broadcast media.

Affiliation system

Major league clubs in the modern farm system will enter into affiliation agreements with several teams to develop players at each class-level. Each major-league team has agreements with one AAA team, one AA team, at least two at A level and at least one in a US-based Rookie League.

Class A ball is divided into High-A and Low-A levels. The Florida State League, California League and Carolina League are High-A leagues while the Midwest and South Atlantic Leagues are Low-A. Twenty-one major league teams have a Short-Season A affiliate and a Rookie affiliate. Teams without a Short-Season A affiliate will invariably have at least two rookie franchises. All clubs keep one Rookie team in a US system, like the Gulf Coast League or the Arizona League. Teams can have several additional Rookie League clubs, depending upon whether the teams participate in the rookie leagues in the Dominican Republic, Venezuela or Mexico. In some cases in the Dominican Summer League, teams may also split control of a rookie club.

Affiliations are contracts that can be drawn up from one to five years. The major league club pays player salaries. The minor league club handles all other operations and operational expenses.

Affiliations between teams change for financial or competitive reasons, or as the result of a move. The New Orleans Zephyrs of the Triple-A Pacific Coast League were affiliated with the Houston Astros through 2004. However, this changed for 2005 because Nolan Ryan's minor league baseball business expanded. The Round Rock Express, a Class-AA club in the Austin suburb of Round Rock, was moved to Corpus Christi and renamed the Corpus Christi Hooks. The Edmonton Trappers, which had been purchased by Ryan in 2003, moved from Canada to Round Rock to become the new Triple-A edition of the Express. The Canadian franchise had been affiliated with the Montréal Expos, now the Washington Nationals. Houston, with its relationship with Nolan Ryan (the Astros are one of three teams that have retired the Hall of Famer's jersey number), and its ability to improve its fan base across a wider area in Texas, moved its AAA affiliation to Round Rock. The Zephyrs, to remain in the affiliated system, had to sign with the Nationals or find another club who was willing to swap affiliations for the Nationals.

As of 2006, the longest continuous link between major-league and minor-league clubs is the link between the Orioles and their Rookie-level Appalachian League affiliate, the Bluefield Orioles. This affiliation has existed since 1958.

Extant farm system

 **Open**

The Pacific Coast League, from 1952-1957, was the only minor league to obtain this classification. At this time, the major leagues only extended as far west as St. Louis and as far south as Washington, DC. This classification severely restricted the rights of the major leagues to draft players out of the PCL, and at the time it seemed like the PCL would eventually become a third major league. The PCL would revert back to AAA classification in 1958 due to increasing television coverage of major league games and in light of the Dodgers and Giants moving to Los Angeles and San Francisco, respectively. No minor league since then has received open classification and it is unlikely to happen in the near future because the two current major leagues do not operate as separate entities as they did in the past.

AAA

Teams are typically in the largest metropolitan areas without Major League Baseball franchises (Portland, Buffalo, Rochester, Las Vegas, Columbus, Charlotte, Louisville, Fresno, Nashville, Norfolk, Raleigh/Durham, Richmond, Indianapolis, Des Moines, Austin, Memphis, Sacramento and New Orleans). AAA leagues usually hold the remaining 15 players of the 40 man roster who are not eligible to be on the major league club. It is often referred to as a "parking lot" because many major-league caliber players (especially if they had chosen to sign with some of the leagues' worst teams) are held in reserve at the minor league level for major league emergencies (since they would not have to clear waivers to be called up). Some players who are called AAAA or "Four A" players will play here. This term stems from the players' ability to play well at the AAA level but not in the major leagues. A recent example of such a player is Anderson Hernandez of the New York Mets. Still, some of the top prospects might be assigned here if they are not quite ready for the major leagues, with the potential to be called up later in the season. Players at this level from the 40-man roster of a major-league team can be invited to come up to the major league club once the major-league roster expands on September 1, although teams will usually wait until their affiliates' playoff runs are over, should they qualify. For teams in contention for a pennant, it gives them fresh players. For those not in contention, it gives them an opportunity to evaluate their second-tier players for the next season under game conditions.

AA

This is the fastest-moving, most fluid group of players, usually located in mid-sized cities such as Portland, Maine. Many will jump to the major league from this level, as many of the top prospects are put here to play against each other, rather than against players with major league experience often seen in AAA. A small handful of players might be placed here to start, usually veterans from foreign leagues with more experience in professional baseball. The expectation is usually that these players will be in the majors by the end of the season, as their salaries tend to be higher than those of most prospects. Unlike the Major League and the class AAA level, 2 of the 3 Class AA leagues have their season divided in to two parts, the Eastern League being the exception. One team may clinch a spot in the playoffs by winning the division in first half of the season, then the teams' records are cleared and another team will also clinch a playoff slot during the second half. Wild cards are used to fill out the remaining teams; usually, four teams qualify for the league playoffs. This system is used at the Class A level as well.

A

Usually located in small or mid-sized cities or suburbs of large cities (Asheville, North Carolina; suburban Myrtle Beach, South Carolina; etc). They usually have particular issues to work out; pitching control and batting consistency are the two most frequent reasons for a player to be assigned to Class A baseball.

The class has been divided into two levels since Minor League Baseball made an adjustment in 2002, although most experts still recognize three because players are promoted by major league clubs as they always have been:

"High" A

One level below Double-A, the California League, Florida State League, and the Carolina League remain at a higher level of play. High-A teams are generally located in large and mid-size cities (San Jose, CA; suburban Roanoke, VA; etc). This is often a second or third promotion for a minor-league player, although a few high first-round draftees, particularly those with college experience and players burning up the foreign rookie leagues, will jump to this level. These leagues play a complete season like AAA and AA, April through early September. Some younger Japanese, Taiwanese, Korean and Australian baseball players get their start at this level as do some of the aforementioned top American "rookie" prospects. Many of these teams, especially in the Florida State League, are owned by major league parent clubs and use their spring training complexes.

"Low" A

Full season leagues like the South Atlantic League and Midwest League are a mix of high-quality first-season rookies from the previous year's draft and undrafted signings, as well as players moving up from the Short-Season leagues. This class of baseball is found in cities such as South Bend, Indiana and Lexington, Kentucky.

Short-Season Leagues

As the name implies, these leagues play a shortened season, starting in June and ending in early September (thus, there are only a few off-days during the season).

Consists of the New York-Penn League and Northwest League and is the highest level short-season affiliate for 22 Major League organizations. The remaining 8 MLB clubs have their highest level short-season affiliate in either the Appalachian or Pioneer Leagues. In many instances players drafted out of college will begin their careers at this level, while high-school draftees will begin their careers in either an Advanced-Rookie or Rookie League.

The late start to the season is designed to allow college players to complete the College World Series, which runs through late-June, before turning professional, give major-league teams time to sign their newest draftees, and immediately place them in a competitive league. Players in these leagues are a mixture of newly-signed draftees and second-year pros who weren't ready to move on, or for whom there was not space at a higher level to move up. Second-year pros tend to be assigned to extended spring training until the short-season leagues begin. For many players, this is the first time they have ever used wooden baseball bats, since aluminum bats are most common in the amateur game, as well as the first time they have played every day for a prolonged basis, as amateur competitions typically regulate the number of games played in a week.

Rookie

Advanced Rookie League

Composed of the Appalachian League and the Pioneer League, this level is a mix of recent draftees and second-year players. Advanced Rookie teams are usually in small cities such as Danville, VA and Casper, WY. For some Major League organizations, such as the Milwaukee Brewers, this serves as their highest level short-season affiliate. The Brewers have a team in the Pioneer League, the Helena Brewers, and a team in the Arizona League, the Phoenix Brewers, but do not have an affiliated club in either the New York-Penn or Northwest Leagues.

Rookie League

The lowest level of Minor League Baseball, the leagues here are also short-season leagues. In the United States, team rosters of the Gulf Coast League and the Arizona League consist of newly-signed draftees and a few players brought in from the Dominican Summer League, Venezuelan Summer League, or Mexican Academy League of the season prior. It is considered a low-pressure learning environment for players, as there are few spectators. Some players in the foreign rookie leagues will stay a year or more longer now because of the shortage of United States H2-B immigration visas caused by changes in immigration law after 9/11.

Defunct levels

Until 1963, there were also Class B, C, and D leagues (and, for half a season, one E league). The Class D of that day would be equivalent to the Rookie level today. The other class designations disappeared because leagues of that level could not sustain operation during a large downturn in the financial fortunes of minor league baseball in the 1950s and 1960s caused by the rise of television broadcasts of major league sports across broad regions of the country.

Determining where players should go

A major league team's Director of Player Development determines, in coordination with the coaches and managers who evaluate their talent, in Spring training. Players both from the spring major camp and minor league winter camp are placed at end of the spring training season by the major league club on the roster of a minor league team.

The Director and the General Manager usually determine the initial assignments for new draftees, who typically begin playing professionally in June after they have been signed to contracts.

The farm system is ever-changing: Evaluations of players are ongoing. The Director of Player Development and his managers will meet or teleconference regularly to discuss how players are performing at each level. In addition to personal achievement, injuries, and high levels of achievement by players in the classes above and below all steer a player's movement up and down in the class system.

Players will play for the team to which they are assigned for the duration of that season unless they are "called up," promoted to a higher level; "sent down," demoted to a lower class team in the major league club's farm system; or "released" from the farm system entirely. A release from minor-league level used to spell the end of a minor league player's career. In more modern times, with a more powerful independent baseball system, many players will "park" a career for a season or two in the independent leagues, which are scouted much more heavily. Many will get a second or third look from the major league scouts if they turn their career around in the indies.

Variations in the system

There are variations to the Farm System's classes that should be noted:

- Rehabilitation (Rehab) Assignments - Players on the Disabled List (DL) can be sent to the minor leagues for rehab work. Players are sent to minor league clubs by geography and facilities, not by class for these reassignments. Curt Schilling's recovery from an ankle injury in 2005 saw him rehab in Pawtucket, Rhode Island at the Triple-A Pawtucket Red Sox, very close to the home club in Boston. Minnesota Twins prospect Jason Kubel, who blew out his knee in the Arizona Fall League in 2004, reported to Minnesota's Class-A Florida State League team, the Fort Myers Miracle which is based in their well-equipped Spring Training facility in Fort Myers, Florida.
- Minor League Free Agency - Like major leaguers, minor league players also enjoy free agency. Their contracts expire after three years if they are on the 40 man roster, and unless their contracts are renewed by mutual agreement, they are released from any obligation to the major league club. Those who can't find the right deal with an affiliated baseball club may also take a season in independent baseball before returning to the farm system of another major league club. This is done because players, in the world of free agency and high-dollar salaries, often find their careers "stuck." Major league clubs will often trade for a big dollar position player rather than call someone up from the minor leagues. This can leave position players in the Triple-A and Double-A levels of the farm system with no ability to move up. They become 'spare parts' players unless they can find a new club that views their skills differently.
- Class System Variations - The classification system today is a very rough rule of thumb, particularly in the "readiness" category. There are players who start at all levels of the farm system, although launching from Triple-A is the most rare. More and more players are taken from Class AA to the majors without time in Class AAA. Triple-A has two appropriate nicknames: It's been dubbed the "parking lot" by some sports writers because players can easily get trapped into being reserves for injured major leaguers. It's also been called the "third major league," because the level of play is exceptional, players play harder because they want to prove something to those judging their talent, and because they draw as well as, if not better than, some of their major league counterparts. The Marlins may have won the 2003 World Series, but up until playoff time, their Triple-A Albuquerque Isotopes franchise was outseating the major league club most nights of the week. The independent leagues also play a role, draining off some talent looking for a change, while some players, particularly foreigners, may elect to play in Japan or another country.

Appendix 4
History of Minor League Baseball

The National Association of Professional Baseball Leagues, now known as Minor League Baseball, was formed on September 5, 1901. Minor League Baseball celebrated its centennial season in 2001. The 100th season was a remarkable one as the teams collectively attracted 38,808,339 fans, the second highest total in history. That total was surpassed in 2003 when attendance reached 39,069,707. The all-time record of 39,640,443, set in 1949, was finally broken in 2004 when 39,887,755 fans attended regular season games. Almost every player who ever played Major League Baseball got his start with a team in the National Association. All Major League umpires got their start in NA games

Minor league baseball refers to professional baseball leagues in North America that compete at levels below that of Major League Baseball. All the minor leagues are operated as independent businesses, but all of the best-known leagues are members of Minor League Baseball, an umbrella organization for leagues that have agreements to operate as affiliates of Major League Baseball. Several leagues, known as independent leagues, do not have any links whatsoever to Major League Baseball, and thus are not members of Minor League Baseball (the organization). The most prominent of these leagues is the Northern League.

Each league affiliated with Minor League Baseball is composed of teams that generally are independently owned and operated, but always, with the exception of the Mexican League, directly "affiliated" with (and occasionally named after) one major-league team; some affiliations stay relatively constant, while others change from year to year. For example, the Omaha Royals have been the Class AAA affiliate of the Kansas City Royals since the Royals joined the American League in 1969, but the Columbus Clippers changed affiliations for the 2007 season from the New York Yankees to the Washington Nationals. However, a small number of minor league teams are directly owned by their major-league parent, such as the Springfield Cardinals, owned by the St. Louis Cardinals, and all of the Atlanta Braves' affiliates except for the Myrtle Beach Pelicans; this effectively locks these teams down during affiliation shuffles.

The purpose of the system is to develop players available to play in the major leagues on demand. Today, 20 minor baseball leagues operate with 246 member clubs in large, medium, and small towns, as well as the suburbs of major cities, across the U.S. and Canada. Minor league baseball also goes by the nicknames the "farm system," "farm club," or "farm team(s)," because of a joke passed around by major league players in the 1930s when St. Louis Cardinals general manager Branch Rickey formalized the system, and teams in small towns were "growing players down on the farm like corn."

Appendix 5 The Business of Baseball

Kurt Badenhausen, Michael K. Ozanian and Christina Settimi notyed in their April 2007 article for Forbes.com:

> Baseball games can turn quickly with one swing of the bat. Baseball's finances can change quickly too. Three years ago, the 30 Major League Baseball (MLB) teams posted an operating loss (in the sense of earnings before interest, taxes, depreciation and amortization) of $57 million. Last season, they earned a record $496 million. Despite its ongoing steroids scandal, baseball has made a big comeback thanks to labor peace, new ballparks, tight races to qualify for the postseason and improved marketing.
>
> In 2006, a record 76 million fans poured through the turnstiles at big league parks. The New York Yankees led the league with attendance (the fourth consecutive year the Bronx Bombers have done so) with 4.2 million, followed by the Los Angeles Dodgers (3.8 million), New York Mets (3.4 million) and St. Louis Cardinals (3.4 million). With the average ticket price of a big league game increasing 5% last season, to $22, gate receipts (including premium club seating) came in at $1.9 billion, 8% above 2005.

Forbes (2007) provides the latest information on the business of baseball.

RANK	TEAM	CURRENT VALUE ($MIL)	1-YR VALUE CHANGE (%)	DEBT/VALUE (%)	REVENUES ($MIL)	OPERATING INCOME ($MIL)
1	New York Yankees	1,200	17	79	302	-25.2
2	New York Mets	736	22	83	217	24.4
3	Boston Red Sox	724	17	33	234	19.5
4	Los Angeles Dodgers	632	31	67	211	27.5
5	Chicago Cubs	592	32	0	197	22.2
6	St Louis Cardinals	460	7	53	184	14.0
7	San Francisco Giants	459	12	32	184	18.5
8	Atlanta Braves	458	13	0	183	14.8
9	Philadelphia Phillies	457	8	38	183	11.3
10	Washington Nationals	447	2	56	144	19.5
11	Houston Astros	442	6	12	184	18.4
12	Seattle Mariners	436	2	23	182	21.5
13	Los Angeles Angels of Anaheim	431	17	8	187	11.5
14	Baltimore Orioles	395	10	38	158	17.1
15	Chicago White Sox	381	21	10	173	19.5
16	San Diego Padres	367	4	48	160	5.2
17	Texas Rangers	365	3	73	155	11.2
18	Cleveland Indians	364	4	27	158	24.9
19	Detroit Tigers	357	22	59	170	8.7
20	Toronto Blue Jays	344	20	0	157	11.0
21	Arizona Diamondbacks	339	11	68	154	6.4
22	Colorado Rockies	317	6	28	151	23.9
23	Cincinnati Reds	307	12	13	146	22.4
24	Oakland Athletics	292	24	31	146	14.5
25	Minnesota Twins	288	33	31	131	14.8
26	Milwaukee Brewers	287	22	42	144	20.8
27	Kansas City Royals	282	18	14	123	8.4
28	Pittsburgh Pirates	274	10	37	137	25.3
29	Tampa Bay Devil Rays	267	28	15	134	20.2
30	Florida Marlins	244	8	36	122	43.3

Appendix 6
"Reaching Back" To Former African American Players To Help *"Reach In"* African American Communities

An article on March 3, 2008 in the New York Times conveyed some very positive news. It showed an example of how one New York baseball team is reaching back to former African American players to get them involved. The story is about Darryl Strawberry. He is a player who has seen hard times and is in a position to help steer young players on the right road. This kind of involvement is a key for reviving baseball in inner cities. More former African American players must similarly be called upon to share their knowledge of baseball and of the world.

The New York Times article read:

> PORT ST. LUCIE, Fla. — The Mets' newest hire looked fit enough to take batting practice Monday. In a clubhouse that has taken on the look of a triage center, Darryl Strawberry appeared like a hallucination, looking so resplendent in his Mets jersey that it was like 1986 again.
>
> At 46, Strawberry is not making a comeback as a player. His latest rebirth, while revolving around baseball, is more personal than professional. The Mets have hired Strawberry essentially to be a big brother. He will serve as a special instructor during spring training and as an ambassador once the season starts, traveling within the New York metropolitan area and to the club's minor league affiliates.
>
> "I'm just glad to be back," said Strawberry, the No. 1 overall pick by the Mets in 1980. A thrice-married father of five, he added: "I'm going to give these young kids the same advice I give to my own boys about focus, choices, decisions. What it's like to excel at a high level and really take care of yourself more than anything. What they have to deal with — the pressures and temptations of life."
>
> Strawberry, an eight-time All-Star, helped the Mets win the World Series in 1986. Toward the end of his 17-year career, he was part of the 1996, 1998 and 1999 Yankees teams that won World Series titles. He knows only too well the pressures and temptations of the sporting life, having waged a decades-long battle with drug and alcohol addiction.

Starting in 2002, Strawberry spent nearly a year in prison in Gainesville, Fla., for violating probation from a 1999 cocaine possession charge. He recently agreed to pay the I.R.S. more than $430,000 stemming from a conviction for tax evasion.

Strawberry looks like the picture of health, no small blessing given that he was found to have colon cancer in 1998 and sat out the postseason after having surgery. He had a kidney removed in 2000 after the cancer came back.

"I'm going to hit 35 and drive in 100," Strawberry joked after taking a seat next to Mets General Manager Omar Minaya in the home dugout at Tradition Field. He said his life took on new meaning two years ago, when he visited a school for autistic children outside St. Louis. His sister-in-law is a teacher there, and Strawberry said he was moved by what he saw. "I looked into the kids' eyes and I felt something," he said. "I've been in pain before so I know what it feels like."

In 2006, Strawberry and his third wife, Tracy, created the Darryl Strawberry Foundation to increase global awareness of autism. Last year, Strawberry participated in a charity golf event that raised $100,000 to fight autism. "I never realized what children with autism went through until I went in there and saw it," Strawberry said. "It touched me. It's made a big difference in who I am and how I see things."

He is back in baseball, but insists that the sport no longer defines him. Given everything that Strawberry can bring to the conversation in his role as a big brother, perhaps nothing is more needed than his perspective on life...